Under the Mantle

Marian Thoughts from a 21st Century Priest

Donald H. Calloway, MIC

Available from:
Marian Helpers Center
Stockbridge, MA 01263

Prayerline: 1-800-804-3823
Orderline: 1-800-462-7426
Websites: fathercalloway.com
marian.org

Imprimi Potest:
Very Rev. Kazimierz Chwalek, MIC
Provincial Superior
The Blessed Virgin Mary, Mother of Mercy Province
January 6, 2013
Epiphany of the Lord

Library of Congress Catalog Number: 2013932408
ISBN: 978-1-59614-273-2
First edition (5th printing): 2016

Cover photo and inside page image sculpture of St. Juan Diego
by Timothy P. Schmalz
Design by Kathy Szpak
Editing and Proofreading: David Came and Andrew Leeco

Acknowledgments: Marian Fathers of the Immaculate Conception,
Mr. & Mrs. Donald and LaChita Calloway, Matthew Calloway, Ileana E. Salazar,
Teresa de Jesus Macias, Cana Salazar, Sophie Salazar, Jason Zasky

A special thank you to Timothy G. Lock, PhD, FTI,
a licensed clinical psychologist, for his thorough review
and professional insights for Chapters 8 and 9.

Printed in the United States of America

MARIAN PRESS
STOCKBRIDGE MA 01263
PRO CHRISTO ET ECCLESIA

2016

To the Immaculata,
My Dove of Beauty

Arise, my love, my fair one,
and come away.
O my dove, in the clefts of the rock,
in the recesses of the cliff,
let me see your face,
let me hear your voice,
for your voice is sweet,
and you are lovely.

Song of Songs 2:13-14

Contents

Introduction

THOSE FORGIVEN MUCH, LOVE MUCH (cf. Lk 7:36-48). Well, anyone who has heard my conversion story knows that I've been forgiven very much! And the way I've been trying to show my love and gratitude to God is by following Jesus' command to prodigals like me, namely, to go out and tell the whole world how much he has done for us in his mercy (cf. Mk 5:19).

"Tell the whole world." I mean that literally. Since I was ordained a priest on May 31, 2003, I haven't stopped travelling the whole world, telling my story to hundreds of thousands of people. As great as this has been, I have to admit that life on the road isn't easy! And it's simply been impossible to accept all the gracious invitations from people who have asked me to speak. Well, love finds a way, so I had the opportunity in 2010 to write my conversion story down in a book called *No Turning Back: A Witness to Mercy*, which enabled me to tell even more people of the wondrous workings of God's great love and mercy in my life.

I have to admit, I like this book thing. It's certainly an easier way to spread the word of God's love than simply by living out of a suitcase, eating Pop Tarts and trail mix for my meals. Now, don't get me wrong. I'm still going to keep getting out there to give my witness. "The love of Christ impels me" (2 Cor 5:14). And if you want me to come speak at your parish or event, feel free to ask! (See the last pages of this book for more information.) But I'm excited to offer even more of the message I've been spreading for the last 10 years, especially for those people whose invitations I've had to turn down due to being overbooked.

Here's what I mean by "more of the message." As I've been going around telling my story, I have found that the organizers of the events where I've been invited to speak would often ask me to give more than one talk. In fact, sometimes they'd ask for as many as five talks! Obviously, I couldn't just say, "No." So, over the years, I've developed about nine talks that people have really seemed to be blessed by, thanks be to God. And that brings me to what this book is all about.

The nine chapters of this book are a compilation of my favorite talks from the road. Of course, the Person of Jesus Christ is *the* most important topic. But sadly, many people today don't believe in him, think he's a myth, and consider the religion he founded to be the cause of all the world's troubles. I once believed that myself! But nothing could be further from the truth. That's why, as a 21st century priest, I want to help those who are living in these crazy times rediscover the awesome truths of the Catholic faith — the Eucharist, the Church, the papacy, Confession, the priesthood, and the Cross. These topics, and others, are the themes of this book.

And as a Marian priest, I firmly believe that there is a tried and true method, taught by God himself, for bringing people back into a belief in Jesus Christ, and back into a love for the truthfulness of his teachings and the Church he founded. That method is Mary. Lovely, beautiful, crown of creation, masterpiece of beauty, demon-crushing, heresy-conquering, humble, handmaid of the Lord, Mary!

Like so many in our times, and in times past, I came to know and love Jesus through Mary. I am a 21st century priest because God has placed me *under the mantle*. There, I find my strength, my purpose, my life, my sweetness, and my hope. And God is placing many more under this most loving maternal mantle. Jesus is raising up a new generation of Catholics today. Ask almost anyone who has experienced a conversion or reversion to the Catholic faith today, and you will almost inevitably hear that the Virgin Mary played a major role in bringing them home. And how could she not? She is the mother of God's children, the heart of the mystery of salvation, and the nexus of the mysteries of Christianity.

Without Mary, we would not have Jesus. Without Mary, we would not have the Church. Without Mary, we would not have the Sacraments. Without Mary, we would not have the New Testament. Without Mary, we would have absolutely zilch! Seriously. I mean every word of that. And this is why every theme that is presented in the nine chapters of this book has, as its guiding principle, Mary. Pure and simple. There is no better way to rediscover Jesus and his Church than through Our Lady.

Each chapter in this book is divided into three subsections so as to bring to light various aspects of the topic at hand. Importantly, this is also why you will discover at the end of each subsection powerful quotes about Our Lady from saints, blesseds, venerables, servants of God, and popes. I refer to these amazing quotes as *Marian Gems*. These quotes will blow you away! It has taken me years to acquire them all, and I know that you will benefit from them greatly.

In addition, many of the analogies I present in *Under the Mantle* may not be familiar to you. Perhaps you have never heard Our Lady described as the "Woman of Our Dreams" (chapter 1), or the Catholic Church as "God's Rehabilitation Center" (chapter 3), or Confession as a "Spiritual Diaper Change" (chapter 4). Yet, as limited as analogies always are, they nonetheless help make the point that is being conveyed. *Therefore, please read this book slowly.* If you read it too fast you are going to miss very important points.

What you're about to read are fundamental, unchanging, beautiful truths communicated in the language of a 20th century man who has become a 21st century priest. I have the degrees to go all academic and technical, and I have done that in some of my other books. But this book seeks to present deep theological truth to Joe Six-pack in the pew. It's simple, yet life-changing truth — logical and reasonable truth that will give you a spiritual kick in the pants. And we could all use a spiritual kick in the pants today.

The purpose of this book is to bring readers into a greater love for Jesus through Mary, and to rediscover and fall in love with Catholicism anew and afresh. Catholicism is about being in love and accepting an invitation to the eternal wedding with the bridegroom, Jesus Christ, the lover of your soul. And Mary's role in all this is of paramount importance. She shows us the way and helps us keep our romance with God alive.

Mary made the Heart of God for us, and God has given Mary, as our spiritual mother, the role of making sure that her children come to know and love his divine Heart. This is why I am absolutely convinced that it is only through Our Lady that we are going to rediscover what it means to be a true follower of Christ, a true Catholic, in the 21ˢᵗ century. Mary is an absolutely necessary part of the New Evangelization.

God is doing something amazing in our times, but so many don't understand it or see it. I want to help you see it. It's happening through Mary, and Jesus desires all of his disciples to live under the mantle and experience it. That's where we find our safety, our refuge, and our protection — *under the mantle* of the Blessed Virgin.

Satan does not want you to live *under the mantle* of Our Lady. This is why he and his diabolical cohorts have been deviously trying to *dis-mantle* Christianity, seeking to snatch souls away from Mary, luring them out from under her mantle, and depriving them of the fullness of the message of Jesus Christ. But if you remain securely *under the mantle* of Our Lady, not even Satan can touch you.

I sincerely hope that as you read this book, you come to understand what living *under the mantle* means and how God desires this for you. My ardent prayer is that you fall madly in love with Jesus and his Church — all through Mary.

Fr. Donald H. Calloway, MIC, STL
Vicar Provincial
The Blessed Virgin Mary, Mother of Mercy Province

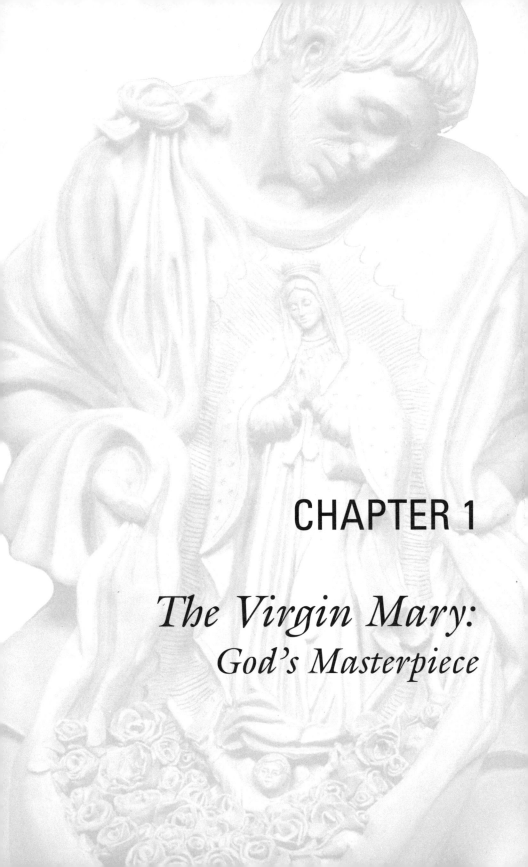

CHAPTER 1

The Virgin Mary:
God's Masterpiece

The Woman of Our Dreams

I'D LIKE YOU TO IMAGINE FOR A MOMENT that you are the eternal Son of God. All powerful, possessing all wisdom and goodness, and full of mercy; you are, in fact, love and mercy itself. As God, you know that the world you created will fall, and so with the other two Persons of the Blessed Trinity, you devised a plan *ahead of time* to save the world. The plan is this: You will enter into the world, sacrificially love fallen mankind, forgive them, and elevate them to a life of grace and sonship with your Father. Specifically, you are going to take on human nature, become a man, establish a Church, sacrifice yourself as a victim, rise from the dead, and send fallen mankind the Holy Spirit to sanctify them and bring them to paradise.

But you are not a magical God. You are not going to enter the world already developed and 33 years old. No. You are going to enter the world through a woman. That woman will be your mother.

Now, remember, you are God.

Would you who are all-powerful, having the capability of fashioning your own mother, make her have any flaws whatsoever? If you had the power to create your own mother, would you make her anything less than a masterpiece of feminine beauty and genius?

I didn't think so.

What son, if he could precede his mother, would make his mother have any defects? What son would want his mother to be a sinner? Any good son would desire that his mother have the superlative of every virtue: She would be the most kind, loving, humble, gentle, merciful, tender, and compassionate of all creatures. She would have the most of everything good and lovely. She would, in fact, be the most holy human person who ever lived; she would be conceived and born immaculate, having nothing to do with darkness, death, and evil. Nothing would compare with her, and outside of the Holy Trinity, no one would be greater than she is.

She would even be a virgin-mother. As her divine Son — if I were God — you can guarantee I would do this for my dear mother. But not just that. I would want her to have every privilege possible: sinless, immaculate, virgin, mother, queen, princess, and pattern of creation and human perfection. Plus, if I were God, I would figure out some way of making her not just my mother, but the mother of everyone. Such a wonderful mother should be shared with everyone.

Well, the reality, my friends, is that we are not God. We are incapable of such things. But in coming into the world to save us, the Eternal Word prepared a worthy dwelling place for his Incarnation to take place. He made his own mother. And she is a masterpiece.

And what makes this mystery even more amazing is that Jesus actually figured out a way of sharing the masterpiece of Mary's motherhood with us! He is not a selfish God. On the contrary, as a most loving Son, he is so proud of his mother that he wants her to be everyone's mother. Thus, he made her the spiritual mother for all who are adopted into his sonship.

But let's not stop there.

If you were God, why not make her the most commonly portrayed woman in art in the history of the world!

Make her name so lovely that every culture would have a variation of it. It would, in fact, be the most common female name in human history.

You might also see to it that a book was written, a book that your Holy Spirit inspired and co-authored, that would tell all generations to call her blessed (cf. Lk 1:48).

You might even anticipate her solemn entrance into human history by promising that it would be her tender and delicate heel that would crush your enemy, forever defeating the darkness of Satan (cf. Gen 3:15).

Why, you might even be so bold as to have made preparations in the beginning of time for all to honor her through establishing universal Commandments that must be observed by all. One of these Commandments would be that sons and daughters, in order to please you, must honor their father and mother (cf. Ex 20:12). In your divine wisdom, you established it this way so that when you shared your mother with others (cf. Jn 19:26-27), making her their spiritual mother, they, as her sons and daughters, would necessarily have to honor her in order to please you.

This would be a most brilliant plan. A plan only God could do.

And God did.

That's exactly what he did.

But let's take it even a step farther.

Similar to the Word (Jesus) creating his own mother, God the Father also created his most perfect daughter. If you were God the Father and could fashion your own daughter, would you not want your daughter to be the most beautiful, pure, and lovely girl of all? I know I would. Any father would. Every good father wants to guard his daughter and protect her from anything that could harm her. And this is exactly what God the Father did in creating the mystery of Mary. She is a princess.

This princess has received a plentitude of his grace. She is "full of grace" (Lk 1:28). God the Father protects her with a jealous and all-powerful love. If anyone attacks or threatens his little girl, they are in big trouble.

And there's one last step in understanding the Trinitarian masterpiece that is Mary.

The Holy Spirit, in creating Mary, fashioned the perfect bride.

Mary is the perfect spouse of God. Once again, if you or I could create our own spouse, we would create a spouse without any flaws or imperfections — one good and virtuous and worthy of praise. As a man, I would create a masterpiece of feminine beauty. She would be the woman of my dreams. Angels would bow down in her presence, and everyone would be subject to her, sing songs about her, and praise her loveliness and unique beauty. All darkness and demons would flee at her presence, and the very fragrance of her person would make grown men cry. My lady would be the best!

Well, just so, the Holy Spirit fashioned the perfect bride. She is the beautiful dove of God, the dove of beauty, and there can't possibly be a more lovely and perfect woman.

Mary is the masterpiece of God. She is the perfect mother, daughter, and spouse. She is the perfect woman. She is the perfect creation, and no other created thing compares to her. She is the Immaculata. God made her. God lives in her, and through her and with her, he crushes the darkness.

Understand God's masterpiece from this perspective: Every artist desires to take delight and find rest in his creation and, if it were possible, even make his vision — his dream — become a reality. In other words, if an artist or sculptor could make his creation come alive, he would. Michelangelo, for example, after having sculpted the famous statue of Moses, is rumored to have considered it so real that he struck the statue with a tool and cried out, "Speak!" For man, of course, this is impossible. But not with God. God is the greatest artist, and with him, all things are possible.

As a matter of fact, God's dream creation became a reality in the person of the Immaculata.

And God so delighted in this masterpiece that he took up an abode in her body and soul and allowed himself to become flesh through her, finding rest and delight in her loveliness. This masterpiece is worthy of giving God flesh. The Word lived in her body for nine months, and the Holy Spirit lives in her forever! Through her, God was born to bleed. God desired to bleed for her because he is madly in love with her.

He loves her so much that he gives her everything, even victory over his enemies.

How appropriate it is then that when we see images of the Immaculate Virgin, she is shown stepping on and crushing the head of the ancient serpent — Satan. This is why Christian art often depicts Mary as pregnant with the divine Child. God abides in her; he lives in her. She is the tabernacle of his presence and the Holy of Holies. Of herself, she does not have the power to conquer Satan and do such great things because she is a creature, but God desires to crush the darkness *through* her. He could do it all by himself, but because he is so in love with Mary, he has chosen only to defeat Satan through her. By living in her, he gives her a unique participation in the mystery of salvation, and together, they defeat the enemy.

Therefore, if we want to conquer sin and evil, we must make a decision to live *under the mantle* of God's masterpiece: the Immaculata. If God himself lives in her and conquers evil through her, who are we to think that we do not need her!

As a matter of fact, as God's masterpiece, the mystery of the Immaculate Conception assures us of the victorious redemption of Christ. When God wants to give us his best gifts, it seems his divine paternal love can't wait to give them to us. As a provident Father, he is always planning *ahead of time*.

Let me explain: The Immaculate Conception of Mary is a gift flowing from the sacrifice of Jesus on Calvary; it is the most perfect fruit of his redeeming love. Yet, historically, Mary is given this tremendous privilege even before the Word becomes flesh, and way before he is crucified on the Cross — the event that wins for us *all* the graces of redemption, including Mary's Immaculate Conception.

God is so in love with Mary that he anticipates the priestly sacrifice of Jesus on the Cross and already applies its perfect fruit to Mary's Immaculate Conception. And this is all possible because God doesn't need to do things according to our time frame. He knows that the sacrifice of Jesus will most definitely happen, so he already gives the perfect fruit of that sacrifice to Mary, his beloved daughter and mother of his Son. It is done because she was created to precede, as mother, and prepare the world, as our spiritual mother, for the coming of the redemption of the Eternal Son.

Mary's Immaculate Conception is the guarantee that our redemption is coming and *will* happen. The reason is because without the sacrifice of Jesus on the Cross, Mary cannot have the gift of having been immaculately conceived. She is free of sin in anticipation of the merits of Christ, and if Jesus does not die on the Cross *for her*, we have an ontological and theological problem; that is, Mary cannot be the Immaculata without the sacrifice of Jesus.

For this reason, popes and saints have noted that Mary's Immaculate Conception is like the white dawn preceding the coming of the Sun (Son). She is white because she is pure and without sin, and just as the first streaks of light on the horizon tell us that the Sun is rising, so it is with Our Lady. She comes before Christ, dispels the darkness, and prepares the world for the Light of the Eternal Son.

How amazing are God's ways. The dream has become reality!

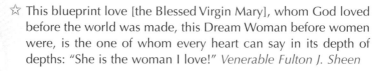

☆ ☆ ☆ Marian Gems

☆ This blueprint love [the Blessed Virgin Mary], whom God loved before the world was made, this Dream Woman before women were, is the one of whom every heart can say in its depth of depths: "She is the woman I love!" *Venerable Fulton J. Sheen*

☆ The Immaculate Conception is the promising dawn of the radiant day of Christ. *St. John Paul II*

☆ For as the dawn is the end of night, and the beginning of day, well may the Blessed Virgin Mary, who was the end of vices, be called the dawn of day. *Pope Innocent III*

☆ He hath regarded the humility of his handmaid; for behold from henceforth all generations shall call me blessed. *Luke 1:48*

☆ *De Maria Numquam Satis* (Of Mary, Never Enough). *St. Bernard of Clairvaux*

☆ All of his divine attributes, in a manner of speaking, attempted to outdo one another in order to create a first-class masterpiece. *Servant of God (Fr.) Joseph Kentenich*

☆ If you could have preexisted your mother [....] would you not have made her the most perfect woman that ever lived — one so beautiful she would have been the sweet envy of all women, and one so gentle and so merciful that all other mothers would have sought to imitate her virtues? Why, then, should we think that God would do otherwise? *Venerable Fulton J. Sheen*

☆ Have no fear of loving the Blessed Virgin too much, you will never love her enough, and Jesus will be pleased since the Blessed Virgin is his Mother. *St. Therese of Lisieux*

☆ Maintain an earnest admiration for the Immaculate. Never be afraid that you might exalt her too much, she who will shine throughout eternity as God's masterpiece, as the most wonderful of his creatures, as the brightest mirror of the divine perfections. *Venerable Pope Pius XII*

☆ She is Heaven's masterpiece, the Empress of Heaven, its joy and its glory, in whom everything is heavenly. *St. John Eudes*

☆ He who is not awestruck by this Virgin's spirit and who does not admire her soul is ignorant of how great God is. *St. Peter Chrysologus*

☆ Mary is the epitome of beauty. Masterpieces are never partial beauties, but a synthesis of the beautiful: Mary is the creature most clearly revealing the divine Trinitarian presence. *Blessed Pope Paul VI*

☆ The Virgin Mary, among all creatures, is a masterpiece of the Most Holy Trinity. *Pope Benedict XVI*

☆ The most beautiful creature of all, the one in whom all the marvels and supernatural order are gathered, is Mary. She is God's masterpiece. *Blessed James Alberione*

☆ The Eternal Father delights in regarding the Heart of the Blessed Virgin Mary as the masterpiece of his hands. *St. John Vianney*

☆ The Immaculate Conception of the Virgin is a pledge of salvation for every human creature. *St. John Paul II*

The Immaculate Blueprint

AS THE DIVINE ARCHITECT, GOD WORKS IN AN ORDERLY WAY. When he created the heavens and the earth, it wasn't mindless activity. He had a plan. And that plan has a blueprint and model — a prototype.

Naturally, God could have created the world in an entirely different way than he did, with a different system of doing things and with different creatures — but he didn't. What he did create is our universe with all of its beauty and wonder, with countless stars and galaxies. And since he is a God of order, he had a perfect model in mind when he fashioned all of creation. That perfect model, first and foremost, is his Eternal Word. And in the fullness of time, that Word became flesh and took on human nature, and we worship him as the Second Person of the Holy Trinity. He is Jesus Christ our Lord. He is truly God and truly man. However, he is not a human person. He is a divine Person. He has two natures, divine and human, but his personhood is divine. In other words, he does not have a split personality. And this is important to remember.

Though Jesus Christ is our ultimate model, the one through whom all things came to exist (cf. Jn 1:3), we nonetheless are never going to be able to share in his divine personhood. After all, we are not God, and we never will be. In heaven, we will share in the divine nature (cf. 2 Pet 1:4), but we will not be divine persons. Thus, in addition to Jesus, a divine Person, we also need a perfect, created model that we can be completely formed into, a human person who is a perfect blueprint as a creature for all other human persons. This human person must be so holy and flawless that, as a creature, this person will serve as the universal blueprint for all peoples for what it means to be pleasing to God. Such a model and prototype will help us aspire to full conformity to Christ, until the time that we are so united with him that we are taken up into paradise to live forever with the lover of our souls.

The created blueprint, model, and prototype for what it fully means to be a holy human person is the Blessed Virgin Mary. She is the one who most conforms us to Christ, our God. She makes the living of Christianity real, concrete, and possible. And in her historical and personal reality, she shows us that Christianity is not just a theory, a possibility, or a clever myth. Christianity is real, and it can — and did — produce a perfect human person, a perfect creature. Her name is Mary. She is our sinless model.

Not only did God give this great gift of sinlessness to the Blessed Virgin at the moment of her conception, but Mary herself so fully cooperated with God's plan that she never committed any personal sins. God preserved her from original sin in light of the merits of Jesus Christ and his sacrifice on the Cross, and she remained faithful at every moment of her life. She is the most fully redeemed human person, having experienced the goodness of God's mercy more than anyone else because God looked with favor on the humility of his handmaid (cf. Lk 1:48).

As the Immaculate Conception, she lives in perfect conformity to the will of God, and she becomes for us — in her human person and in her complete fidelity to God's plan and will — the model and the pattern or blueprint for what it means to be a fully redeemed human person in love with Jesus Christ.

That is why she acts as Mediatrix between Jesus and us. Of course, Jesus is the one Mediator between God and man (cf. 1 Tim 2:5). But God has also established, in his divine wisdom, a mediatrix between Jesus and us. And we need this mediatrix. Those who do not think this is necessary need to look more closely at the reality. I mean, if we need parents to mediate life to us, the Bible to mediate God's message to us, the Church to interpret those sacred pages as a mediatrix for us, and the Sacraments to mediate sanctifying grace to us, who are we to think that we do not need the *person* of Mary as our Mediatrix with Jesus? Without her, we would not have Jesus, the New Testament, or the Church. She brings us to Jesus, and she also brings Jesus to us. God set it up that way.

And because this is true, Mary is not an option in our spiritual lives but a necessity. She is both our spiritual mother and our model.

Since God desires that we become holy and without sin, "that he might present the church to himself in splendor, without spot or wrinkle or any such thing, that she might be holy and without blemish" (Eph 5:27), we have to seek to be conformed to the pattern that God set up for us. *We have to become immaculate.* And the immaculate mold through which this happens is not a thing, but a person — she is our spiritual mother, the Immaculata. This is why the only true and complete way to be pleasing to Jesus is to love, honor, and become like his mother.

To use an analogy and a play on words, God has *Maryed* (married) humanity. The divine lover has espoused himself to mankind. And God is not a polygamist. There is only one bridegroom and one bride. The bridegroom is God and the one bride is Mary. If we, therefore, want to be faithfully married (*Maryed*) to God, we have to fit into the pattern of what it means to be espoused to him, namely, Mary. This is why I will often emphasize in this book that the Church is patterned off of Mary. The Church is the bride of God after the example of Mary, and there is only one true Church because there is only one true bride.

Actually, the marriage analogy should be somewhat familiar to us. Saint Paul talked about it in his second letter to the Corinthians. To the Corinthian community, he remarked: "I betrothed you to Christ to present you as a pure bride to her one husband" (2 Cor 11:2). Notice that he was referring to *all* the members of the Corinthian community, women *and* men. In our souls, all of us, both women *and* men, have the feminine dimension of receptivity. God is the bridegroom, so the souls of all human persons are called to be spiritually espoused to him. He is the initiator, we are the receivers. And all of this is spiritual, of course.

In a certain sense, Christianity would be nothing more than an idea or a philosophy without the concrete proof that it works, and this is evidenced in a concrete and perfect human person, one who has been fully redeemed and experienced the goodness and mercy of God in the most exemplary way, becoming the prototype for all others. Mary is this human person. All has been perfectly accomplished in her. And for this reason, no one ever lives Christianity as Jesus wants it lived unless they are living it within a Marian framework, a Marian modality, a Mariasphere.

If you had the opportunity to ask the founder of any religious community what is the basis of the community's charism, I'm sure they would tell you that Mary is their model for loving and serving Jesus, though the particulars of their mission and apostolate may vary. If you asked St. Francis, for example, I guarantee he would tell you that he desires that all of his little brothers strive to conform their souls, and the souls of those they serve, to Mary. This is what makes souls pleasing to Jesus.

Similarly, if you asked St. Benedict, St. Dominic, or St. Ignatius of Loyola — the founders of the Benedictines, Dominicans, and Jesuits respectively — all would say that the members of their communities seek to imitate and become like Mary, because she is perfect and the most conformed to Jesus. This aspect is *always* written into their Constitutions that they vow their lives upon. It has to be because there is no other model or pattern for following Christ than Mary.

As a matter of fact, being like Mary in her virtues is a pre-requisite for being canonized or beatified in the Catholic Church. It's impossible to become holy if you are not patterning yourself off of the very blueprint that God set up for what it means to be a holy and virtuous human person. And that's why no one outside the Catholic Church is ever beatified or canonized. Anyone who does not love and imitate Mary in her virtues cannot become holy.

In days of old, having Mary as a model was widely known and practiced. Consider how many sisters in religious communities would take the name Sr. Mary Francis, or Sr. Mary Augustine, or Sr. Mary Joseph, or Sr. Mary Catherine. If you want to be holy and share a life of union with the Heart of Christ, you have to seek to become like Our Lady. The saints all know this; it's how they became saints.

And many saints have been given special graces at select times in the Church's history to remind people of this — so we don't forget or go looking for blueprints or models other than Our Lady. It's also why many saints have said that the real heart of Christianity is to become an *altera Maria* — that is, *another Mary*, for Jesus. All that Jesus really wants to hear from his followers is what was first said by his mother, namely, *fiat* (cf. Lk 1:38). *Fiat* basically means *let it be done to me*. That word is the greatest word ever uttered by a creature, and there will never be any word said by a creature that will outdo it. And that one word is all that the divine bridegroom wants to hear from his bridal Church — *fiat* — "let it be done to me according to your word."

Saint Louis de Montfort, one of my favorite saints, noted that the essence of Christianity is to become liquefied by the Holy Spirit and poured into the Mary mold. It's an analogy, of course, but it beautifully illustrates that the one perfect mold for what it means to be a Christian, and of what it means to be pleasing to Jesus, is Mary Immaculate.

Saint Maximilian Kolbe, another one of my favorite saints, even boldly stated that we should strive to be *transubstantiated* into the Immaculate. Typically, we only think about the word "transubstantiation" as being associated with the Eucharist. The host is changed from being a piece of bread into the Body of Christ through transubstantiation. What the profound thought of St. Maximilian teaches us is that we have to become another Mary — without sin and without spot or wrinkle or any darkness. We have to be, as it were, transubstantiated into the Immaculate. This is profound, but it is exactly what Jesus came to do, and exactly how Jesus wants Christianity done.

Consider the fact that at the beginning of every secular New Year (January 1), countless individuals make New Year's resolutions: "I'm going to lose weight" or "I'm going to exercise" are two common examples. There's nothing wrong with these resolutions, but they usually don't last long. But if God could tell us what his New Year's resolution would be for us, I wonder what he would tell us?

Well, actually, he kind of has.

On January 1 every year, the Church celebrates the solemnity of Mary, the Mother of God. When I was a seminarian, I thought to myself: I wonder if this is God's way of telling us that this is what he desires for us for the New Year, that we resolve to become more like Mary? To love her and imitate her virtues of being more kind, humble, patient, merciful, etc. This is the universal resolution God desires for us, all of us. Children can do it and the elderly as well. And we can actually keep this resolution. Eventually, all our bodies are going to grow old and fat, but this resolution is ageless and very pleasing to God.

Lastly, so you don't just remember this "resolution" once a year, here's a little something that will help you daily remember that God wants you to be like Mary: Many people today, sadly, go to palm readers looking for answers and direction in life. Obviously, that stuff is nonsense, dangerous, and dumb, not to mention sinful and dabbling in darkness. But what if God has already told you the direction in life he wants you to follow, and it is engraved on your hands?

Go ahead, take a look at the palm of your hands.

Do you not see the letter *M*?

It's there.

God put it there.

You have been branded.

Just as we are engraved on the palms of God's "hands" (cf. Is 49:16) and he took on our nature, we all have an *M* on our hands so that we can seek to become like Mary. It may be a silly analogy, I know, but you will never look at your hands the same way again. They are now a daily reminder to you that God has marked you to become like Mary.

God is not selfish with his masterpiece. He desires to share her loveliness with us and make her the blueprint for following him and doing his will. After all, Jesus himself said that those who do the will of his heavenly Father are like his mother (cf. Mt 12:50).

☆ ☆ ☆ Marian Gems

☆ We want her [Mary] to think, to speak and to act through us. We desire to belong to the Immaculate to the extent that nothing will remain in us that is not her, so that we may be annihilated in her, transubstantiated into her, changed into her, that she alone remains, so that we may be as much hers as she is God's. *St. Maximilian Kolbe*

☆ After the love which we owe Jesus Christ, we must give the chief place in our heart to the love of his Mother Mary. *St. Alphonsus Liguori*

☆ In the Immaculate Conception, the Eternal Father prepared her to be the Mother of Mercy by preserving her from original sin and filling her with sanctifying grace and the infused virtues, which he poured out on her as on no other human creature. *Blessed Michael Sopocko*

☆ Our Lady's love is like a limpid stream that has its source in the Eternal Fountains, quenches the thirst of all, can never be drained, and ever flows back to its Source. *St. Marguerite Bourgeoys*

☆ The name of the Mother of God contains all the history of the divine economy in this world. *St. John Damascene*

☆ Mary is the living mold of God. *St. Augustine of Hippo*

☆ Saints are molded in Mary. There is a vast difference between carving a statue by blows of hammer and chisel and making a statue by using a mold. Sculptors and statue-makers work hard and need plenty of time to make statues by the first method. But the second method does not involve much work and takes very little time. Saint Augustine speaking to our Blessed Lady says, "You are worthy to be called the mold of God." Mary is a mold capable of forming men into the image of the God-man. Anyone who is cast into this divine mold is quickly shaped and molded into Jesus and Jesus into him. At little cost and in a short time he will become Christlike since he is cast into the very same mold that fashioned a God-man. *St. Louis de Montfort*

☆ It was fitting that this Virgin should shine with a purity so great that, except for God, no greater purity could be conceived. *St. Anselm of Canterbury*

☆ If Christ is the most perfect Reconciler, he must have merited that someone be preserved from sin. Such a person is none other than his mother. *Blessed John Duns Scotus*

☆ Nothing is too much when it comes to honoring the Immaculate Virgin. *St. Faustina Kowalska*

☆ A devotee of Mary will be saved; a great devotee of Mary will become a saint. *Blessed James Alberione*

☆ The Immaculate must be the Queen over all nations, and this as soon as possible, and not only over all taken together as a whole, but over each person individually. Whoever goes contrary to this and refuses to believe in her love, will perish. *St. Maximilian Kolbe*

☆ I thank you, Lord, for having given me such extraordinary feelings of love for the Immaculate Conception of the Blessed Virgin Mary. *Blessed George Matulaitis*

☆ Only by being another "Mary" for Jesus will they [souls] be capable of being transformed. *Servant of God Mother Auxilia de la Cruz*

☆ It would be more advantageous for the world to be without the sun, moon, and stars than to be without Mary. Mary is of greater benefit to the world than the sun and moon and stars of the firmament. *St. Lawrence of Brindisi*

☆ *Immaculata Virginis Mariae Conceptio, sit nobis salus et protectio* (May the Virgin Mary's Immaculate Conception, be our health and our protection). *St. Stanislaus Papczynski*

Total Consecration

ALL THAT HAS BEEN SAID SO FAR ABOUT MARY — that she is our spiritual mother, God's masterpiece, the Immaculate blueprint, and the pattern of what it means to be a holy human person — leads us to total consecration.

If we want to defeat the darkness of Satan, the darkness within ourselves, and the darkness in the world, we must consecrate ourselves to Our Lady because she alone is the one God designed to crush the head of Satan (cf. Gen 3:15). If we are on her side, we are on the winning side; but if we are not on her side, we are on the losing side.

Consecration means the setting aside of something for a holy purpose. Sometimes *consecration* is also called *entrustment*. The idea behind both Marian consecration and Marian entrustment is basically the same: namely, the giving of oneself *completely* to Jesus through Mary.

Since God has given Mary special and unique privileges and placed her at the heart of Christianity as its mother, it is appropriate that we entrust ourselves totally to her, so that she can more fully conform us to Christ. This is her right as a mother. She receives us as gifts from God, and she helps us "grow up" and mature in the spiritual life.

God wants to give us to her, and he has shown us how by doing it himself.

Who, after all, is the first one who is totally set aside for a holy purpose and entrusted to Mary? Jesus, of course. God the Father completely and totally entrusted his divine Son into her hands because she was created with the capacity to receive such a treasure. Thus, she dedicates her entire life to seeing to it that her Son is taken care of, so that he can fulfill his saving mission.

God became dependent on Mary.

And it is the same with us.

We are her spiritual children, and it is her great joy as a mother to see her children grow and fulfill the will of God. In preparation for this great responsibility, God has given her the capacity to receive all of us. She is the Seat of Wisdom and the Queen of heaven and earth. Her spiritual motherhood is universal.

It would be a tragedy and an insult to God to think ourselves "below" such consecration and entrustment. It would be tantamount to saying to God, "It's nice that you entrusted your Son to her, but I can do Christianity another way and don't need her. Thanks, but no thanks." It would not be pleasing to God to say such a thing.

Total consecration is really what it means to live *under the mantle* of Our Lady. If Jesus Christ lived *under the mantle* in order to grow, fulfill his mission, and conquer the darkness, we must imitate him and do the same. We, as her sinful and fallen children, must not deprive her of her maternal rights. She desires to nurture us, teach us, feed us, clothe us, correct us, and discipline us. This is why Jesus initiated total consecration from the Cross (cf. Jn 19:26-27). He entrusts John the Apostle to her, and John the Apostle represents all of us. And like John, we must all strive to become beloved disciples of Jesus through Mary.

When we give ourselves entirely to Mary, we allow her, and give her permission, to use us, and to distribute all of our good works, prayers, merits, and everything we do in our lives for the greater glory of God and the benefit of souls. As the New Eve and mother of Christians, she has been given by God the ability to understand what the needs of all her children are, so she distributes graces to whom she wills and when she wills. She can do this because whatever she does is always in complete conformity to God's will, at all times and in every situation.

We will go deeper into the theology of the Church as the mystical body of Christ in chapter three, but for now, remember this: All that we give to her as our spiritual mother, she can distribute as she sees fit, and where she sees the need, in the mystical body of Christ. God, so to speak, has given her the "mobility" to be able to move quickly and see from a distance what needs to be taken care of. When we give all to her, not only do others benefit, but we benefit as well.

So how do you consecrate yourself to Mary? There are many beautiful ways, and you can even come up with your own. But I highly recommend St. Louis de Montfort's method, which is the most well known. His method is commonly referred to as: *Total Consecration to the Blessed Virgin Mary*. Saint Louis de Montfort's book *True Devotion to Mary* is a theological masterpiece. Trust me, it's one of the best books ever written on Our Lady. From this particular form of Marian consecration, St. John Paul II coined the motto for his pontificate: *Totus Tuus*. This means *All Yours* and just further illustrates that if a very holy Pope gave everything to Mary, we should not hesitate to do the same.

Another awesome way of being consecrated to Mary comes from the heroic and very saintly priest St. Maximilian Kolbe, the martyr of love who was executed in the concentration camp of Auschwitz. During his life, he founded the *Militia Immaculatae*, which offers an exceptional method for consecrating yourself to Our Lady. I highly encourage you to acquire a good book about St. Maximilian Kolbe. You will be in awe of this holy priest's zeal for serving the Immaculata.

There is also the Servant of God, Frank Duff. He was a very devoted son of Our Lady and founded the Legion of Mary. In many ways, his method of Marian consecration is very much based off of de Montfort's, but the genius of his method is that he desired people to come together in prayer groups in order to live their consecration with others. I personally know many people who have benefited from attending Legion of Mary prayer groups and following this method of Marian consecration.

Further, I would be remiss if I didn't also mention the Servant of God, Fr. Joseph Kentenich. I only learned about this very holy priest a few years ago, but I truly believe he was another example of being an apostle of *Marian consecration*. He was on fire with love for Our Lady and founded the Schoenstatt movement, which encourages a type of Marian consecration known as the *covenant of love*. His writings and homilies are profound, and he spoke frequently about the need to become an *altera Maria* and an "apparition of Mary" for the world.

Even in my own religious community, one of my brother priests has recently formulated a very good method for consecrating yourself to Our Lady. His method offers people a blending together of the great Marian spiritualities of St. Louis de Montfort, St. Maximilian Kolbe, St. John Paul II, and St. Teresa of Calcutta. His book is called *33 Days to Morning Glory*, and much like this book, it offers ancient and fresh insights about Our Lady from the perspective of a 21st century priest.

There are just so many ways of giving yourself to Our Lady, but the most important thing is that you do it!

☆☆☆ Marian Gems

☆ As all perfection consists in our being conformed, united, and consecrated to Jesus, it naturally follows that the most perfect of all devotions is that which conforms, unites, and consecrates us most completely to Jesus. Now of all God's creatures Mary is the most conformed to Jesus. It therefore follows that, of all devotions, devotion to her makes for the most effective consecration and conformity to him. The more one is consecrated to Mary, the more one is consecrated to Jesus. *St. Louis de Montfort*

☆ Make every effort, like many elect souls, to follow invariably this Blessed Mother, to walk close to her since there is no other path leading to life except the path followed by our Mother. *St. Padre Pio*

☆ The Immaculata alone has from God the promise of victory over Satan. She seeks souls that will consecrate themselves entirely to her, that will become in her hands forceful instruments for the defeat of Satan and the spread of God's kingdom. *St. Maximilian Kolbe*

☆ Consecrating ourselves to Mary means accepting her help to offer ourselves and the whole of mankind to him who is holy, infinitely holy; it means accepting her help — by having recourse to her motherly heart, which beneath the cross was opened to love for every human being. *St. John Paul II*

☆ O Mary, my Mother, and my Lady, I offer you my soul, my body, my life and my death, and all that will follow it. I place everything in your hands. *St. Faustina Kowalska*

☆ O most loving Virgin, Mother of the Savior of all the ages, from this day onward take me into your service. And in every circumstance of my life, be with me always, most merciful Advocatrix. Except for God, I place nothing above you, and, as your own servant, I freely place myself under your command forever. *St. Odilo of Cluny*

☆ Mary's vastness exceeds our capacity to exaggerate her. Our intelligence really cannot compass her. Necessarily God's masterpiece evades our full understanding so that when luminous glimpses are afforded to us we find the light too much. *Servant of God Frank Duff*

☆ Oh, if all men but knew thy goodness! Certainly, they would consecrate themselves entirely to thee. Thou wouldst give them to thy Son, and thus every day thousands of souls would be saved. *St. John Eudes*

☆ I wish I could consecrate all souls to her, for it is she who leads us to Jesus: it is she that we must allow to live in us so that Christ can take the place of our nothingness: she is the safest, shortest, the most perfect way to lead us to the Infinite, to unite us with uncreated Love until we are lost in him, immersed in the Source of eternal bliss. *Blessed Dina Belanger*

☆ We entrust ourselves to Mary because she dries our tears with compassion and with kindness comforts our hearts. *St. Luigi Guanella*

☆ I wish to love the Mother of God as God himself loved her and still loves her. Imagine the boundless confidence God himself had in entrusting his only Son to her. And she remained ever faithful. *St. Vincent Pallotti*

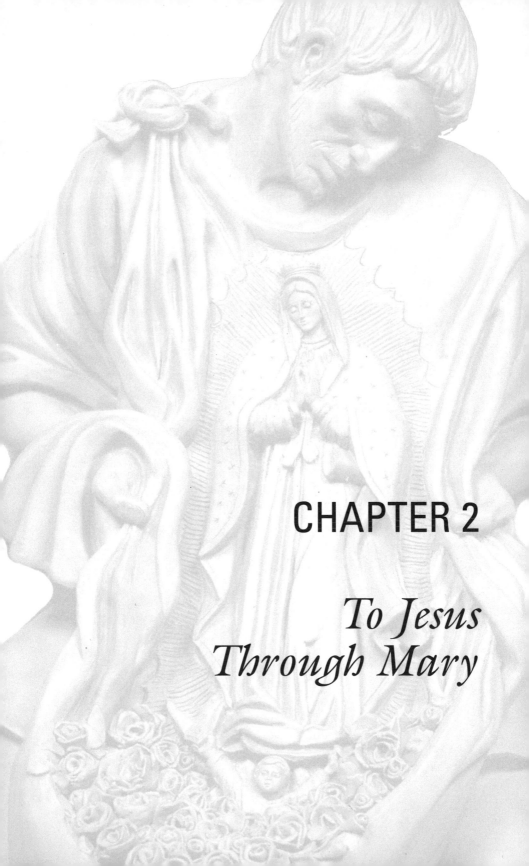

CHAPTER 2

To Jesus Through Mary

'Who Do You Say That I Am?'
(Mt 16:15)

IF YOU KNOW MY STORY, THEN THIS CONFESSION WILL COME AS NO SURPRISE: For the first half of my life, Jesus was an enigma to me. In fact, up until the time I was 20, I didn't know who he was, and I surely didn't believe in him. Back then, if someone had asked me, "Who do you say that Jesus is?" I would have said, "Who cares? He's not even real, dude. He's a myth."

At the age of 10, I was baptized in an Episcopalian church in southern Virginia. But it was largely a formality because the only reason it was done was to acquire the certificate that stated I had been baptized. As a matter of fact, no photos were taken, no family members invited, and we never went back to church again. So you can understand, then, why Jesus was about as real to me as a character in a children's book, on a par with the Easter bunny, the tooth fairy, or Jack and the beanstalk. In my mind, Jesus was nothing more than a magical, mythical character that you remembered once or twice a year.

The "once or twice a year" part I liked because I got presents and a break from school. Even most adults liked that aspect of it because they, at least, got a day off of work. But once the "day" was over (Christmas or Easter), you put the lawn ornaments back in the garage and got on with reality. As far as I was concerned, if you continued to believe in the Easter bunny, the tooth fairy, or Christianity when you reached your teens, you were in need of treatment. Clearly, anyone who grew up to be an adult and still believed in a bunny rabbit that popped out chocolate eggs, a tooth fairy who delivered money under a pillow, or a man who walked on water needed supervision and psychiatric care. Such fairytales were for children.

Sure, like most Americans, every now and then I would see some guy on television on a Saturday or Sunday morning preaching about Jesus. They always seemed to be on at the same time as cartoons like Scooby Doo or Bugs Bunny, or other fictional programs intended for children. So it always seemed weird to hear a grown-up preaching as though a fairytale were real. Anyone who grew up to be a 50-year-old man making a living off of telling others that fairytales were real was to be avoided; something was wrong with him in the head. As far as I was concerned, these people needed medication. Strong medication. Hadn't their parents and friends told them this was not real?

Sadly, I think that's how a lot of teenagers experience Christianity today. They don't have a relationship with Jesus and don't *really* believe in him, and neither do their parents. Many don't even think he's real, or even care. Even if their parents claim to be Christians, they give a totally different example by their words and actions. And now that our culture is more secular than ever, things are even worse nowadays than when I was a teen. In some schools, you don't even have to say "under God" anymore when reciting the Pledge of Allegiance. Even many, if not most, of the textbooks used in schools today have re-defined history from being A.D. (*Anno Domini* – Year of the Lord) to being C.E. (Common Era). The "scholars" and "learned ones" of our times don't want history centered on the person of Jesus Christ, especially not in the classroom.

Fortunately for me, when I was going on 20, I had a radical conversion, receiving a divine 2x4 across the face; a spiritual kick in the pants, if you will. There were many reasons for my conversion, but in large part, it was due to reading a book about the Blessed Virgin Mary that my parents had placed on the bookshelf outside my room — my parents had converted to Catholicism a few years earlier.

Looking back on it now, I can see why God revealed himself to me through Mary. As a young man, I held Christianity and its teachings in disdain, and I pretty much lived to enjoy the pleasures of the feminine. Jesus could have appeared to me face-to-face, and I would have pushed the "phantasm" aside and chalked it up as a bad psychological moment. But put an exquisitely beautiful woman in front of me, and I'm all ears! God totally knew what he was doing.

In retrospect, as an American teenager, my knowledge of Christianity was sad. Up until I was almost 20, I wasn't even aware that Jesus had a mother. Remember, in my mind, Jesus was a myth, a fairytale. Myths don't have mothers. The Easter bunny didn't have a mother. Neither did the tooth fairy. So when I picked up that book off my parents' bookshelf and read that the most beautiful woman who ever lived was the mother of Jesus, my immediate reaction was, "What are you talking about?"

Long story short, during the initial days of my conversion, I was being led to discover the truth of Jesus Christ through having been baited and lured in by the loveliness of Mary. At first, though, it was hard for me to make the transition from thinking that Christianity was nothing more than a fairytale. But then it dawned on me that if the Virgin Mary and Jesus were real, and if Mary was truly the mother of Jesus, then it made total sense that nobody would know him better than her. *That was the fundamental turning point of my conversion.*

I was just so floored by the reality that there could be such a beautiful and captivating woman — that she could be so religious, so Christian, and even declare that she was the mother of a *real* and *living* Jesus. Jesus Christ might be a myth — that's what I grew up thinking — but the very fact that this beautiful woman was so into him and seemed to really know what she was talking about made me want to look into this "Jesus" a little more. And it wasn't just any Jesus; I'd heard all about the portrayals of Jesus on television. I wanted to know about *her* Jesus.

What happened was that Mary helped peel away my misconception that Jesus was the big mythological geek maker in the sky. As such, I thought he only wanted to make people memorize the Bible and would then probably throw them into an eternal lake of fire anyway, because they weren't among the chosen ones. Of course, coming to this change in thinking was not easy. All my life, I had heard contradictory messages about who Jesus was. I grew up listening to songs like "Personal Jesus" by the English band Depeche Mode, which tells us that Jesus is whoever you want him to be. So I had many legitimate questions as I continued in my conversion.

Like, for example, why were there so many different Christian churches, each claiming to have the "real" Jesus and the authentic Christian message? I was totally convinced that the Catholic Church was where God wanted me to be, so I was already enrolled in the RCIA program (Rite of Christian Initiation for Adults) and in the process of becoming Catholic. But I just had to visit some of the other places and see what they were all about. Why weren't they Catholic, I wondered? It made no sense to me at all why there wasn't just one church. So, I decided to visit some.

Boy, was that an eye opener! In many of them, the preaching was dynamic, there was great fellowship and community, and some had awesome, pumping music, not the lame stuff I heard occasionally on the radio. But as I listened more attentively to the preachers, I realized that the message at these churches sounded really familiar. In many ways, it was the fairytale story I was used to hearing. I heard them preaching a more mythical understanding of who Jesus was, rather than a Jesus who lived with his mother for 30 years. As a matter of fact, I never even once heard them say anything at all about the mother of Jesus. And what I noticed was that certain things I was reading about in the New Testament, teachings that seemed to be quite important and yet mysterious, were not mentioned or taught at all. Why were these important aspects of Jesus' words not being presented? Where was the explanation of the *mysteries* of Christianity?

Mystery, in the Christian tradition, does not mean magical or mythical. It means a *certain* and *true* reality that goes beyond our ability to completely comprehend it (not against our ability to comprehend it). I didn't hear anything about the Eucharist (the Last Supper-Mass), the Sacraments (in particular, Confession), the Church, the papacy, the saints, sacramentals, nuns, priests, redemptive suffering, etc. Sadly, a lot of what I heard being preached made Christianity seem more magical and mythical than real. It often went something like this: "If you're suffering, it's because you lack faith; and if you don't have wealth, it's because you haven't claimed it due to your weak faith." In addition, many important theological and moral issues were not being taught. Then, if they were being presented at all, each minister offered a different interpretation. That seemed like chaos to me.

What visiting all those churches made me realize was that I had been given a great treasure in being invited by God to become a member of the Catholic Church — even my daily reading of the New Testament was pointing me to the truthfulness and uniqueness of the Catholic Church. As a result, I began to devour every book I could find that unpacked the teachings of the Catholic Church. And that's when I discovered something truly remarkable.

I discovered that Mary is *always* at the core of knowing the real Jesus and his authentic teachings. And the Catholic Church has the real Jesus — Jesus in his fullness — because they have the mother of Jesus. They love her, honor her, and listen to her maternal command, "Do whatever he tells you" (Jn 2:5). Thus, it all began to make total sense to me that in order to know, love, and follow the real Jesus, you have to know and love his mother. After all, if a person doesn't learn about Jesus from his mother, how can they be sure they have the real one?

So as I went deeper in my relationship with our Lord, I made sure to ask the Virgin Mary to shield me from the temptation to create my own personal Jesus. I asked her to teach me about *her* Jesus and *his* Christianity, not the one that other people were trying to push on me. And she did. She did it through the Catholic Church.

Here's an example of how she helped me: As part of my conversion zeal, I desired to learn more about the Bible, where it came from, and why there were so many versions. And wouldn't you know it, I learned that the Bible didn't just pop out of the sky like some mythological fairytale, which was the impression I had from the televangelists and other churches. I learned that God used the Catholic Church to determine which books were to be included in the Old and New Testaments. This is an historical fact. It made total sense, too, because where there is Mary, there is the real and complete Word, the real and complete Jesus. Mary doesn't want us to have anything less than the fullness of the Word. She doesn't want us to have part of the Word, or half of the truth. Mary is the Mother of the Word, and she wants us to have it all.

Thus, I didn't want the King James Version. Who the heck is he? I wanted the King Jesus Version! The one with all the right books, with nothing taken out or added in. After all, the Book of Revelation itself has a stern warning for those who add to or take away things from the sacred text (cf. Rev 22:18-19). Thus, I was so relieved to know that I had been led to the place that not only had the real and complete Jesus but also the real and complete Bible. Catholicism just made sense.

Sadly, though, even in light of the fact that I was totally convinced about Catholicism being the authentic way to Jesus, and was well on my way to becoming a Catholic, I was seriously bummed out by many of the Catholics that I met. They were a sorry people.

Many of them didn't really care about the teachings of the Church, the importance of Confession, vocations to the priesthood, or what the Pope had recently taught. Many of them didn't even have a relationship with Mary at all. And the fruit of that was evident in that many of them didn't really care all that much about Jesus either. Oh, they went to Mass and got all the "certificates," but so many were totally clueless about their faith and its holy teachings.

I met Catholics who were pro-choice, in favor of homosexual marriage, contraception, abortion, women priests, and cohabitation. I met some interesting people during my days of becoming a Catholic! At times, I felt like Jeremiah the prophet, that is, kind of duped (cf. Jer 20: 7-18). What was going through my mind at that time was something like this: "Thanks for revealing the fullness of truth to me, God, and for being so merciful to me and showing me the real Jesus through the Catholic Church. But your children seriously stink!"

So what the heck happened that caused so many modern Catholics to turn away from loving Jesus and his Church? The answer is heartbreaking. They had forgotten Mary.

If you don't know Mary, you won't really know Jesus and appreciate what he desires to give you. Without a relationship with Mary, it's very easy to create your own personal Jesus, your own personal Christianity, or worse yet, make Jesus into another "important spiritual teacher," maybe even reducing him to the same level as Mohammed, an "enlightened" Buddha, or some vegan guru in Sedona, Arizona, who navel gazes to find inner tranquility. You might even put a bumper sticker on your car that says, "Coexist."

I met so many Catholics who were fascinated and preoccupied with studying other religions and their spiritual practices, but they didn't pray the Rosary or read the Bible. Some even tried to "enlighten" me with their reinterpretation of ancient Judeo-Christian truths. And I became quickly aware that at the core of this deviancy seemed to be that they did not know and love Our Lady. When you don't know and love Mary, you end up with either a "personal" Jesus or a false god; the uniqueness of the real Jesus *and* his Church are abandoned in favor of a more comfortable and, oftentimes, politically correct spirituality.

Knowing and loving Mary makes all the difference for knowing who Jesus really is, understanding the uniqueness of the one Church he founded, and being able to recognize the deficiencies of all other religions and versions of Christianity. While all other major world religions have elements of the truth, they do not have the fullness of the truth about God, and cannot save. While other versions of Christianity surely teach Jesus Christ, they also are man-made and do not have the fullness of truth about Jesus. The latter may come across as arrogant and judgmental, but even outside of anything theological, it's just the plain, simple, and historical truth. Anyone who denies this is ignorant of history.

If you know and love Mary, you will know that loving God means you can only believe in and worship the Holy Trinity. Even simple logic tells you that there can only be one Supreme Deity. Thus, Christianity is all or nothing. In other words, you can't believe in Mary's divine Son, Jesus Christ, and be getting a little Buddha on the side.

Yet sin is so attractive and so pleasurable that I myself in my youth was blinded by its enticing ways, ways that made me justify my sinful pleasures and shut off right reason. Thus, I became a devout believer in the dogmatic secular "truth" that all religions are the same, that our ancestors were basically nothing but a bunch of monkeys. That's what I was taught in school — that's what everybody is taught in public school! We are not taught that we are a special creation, created by a loving God, and that the heavens and the earth were made for us. We are told that we are the problem. Mankind must be reduced through population control. And the Christian religion, in particular, is the enemy of the state and society.

Case in point: I remember a biology teacher once in junior high making fun of Christians who believed they were created by a Father in heaven and were special in the universe. He said to the class: "Science has proven you're nothing but upright apes; get over yourselves!" And to further illustrate his point that day in class, he said that the Incarnation of Jesus was stupid, pointless, and a waste of time because as upright apes, we are still evolving and will eventually move beyond what we currently define as "human" into some other life form. Thus, we needed to leave the "salvation" offered by a celestial savior to rot on the cross of the mythological religion that ignorant humans have created.

Needless to say, that dude had issues. But the first 20 years of my life bear strong witness to the effects of what repeatedly being told you're nothing but a monkey can do. I become a brainless, irrational, pleasure-seeking beast. The animal they told me I was, I, in fact, became. And life itself became meaningless, and the Incarnation of God pointless.

I laugh at all that ideological junk I was taught in junior high now, but in the days of my youth, I actually thought the Catholic Church was against reason and science and that Christians were irrational. Little did I know that it was largely the Catholic Church that educated and formed Western Civilization. Oh, I could go on and on about all that the Catholic Church has contributed to the various fields of science, but all you have to do is look up the facts in the real history books — not the revisionist history books, but the good ones.

Speaking of history, the downgrading of the uniqueness of Jesus and his Church in the lives of many modern Catholics only happened after something else occurred first. You can't redefine the God-man and downgrade him to the status of a wise guru or an "important spiritual teacher" until you first downgrade his mother, because a mother always precedes a son. Mothers always come first.

It's an historical fact that a major downgrading of Mary unfolded in the 1960s and 1970s. She was abandoned, kicked out of parishes, schools, seminaries, convents, and even the home. For fear of messing up ecumenical and inter-religious dialogue, not riding the wave of modern historical-critical and feminist research being done on the Bible, and a whole host of other anthropological, moral, and theological issues, Mary was downgraded and pushed into the background. It was all for the reason that a new model for what it meant to be church, a human person, and a follower of Christ, was in the making. And in order to fashion a new model, the old model had to be deconstructed. Mary had to go away. And that's exactly what happened.

We are still reaping the fruit of this ideology today. And the fruit of it all? You end up losing the real Jesus. And when you lose Jesus, you lose everything. Everything gets questioned: marriage, sexuality, contraception, abortion, the papacy, the uniqueness of Christianity, the male-only priesthood, the Real Presence of Jesus in the Eucharist, etc. The lesson to be learned from those troublesome times is that downgrading Mary always means downgrading Jesus, and eventually it means losing everything.

The blessed result of my conversion *through* Mary, though, was that I learned I could trust the Catholic Church to give me the real Jesus, even if the Catholic Church was full of "stinkers" (sinners). After all, God had invited me into his covenant family, and I am the worst stinker of them all.

Thus, I came to believe and remain absolutely 100 percent convinced that the only way Jesus Christ wants Christianity practiced is called Catholicism. And the Catholic Church is the only Church he founded. Coming to know this, I knew I didn't want to belong to some church that was started by some German dude in the 16th century, nor did I want some version of Christianity that was started in Alabama by Bubba so-and-so in 1970-something. I wanted the Church started by Jesus Christ himself because only Mary and the Catholic Church fully reveal who Jesus is.

Only the Catholic Church echoes what Mary teaches us about Jesus — because both Mary *and* the Catholic Church are our mother. And this is the crux of the issue concerning how we find out about who Jesus really is. Christianity is all about Jesus Christ, but if you don't know Mary and the Catholic Church, you will never truly know Jesus Christ in his fullness.

He is the Son of God *and* the Son of Mary.

☆☆☆ Marian Gems

☆ Let those who think that the Church pays too much attention to Mary give heed to the fact that Our Blessed Lord himself gave ten times as much of his life to her as he gave to his apostles. *Venerable Fulton J. Sheen*

☆ God could have given us the Redeemer of the human race, and the Founder of our Faith, in another way than through the Virgin, but since Divine Providence has been pleased that we should have the Man-God through Mary, who conceived him by the Holy Ghost, and bore him in her womb, it remains for us to receive Christ only from the hands of Mary. *Pope St. Pius X*

☆ As no man goeth to the Father but by the Son, so no man goeth to Christ but by his Mother. *Pope Leo XIII*

☆ God alone excepted, Mary is more excellent than all, and by nature fair and beautiful, and more holy than the Cherubim and Seraphim. To praise her all the tongues of heaven and earth do not suffice. *Blessed Pope Pius IX*

☆ If we have a box in which we keep our money, we know that one thing we must always give attention to is the key; we never think that the key is the money, but we know that without the key we cannot get our money. Our Blessed Mother is like the key. Without her we can never get to Our Lord, because he came through her. She is not to be compared to Our Lord, for she is a creature and he is the Creator. But if we lose her, we cannot get him. That is why we pay so much attention to her; without her we could never understand how that bridge was built between heaven and earth. *Venerable Fulton J. Sheen*

☆ If we want to be Christians, we have to be Marian. *Blessed Pope Paul VI*

☆ If you do not understand Our Lady, you do not understand Christianity, because Christianity puts her in a most extraordinary position. *Servant of God Frank Duff*

☆ Never be afraid of loving the Blessed Virgin too much. You can never love her more than Jesus did. *St. Maximilian Kolbe*

☆ He [Jesus] became man of her; and received her lineaments and her features as the appearance and character under which he should manifest himself to the world. He was known, doubtless, by this likeness to be her Son. Thus his Mother is the first of the Prophets, for, of her, came the Word bodily; she is the sole oracle of Truth, for the Way, the Truth, and the Life vouchsafed to be her Son; she is the one mold of Divine Wisdom, and in that mold it was indelibly set. *Blessed John Henry Newman*

☆ The reason why Mary became his mother and why he did not come sooner was that she alone, and no creature before her or after her, was the pure Vessel of Grace, promised by God to mankind as the Mother of the Incarnate Word, by the merits of whose Passion mankind was to be redeemed from its guilt. The Blessed Virgin was the one and only pure blossom of the human race, flowering in the fullness of time. *Blessed Anne Catherine Emmerich*

☆ Among creatures no one knows Christ better than Mary; no one can introduce us to a profound knowledge of his mystery better than his Mother. *St. John Paul II*

☆ If the place occupied by Mary has been essential to the equilibrium of the faith, today it is urgent, as in few other epochs of Church history, to rediscover that place. It is necessary to go back to Mary if we want to return to that "truth about Jesus Christ," "truth about the Church," and "truth about man." *Pope Benedict XVI*

☆ Jesus, in the manger you didn't take the gifts for yourself that were offered. You left them all for Mary, your mother. *Servant of God Mother Auxilia de la Cruz*

Mary Christmas

SHORTLY AFTER MY ORDINATION TO THE PRIESTHOOD IN 2003, I was driving down the Massachusetts Turnpike and saw the most phenomenal bumper sticker I've ever seen. I have no idea who was in the car or where they got the sticker, but it was sweet. It read, "Wise men *still* find Him with His mother!" You got to love it! I probably did freak out the guy driving the car, though, because I was tailgating him trying to read it. Then, when I saw what it said, I tried to catch up with him in order to give him a blessing and a huge thumbs up. But my exit was coming up, and I had to get off the turnpike.

Ever since I saw that bumper sticker, I've come up with a few others that would be pretty sweet to see on a car someday. For example, "*Catholics, the more the Mary-er.*" Or, following the example of the bumper stickers you see that say, "*Keep Christ in Christmas,*" I've thought about making one that says, "*Have a Mary Christmas!*" As a matter of fact, when I send out Christmas cards now, I always sign them with "MARY CHRISTMAS!" The play on words works perfect in English, but I don't think it does in other languages.

It's funny, but after my conversion to Catholicism, every December when I hear the song "Have Yourself a Merry Little Christmas," I can't help but hear the lyrics of the song through Catholic ears, that is, "Have Yourself a Mary Little Christ Mass." Guess I'm silly like that, but the truth is that without Mary, we would not have Christmas. Without Mary, we would not have Christianity.

So it totally breaks my heart to know that there are a lot of Christians who believe that the Virgin Mary was nothing more than an insignificant woman whom God used and then cast aside after Christmas. I'm positive this breaks the Heart of God, too, because it's not how God sees Mary at all. He came to us through her for a reason — to teach us something. Something extremely important.

Let me explain: Imagine you are one of the wise men — the kings from the East. You saw a star and are following it because you have been told that the newborn King is about to be born, and if you follow it, you will find him. Then, imagine you have come to the end of the journey at the cave in Bethlehem and look in and see the manger scene. At that point, you rush in and say, "Woman, what are you still doing here? You are of no significance now, step aside. We want the baby."

That wouldn't be right. That would be kidnapping. Kidnapping is bad. Kidnapping the Baby Jesus is even worse because the Baby Jesus is God, so when you kidnap him, you are kidnapping God. Sadly, this is what many modern scholars and Christians have done. They have stolen Jesus out of the hands of Mary.

If the kings (nations) of the earth want to bring their gold, frankincense, and myrrh to the newborn King — if they plan to worship him and touch him, to receive him and hold him — they have to ask permission from Mary. What person would just rush up to a mother and snatch her child away from her? That's a crime. That's shameful behavior and a big no-no.

Of course, Our Lady is more than willing to give Jesus to us. All anyone needs is the humility to ask her: "May I touch him? May I hold him? May I look upon him and talk to him?" And, of course, she will let you. She wants us to worship him and adore his divine little chubby belly. She delights to show him to the nations and make him known. She is the world's first monstrance (the word *monstrance* means "to show"). That's the reason God did it this way; Mary shows us Jesus. In the Incarnation, Mary even made it possible for us to tickle God!

He could have come into the world already formed as a 33-year-old man, ready to accomplish his saving mission, to mount the Cross on Calvary, and sacrifice himself for us. But he didn't. The fact that he chose to come into the world as Mary's little baby, to learn to walk and talk from her, is extremely important for us. It's important because the members of Jesus' mystical body, the Church, must also be born of Mary and be formed by her. There is no other way. If God did it this way, we must also allow this to be done to us. This is the will of God.

Don't misunderstand me, though — it's all about Jesus Christ. But we must remember that Mary is not on the sidelines or insignificant. She's essential to this mystery. Jesus, the Second Person of the Blessed Trinity, allowed himself to become so small that he lived in Mary's body for nine months and took flesh from her flesh, bone from her bone, blood from her blood. The God who is the Creator of all things and knows all the languages of the earth learned how to speak from her. The God who created our legs learned how to walk from her. He didn't need to, but he did. Once again, God planned it this way.

Jesus, the God-man, learned how to do all these things *through Mary* for a reason — so that he, and the people who would follow him, would be formed by her, taught by her, educated by her, and nourished by her. These are great mysteries of Christianity, and they are essential mysteries. If we are to become true disciples and followers of Jesus and to live a life that imitates his, we cannot remain under the impression that his being born of Mary and spending the first 30 years of his life *under the mantle* of his mother is of no real importance. It had great meaning for him, and it has great meaning for us.

We see this special place of Mary in the life of Christ and in the life of the Christian in a key passage in the New Testament: Galatians 4:4-6. It reads: "But when the fullness of time had come, God sent his Son, born of woman, born under the law, to ransom those under the law, so that we might receive adoption. As proof that you are children, God sent the spirit of his Son into our hearts, crying out, Abba, Father!" This passage, my friends, is what Christianity is all about. Jesus came so that we could have life through being adopted into a filial relationship with his Father. We now have the awesome privilege of being able to call God our Abba, that is, our Dad. It doesn't get better than that!

And Galatians 4:4-6 is an extremely important passage for understanding the necessity of Mary's role in the mystery of salvation, because what it is saying is that God's plan of adoption, in its fullness, came to be through a woman. And it wasn't just any woman, but the mother of Jesus Christ. Through Mary, God took on human nature and made it possible for us to become "partakers of the divine nature" (2 Pet 1:4) and be adopted into God's family. But how precisely does this adoption happen?

We know that the Eternal Word took on human nature by being born of woman (Mary), but how exactly do we become partakers in the divine nature? Did Jesus tell us anything about this specifically? Yes, he did. He would not leave us guessing about something so important. He tells us quite clearly how it happens: "Amen, amen, I say to thee, unless a man be born again, he cannot see the kingdom of God" (Jn 3:3). Our adoption happens through being born again. As brothers and sisters of Jesus Christ, we are only adopted into a true filial (son and daughter) relationship with God the Father through being born again.

It's sad, however, how the teaching of Jesus about the necessity of being born again has been redefined and hijacked by many today. Many Christians claim to be born again, but they disregard *the* necessary person through whom it happens: the woman. Think about it: Do you know of any birth that takes place without a mother? So why do so many people claim they are born again and yet cast aside and ignore the mother through whom it happens? Scripture itself informs us that we are born again through water and Spirit (cf. Jn 3:5) *and* the woman (cf. Jn 19:26-27; Rev 12:17).

Let me explain: You may recall that Nicodemus, a Pharisee, was very confused by the teaching of Jesus about our need to be born again. Nicodemus asked Jesus: "How can a man be born when he is old? Can he enter a second time into his mother's womb and be born?" (Jn 3:4). We can learn a lot from Nicodemus's valid question. Nicodemus is correct to assume that being born again involves a mother, but he is wrong to think it a physical rebirth. So Jesus responds by saying: "That which is born of the flesh, is flesh; and that which is born of the spirit, is spirit. Wonder not, that I said to thee, you must be born again" (Jn. 3:6-7). In essence, what Jesus is saying to Nicodemus and to us is that our rebirth will not come through the womb of a physical mother — the re-entering into our mother's womb — but through a spiritual mother.

Jesus made it pretty clear what he was talking about. It's not physical rebirth but spiritual rebirth. Yet, in order for the birth to have any real meaning and be understood in a filial and familial way, it's obvious that there *must* be a woman involved, or it's not a birth Jesus was talking about but something else. By using the word "born," it's clear that Jesus wasn't talking about something else. He doesn't even need to mention the necessity of having a mother involved. It's understood. So, the question remains, if the rebirth (adoption) happens through a mother, but she is not our physical mother, who is she? And when, where, and how does this rebirth take place?

This is what Catholicism unpacks!

And it's what so many people ignore in their understanding of what it means to be born again. Yes, we are born again — born into God's family. But it *only* happens through a woman, and that woman is our spiritual mother. God is our Father and Jesus is our older brother, but we have to have a common spiritual mother, or the kingdom of God is not a family. And since we become true brothers and sisters of Jesus (sons in the Son), we have to have the *same* mother he has. It's a no-brainer, really. Simply put, our spiritual mother is the physical mother of Jesus. Her name is Mary.

This is why it's necessary to have Mary in our lives; without her, we cannot truly be born again into God's kingdom. If we are going to become brothers and sisters of Jesus, then we must have the same mother. Not physically, of course, but spiritually. That's what God does for us through Mary, and then continues to do for us through the Church, which is patterned off of Mary's fruitful spiritual maternity. If we are not reborn into the life of grace through water-Baptism, the Holy Spirit, *and* this mother, then we are not doing Christianity as Jesus wants it done.

So it is that when people don't understand this aspect of Christianity — Mary *and* the Church as their spiritual mother — they question the importance of the Church's teachings about Mary and even the Church itself. When you don't believe that Mary is your spiritual mother, you strip her of her God-given privileges and honors, insulting her and ridiculing her, not realizing she is your own mother! Likewise, when you don't believe that the Church is your spiritual mother, you seek to downgrade her and consider her unnecessary for salvation.

For example, in regards to Mary, some wonder why the Catholic Church teaches that Mary remained a virgin before, during, and after the birth of Christ. They ask why the Church teaches that Mary had no other children besides Jesus. Such questions may come even from those who in no way mean to disparage Mary but who honestly want to know her better, and they simply find it difficult to understand how this could be.

Actually, for those who approach the mystery of Mary with humility and openness, the doctrine of her perpetual virginity is not that difficult to understand. For example, just as light passes through a window and does not compromise the integrity of the glass, so God came into the world through the virginal womb of Mary and yet left the sanctuary of her womb intact. Mary's womb is a sanctuary, akin to the Holy of Holies in the Old Testament, where only the high priest could enter (cf. Heb 9). Jesus Christ — Light from Light, true God from true God — is the high priest of the New Covenant. Only he enters the inner sanctuary of Mary's womb. He does no violence to the integrity of that sanctuary, but leaves it pure and intact. He can do this because he is God, and, remember, everything he does is done for a reason.

Or, using another analogy to understand Mary's perpetual virginity, we all know that morning dew passes through a flower and yet leaves the integrity of the flower whole and intact. Just so with Mary's immaculate womb and the Incarnation of the Word. She is a perpetual virgin, and yet, paradoxically, God makes her the abundantly fruitful spiritual mother.

The fact that Jesus did not have any brothers and sisters who were born of Mary's physical womb is even evidenced in Scripture. From the Cross, Jesus said to John the Apostle, "Behold, your mother" (Jn 19:27), entrusting Mary to John so that he could take care of her. If Jesus had physical brothers and sisters who were children of Mary, why would he entrust his mother to the Apostle John, whom we know is the son of Zebedee? (cf. Mt 4:21). That would make no sense at all. The reason, of course, is because Jesus did not have other physical brothers and sisters! But through Mary, he desires to have a multitude of spiritual brothers and sisters. There was only one who was born of the physical womb of Mary, but since God desires Mary to be the universal spiritual mother, he himself fashioned her Immaculate Heart as a spiritual womb. In that heart, he desires to give birth to all his children.

Jesus definitely wants Mary to be everyone's mother, but there is no way Mary could be the *physical* mother to all of God's children born throughout history. So Jesus himself devised a wondrous plan to see to it that all who are reborn and adopted into his family come to term through her extended spiritual motherhood, the Catholic Church. This is why the Catholic Church teaches that Mary is a perpetual virgin *and* mother because she is the model — the pattern — of what Jesus was establishing on earth as the visible, ever-enduring, undying presence of Mary's spiritual motherhood, that is, the One, Holy, Catholic, and Apostolic Church, our spiritual mother. Mary, the perpetual virgin and mother, only lived on this earth for so many years, but after she was assumed into heaven, the enduring spiritual motherhood of the Church remained as a visible sign of Mary's motherhood in heaven. Just as the Eucharist is the extension of the Incarnation, the Church is the extension of Mary's motherhood. We are only truly born again and adopted into God's family through her.

Did you know that the Catholic Church calls the baptismal font the womb of Christians? It's where we are born again — where physical water is poured over our heads and the life of grace enters our souls. The baptismal font is comparable to the heart-womb of Mary. We are born there. For God loves Mary so much that he expanded her heart-womb, making it the baptismal font of the Church. He gave it the capacity to contain everyone, so that Mary *and* the Catholic Church could be the New Eve and mother of all the living, allowing us the awesome privilege of crying out to God, saying, "Abba, Father!"

As we are coming to term, our spiritual mother (Mary and the Church) cry out in labor, giving birth to us (cf. Rev 12:2). It hurts her, and her heart-womb is pierced (cf. Lk 2:35) because we are being born through her pain. Mary did not experience labor pangs during the birth of Jesus because she was free of sin as the Immaculate Conception, not having original sin or personal sin. Birth pangs are the result of sin (cf. Gen 3:16). But she endures labors pangs of the heart when giving birth to us because we are being born from darkness to light, from sin to life. And she endures those pangs because she loves us and wants us to be born again and adopted into God's family. She is willing to endure the piercing of her heart-womb and all the pain that goes with it because she is our mother.

In Bethlehem, when Mary gave birth to Jesus, she gave birth not just to the physical body of Jesus but also to his mystical body, the Church. Mary gave birth to the one who saves us, and that saving mystery continues in his mystical body, the Catholic Church. All who are baptized in the name of the Father, and of the Son, and of the Holy Spirit are born of the Marian-Church, whether they realize it or not. This is why even if a person was not Catholic when they were baptized, as long as their baptism was done using the Trinitarian formula, they are not re-baptized if they become Catholic. They were already born of Mary and the Church, and now they are simply coming home. Without Mary and the Catholic Church, therefore, we cannot truly be reborn, receive adoption, and enter *fully* into the family of God. This is why only those members who abide *under the mantle* of Mary and the Church can receive the life-giving food that Mother Mary and Mother Church make: the saving Body and Blood of Jesus Christ.

☆ ☆ ☆ Marian Gems

☆ The life of Jesus Christ in us originates through baptism and faith, thus we are conceived of the Holy Spirit. But, like the Savior, we must be born of the Virgin Mary. *Blessed William Joseph Chaminade*

☆ Jesus is Head of the Mystical Body of which we become members through baptism. If Jesus was born of Mary, all those who are part of Jesus must be born spiritually of her. *Blessed Michael Sopocko*

☆ The ancient Fathers rightly taught that the Church prolongs in the sacrament of Baptism the virginal motherhood of Mary. *Blessed Pope Paul VI*

☆ Since Jesus is the Son of Mary's womb, we, too, are sons and daughters of that holy womb; her pure, virginal heart. *Servant of God Mother Auxilia de la Cruz*

☆ She is the Mother of the Life from whom all men take life: in giving birth to this life herself, she has somehow given rebirth to all those who have lived it. Only one was begotten, but we have all been reborn. *Blessed Guerric of Igny*

☆ The Wise Men found our Lord in the arms of his Mother. So did the shepherds. This is not a coincidence; it is symbolic. *Servant of God (Fr.) Joseph Kentenich*

☆ The Blessed Virgin did not lose the flower of her virginity when she gave birth to the Savior. *St. Anthony of Padua*

☆ If God labored six days in preparing a paradise for man, he would spend a longer time preparing a paradise for his Divine Son. As no weeds grew in Eden, so no sin would arise in Mary, the paradise of the Incarnation. Most unbecoming it would be for the sinless Lord to come into the world through a woman afflicted with sin. A barn door cannot fittingly serve as an entrance to a castle. *Venerable Fulton J. Sheen*

☆ O womb, in which the decree of our liberation was composed! O belly, in which were forged weapons to oppose the devil! *St. Proclus of Constantinople*

☆ For every man who is born again, the water of baptism is like the virginal womb. The same Spirit that filled the Virgin now fills the baptismal font. *St. Leo the Great*

☆ In the Church's liturgy, Advent is a Marian season. It is the season in which Mary made room in her womb for the world's Redeemer and bore the expectation and hope of humanity. To celebrate Advent means: to become Marian, to enter into that communion with Mary's Yes which, ever anew, is room for God's birth, for the "fullness of time." *Pope Benedict XVI*

☆ Behold, "the Mother of Jesus," Mother immaculate, Mother untouched, Mother who never experienced the pains of motherhood, Mother uncorrupt, Mother not deprived of the virtue of virginal chastity. She is spotless, a fitting Mother for the spotless Lamb. *St. Albert the Great*

☆ Hapless are they who neglect Mary under pretext of the honor to be paid to Jesus Christ! As if the Child could be found elsewhere than with the Mother! *Pope St. Pius X*

☆ There is no danger of exaggerating. We can never hope to fathom this inexpressible mystery [Mary's divine maternity] nor will we ever be able to give sufficient thanks to our Mother [Mary] for bringing us into such intimacy with the Blessed Trinity. *St. Josemaria Escriva*

☆ If Mary could make God small, she could also make him big and, indeed, she did. For Mary conceived him and carried him in her womb, and gave him birth, and nursed him, and raised him. What a marvelous work! *St. Lawrence of Brindisi*

☆ If Paul by his care and heartfelt tenderness gives birth to his children again and again till Christ be formed in them, how much more so does Mary! *Blessed Guerric of Igny*

☆ True devotion to Christ demands true devotion to Mary. *Pope St. Pius X*

☆ The Infant Jesus doesn't preach, or perform any miracles; he just receives the sweet caresses of his dearest mother because that is the will of his Father, who is in heaven. *Servant of God Mother Auxilia de la Cruz*

☆ The Church neglects one of the duties enjoined upon her when she does not praise Mary. She deviates from the word of the Bible when her Marian devotion falls silent. When this happens, in fact, the Church no longer even glorifies God as she ought. *Pope Benedict XVI*

☆ While we adore the Child, should we not then venerate his mother, and while we kneel to Jesus, should we not at least clasp the hand of Mary for giving us such a Savior? There is a grave danger that, lest in celebrating a Christmas without the mother, we may soon reach a point where we will celebrate Christmas without the Babe, and these days are upon us now. *Venerable Fulton J. Sheen*

'Eat My Flesh and Drink My Blood' (Jn 6:54)

"EAT MY FLESH AND DRINK MY BLOOD" has to be one of the most shocking statements ever made. To make such a statement, you either have to be a lunatic or God. It's one or the other.

Immediately after Jesus made this bold statement, many of his listeners and even some of his disciples walked away, preferring to think him a lunatic or a liar, rather than God (cf. Jn 6:66). I'm not one to read too much into numbers, but it is interesting that the passage in the inspired Word of God where we learn about those who turn away from the teaching of Jesus concerning his Body and Blood in the Eucharist appears in John 6:66. Make of it what you will.

At any rate, the Eucharist is without a doubt *the* summit of all the teachings of Jesus in all of the Scriptures. I remember the first time I heard a priest say those words — "eat my flesh and drink my blood" — at the first Catholic Mass I ever attended. I thought the priest was off his rocker. "Get some help, brother!" is what I was thinking. Who wouldn't think a man was crazy with that kind of talk? It's crazy talk!

But love does crazy things. Things that often don't make much sense. And divine love does even crazier things. Non-sensible things, I guess you could say. And these mysteries require great faith and trust on our part.

So important is this teaching of Jesus that I really believe I need to quote the entire passage here:

> "I am the bread of life. Your fathers ate the manna in the wilderness, and they died. This is the bread which comes down from heaven, that a man may eat of it and not die. I am the living bread which came down from heaven; if any one eats of this bread, he will live for

ever; and the bread which I shall give for the life of the world is my flesh." The Jews then disputed among themselves saying, "How can this man give us his flesh to eat?" So Jesus said to them, "Truly, truly, I say to you, unless you eat the flesh of the Son of man and drink his blood, you have no life in you; he who eats my flesh and drinks my blood has eternal life, and I will raise him up at the last day. For my flesh is food indeed, and my blood is drink indeed. He who eats my flesh and drinks my blood abides in me, and I in him. As the living Father sent me, and I live because of the Father, so he who eats me will live because of me. This is the bread which came down from heaven, not such as the fathers ate and died; he who eats this bread will live for ever" (Jn 6:48-58).

God's ways are not our ways, and when he makes bold statements repeatedly such as in this one, we have to trust him. God is not a liar. How sad it was that many of his disciples walked away from this teaching. They were depriving themselves of the greatest gift by not believing and trusting the words of Jesus, even if it went beyond their ability to completely comprehend it. Had they but trusted Jesus, they would have realized that although this statement goes beyond reason, it does not go against reason. Faith gives us a greater, higher form of knowledge; it elevates reason and is required to grasp the more mystical and sacramental teachings of Jesus.

These mystical and sacramental teachings of Jesus are so important that he will not change them to suit us. Notice, for example, that Jesus let those who did not accept this teaching walk away. He did not change the teaching to suit their ability to feel comfortable with it. He did not stop them when they walked off, as if he could give them a different, more "reasonable" understanding of the teaching. Jesus did not soothe their lack of comfort with his teaching by saying something like: "Please don't take it literally; I only meant it symbolically. Interpret it the way you would like to interpret it, a way that feels good to you." The fact of the matter is that he did mean it literally, but they were unwilling to trust him and stick around to find out how it could be done. The saving truths that Jesus came to give us cannot be changed because Jesus came to give us the truth in its fullness, and it is only his truth in its fullness that sets us free and gives us eternal life.

Perhaps an analogy will help make this clearer.

Have you ever thought about eating a baby? No, me neither. But why do we say and act like we will when we see a cute, chubby little baby? We instinctively smack our lips and push our noses into the baby's fat little belly, and we make funny noises while saying in gibberish or baby-talk: "I'm gonna eat you up! Yes, I am. Yes, I am!" I've always thought that if a baby had the use of reason at that point, it would scream in terror! But instead the precious baby just laughs and giggles. Sometimes, it even cries with delight as we mimic the act of gnawing on its flesh. We all instinctively do this "crazy" action because little chubby babies are adorable, and we love them. Yet, as cute and adorable as they are, we do not eat them.

But there is one baby, a divine baby, who was born to be consumed. Yeah, I know, it still sounds a little strange, but stay with me because this is at the core of the Christian mystery of salvation. You must allow your understanding and reasoning to be elevated through the acceptance and truth of this mystery. If you do not, you won't really understand Christianity and Mary's essential role in it.

So how does this consuming of the flesh and blood of Jesus take place? It takes place when that same divine Person of Jesus Christ, with the same divine flesh he had as a child, establishes and institutes the mystery of the Catholic Mass at the Last Supper. The divine baby has grown to be the God-man, and he teaches his disciples how the consuming of his flesh and blood is to take place for all future ages. The Last Supper is also, paradoxically, the First Supper because he establishes the consecratory words that will institute the Eucharistic meal till the end of time, namely:

> And he took bread, and when he had given thanks he broke it and gave it to them, saying, "This is my body which is given for you. Do this in remembrance of me." And likewise the cup after supper, saying, "This cup which is poured out for you is the new covenant in my blood" (Lk 22:19-20).

This is the Eucharistic mystery at Holy Mass, as taught by the Catholic Church. In essence, God desires to be consumed so that we can have eternal life. The whole reason for the Incarnation — for God becoming a baby and in time a full-grown man — was so that his flesh would be the instrument of our salvation. We have to eat his flesh and drink his blood to have life. And this is why the full statement of Jesus regarding this most important teaching states this: "Unless you eat the flesh of the Son of man and drink his blood, you have no life in you" (Jn 6:53).

The mystery of the Catholic Mass is the mystery of the re-presentation of the sacrifice of Jesus on Calvary, given to us under the appearance of bread and wine. What looks like only bread and wine has been transformed to become the Body and Blood of Christ. Further, we not only consume this mystery, we love and adore it; we love and adore him!

Furthermore, to prove that he has the ability to do this, it is of great significance that at the Last Supper, Jesus intentionally gave his disciples his Body and Blood *before* he was even histori-cally sacrificed on the Cross. He did this to teach them a most important lesson. And this most important teaching of Jesus (the Eucharist) requires a most important lesson (the lesson of the Last Supper) in order for us to understand it.

The lesson is this: He who can change bread and wine into his Body and Blood before he is even sacrificed on the Cross — and is, in fact, sitting right there in front of his apostles at the Last Supper — can most certainly transform bread and wine into that same Body and Blood after the sacrifice of the Lamb is consummated on Calvary and he is raised from the dead and seated at the right hand of his heavenly Father. In other words, he is not limited by time. So when we "do this in remembrance of him" at Catholic Mass, all future generations are mystically present at the Last Supper, the everlasting Supper, and able to consume his flesh and drink his blood. God is not limited to functioning within our time constraints. God is able to make it possible. For us finite humans, this is impossible, but as the angel once told Mary, "With God nothing will be impossible" (Lk 1:37).

This lesson of Jesus is of such importance that I can't emphasize it enough. The whole *source and summit* of the Christian life, the Eucharistic mystery, is built upon it. Namely, not only at the historical Last Supper were his apostles able to consume his life-giving flesh, but all future disciples and followers of Jesus will be able to consume him, too. If the historical Last Supper was the only chance Christians had to consume his life-giving flesh and blood, that would leave everyone who wasn't there bereft of eternal life! But that's not what Jesus intended. What he intended was for all future generations to be mystically present at the Last Supper, consume him, and have life.

Jesus is not a liar. If he tells us we must eat his flesh and drink his blood to have life, then he provides a way for those who, like you and me, were not historically present for the Last Supper to receive him. And the only way that Jesus established for all future generations to receive him and be transported mystically to the historical Last Supper happens each and every single time Catholic Mass is celebrated. Further, it doesn't *essentially* matter if the music stinks at the Mass you attend, or if the people around you are a bunch of stinkers, or if the priest is a boring preacher and sinful himself — not that those aren't important issues that should be dealt with. What really matters is that Jesus, the Bread of Life, is there. You will not be able to truly consume him anywhere else! You must understand this. You simply must. It's a matter of life and death.

Jesus is our bread — the Bread from Heaven that gives us eternal life. Jesus is so in love with us that he greatly desired to be sacrificed, so that we can consume him and be with him in paradise. You can hear the longing of his Sacred Heart when he says to his disciples: "I have earnestly desired to eat this Passover with you before I suffer" (Lk 22:15). It is this sacrificial meal that will save us, and he longs for us to be saved. He is our Savior and desires nothing but our good.

So desirous of our good is Jesus that he extends his incarnate love by becoming our Emmanuel food, for the Eucharist is the extension of the Incarnation. God is *still* with us bodily in the Eucharist. Our Emmanuel (God with us) truly remains with us in the Eucharistic mystery. He is crazy in love with us, so much so that he makes himself a prisoner of love for us in the tabernacle.

And let's not forget that Mary's womb was the first tabernacle for our Emmanuel, where his saving presence abides. Without her, God's Emmanuel presence among us would not have happened *then*, and without her, it would not be happening *now*.

Part of the mystery of the Incarnation of the God-man is that it intrinsically makes Our Lady the mother of the Eucharist; without her, we would not have the flesh of the God-man to consume. The flesh that Jesus gives us at the Last Supper, on Calvary, and at every Catholic Mass is the same flesh that came forth from her womb in Bethlehem. Interestingly, did you know that in Hebrew the word *Bethlehem* means "House of Bread?" I have also been told that in Arabic it means "House of meat." Isn't that amazing! Once again, God in his divine providence totally knows what he is doing, and he does it to teach us a lesson.

Mary is the mother and the bearer of the Bread from Heaven. As the mother of the Living Bread and the one who gave the Word flesh, she desires nothing more than to see us be united perfectly with her divine Son in Holy Communion. As a good mother, she herself desires to feed us with this most perfect bread — the Bread of Life. For this reason, many saints have stated that Mary's womb is like a fiery oven in which was baked for us the Bread of Life.

A good mother desires to feed her children with the best of foods, and no mother could ever give her children a greater food than the flesh of the God-man, the food that provides eternal life. This is exactly what Mary does for us. She supplies us with the food that gives us eternal health, that is, eternal salvation.

Remember how I stated that everyone "adores" babies? Well, obviously we do not "adore" them in the sense that we burn incense before them and bow down in gestures of worship. No, we "adore" them because they are just so darn cute.

However, with the flesh of Jesus Christ, not only are we blessed to be able to consume him, but we also are privileged to be able to adore and worship him in the flesh in the Blessed Sacrament outside of Holy Mass. This explains why every Catholic Church, patterned off of Mary, has a tabernacle, where his saving presence abides.

Mary's baby we *really* and *truly* adore — we worship him with the worship due to God. Mary's baby is God. And this same Son died on the Cross for us and extended his presence among us through being present in all the tabernacles in Catholic Churches throughout the world. This is the mystery of Eucharistic adoration. We incense him, bow before him, and gaze with love at the mystery of God's adorable love.

The Real Presence of Jesus in the Eucharist is not the presence of a dead person but of the living God. The divine prisoner of love abides in the sacred Host, and he resides in the tabernacle *for our sake* because he loves us and wants to be with us.

When you think about it, all of this gives Satan reason to greatly hate Mary. She prepares for us and feeds us with the Bread from Heaven. Without Mary, we can't have the Eucharist, which means that without Mary, we can't have life. Mary and the Eucharist go hand in hand. Mary and eternal life go hand in hand. She is so united with the Eucharistic mystery that she can validly say of the flesh and blood of Jesus, "This is bone of my bone and flesh of my flesh."

This is why if we abandon Mary, it is only a matter of time before we abandon the Eucharist *and* life. A parish that has no devotion to Mary will eventually displace the tabernacle, making Jesus almost impossible to find. A parish community that does not genuflect in adoration to the Bread that saves us will begin to worship themselves, in part because the tabernacle of his Real Presence is nowhere visible. Today, we need to be reminded that Mary was the first Church architect. She fashioned the body of Christ, and in her body, which is the temple of God, Jesus is always front and center.

Likewise, a religious community that has no devotion to Mary will not have vocations and a future. If religious sisters become radical feminists and fail to see Mary as their model for loving Jesus, they will lose the ability to be spiritually fruitful, become incapable of bringing new life into the community, and eventually fade away. A seminary that does not teach men to honor and reverence Mary will not produce priests according to the Heart of Christ. Such a seminary will be incapable of making saintly priests, because pushing Mary to the side leads to pushing Jesus to the side. If you get rid of Mary, you get rid of life. If you fail to reverence Mary, you cannot truly grow in holiness and conformity to Christ.

But where there is reverence and love shown to Mary, there will be worship and adoration of Jesus in the Eucharist, both at Mass *and* in the tabernacle. In parish churches where Mary is loved, the tabernacle will be prominently located and frequently visited. If a priest celebrates Mass with great love and devotion, I pretty much guarantee he has a filial relationship with Mary. Any loyal and devoted son of such a good mother will treasure the food she has made for him, and he will treat it with care. He receives that heavenly food with gratefulness and wants others to taste of that life-giving Bread that his mother made.

When a priest has a Marian heart, he will not only celebrate Mass with great reverence but will adore the Blessed Sacrament and want others to do the same. Mary is the first adorer of the flesh of Christ in the manger, and she wants all of her children — especially priests — to adore him as the Eucharistic Emmanuel.

☆ ☆ ☆ Marian Gems

☆ The Eucharist began at Bethlehem in Mary's arms. It was she who brought to humanity the Bread for which it was famishing, and which alone can nourish it. She it was who took care of that Bread for us. It was she who nourished the Lamb whose life-giving Flesh we feed upon. She nourished him with her virginal milk; she nourished him for the sacrifice, for she foreknew his destiny. *St. Peter Julian Eymard*

☆ The Flesh born of Mary, coming from the Holy Spirit, is Bread descended from heaven. *St Hilary of Poitiers*

☆ The body of Christ that the most Blessed Virgin bore, fostered in her bosom, wrapped in swaddling cloths, and nurtured with maternal love, that body, I say, and without doubt not any other, we now receive from the holy altar, and we drink his blood as a sacrament of our redemption. *St. Peter Damian*

☆ There is nothing Mary has that is for herself alone — not even her Son. Before he is born, her son belongs to others. No sooner does she have the Divine Host within herself than she rises from the Communion rail of Nazareth to visit the aged [Elizabeth] and to make her young. *Venerable Fulton J. Sheen*

☆ She [Mary] knew her office and her mission: she accomplished these most faithfully, even to the very end, by cooperating with the Son as Coredemptrix. She prepared the Host for sacrifice. *Blessed James Alberione*

☆ So submissive was he to her care that the door that slammed in her face in Bethlehem also slammed on him. If there was no room for her in the inn, then there was no room for him. As she was the ciborium before he was born, so she was his monstrance after Bethlehem. To her fell the happy lot of exposing, in the chapel of a stable, the "Blessed Sacrament," the body, blood, soul, and divinity of Jesus Christ. She enthroned him for adoration before Wise Men and shepherds, before the very simple and the very learned. *Venerable Fulton J. Sheen*

☆ Mary brings us the Bread of Life. From the day of her birth we salute her as the aurora of the Eucharist, for we know that the Savior of mankind will take from her the substance of that Body and Blood which he will give us in the Adorable Sacrament of his love. *St. Peter Julian Eymard*

☆ Because of a food, we were cast out of the loveliness of paradise, but by means of another food we have been restored to the joys of paradise. Eve ate the food by which she condemned us to the hunger of an eternal fast. Mary brought forth the food that opened for us the entrance to the banquet of heaven. *St. Peter Damian*

☆ He [Jesus] was Blessed Mary's food, her Son, the honey of angels, the sweetness of all the saints. Her life was sustained by him whom she fed. The Son, to whom she gave milk to drink, gave her life. *St. Anthony of Padua*

☆ The flesh of Christ is the flesh of Mary, and although it was raised to great glory in his Resurrection, yet it still remained the same that was taken from Mary. *St. Augustine of Hippo*

☆ In a certain sense Mary lived her Eucharistic faith before the institution of the Eucharist, by the very fact that she offered her virginal womb for the Incarnation of God's Word. *St. John Paul II*

☆ From her own womb's immaculate flesh she gave birth to the nutriment of our souls. *St. Peter Damian*

☆ Devotion to our Lord Jesus Christ and devotion to Mary are intimately united. The more we love Jesus Christ in the Blessed Sacrament, the more we love the Blessed Virgin; and the more we love the Blessed Virgin, the more we love the Blessed Sacrament. *St. Mary Euphrasia Pelletier*

☆ ☆ ☆ ☆ ☆ ☆ ☆ ☆ ☆ ☆ ☆

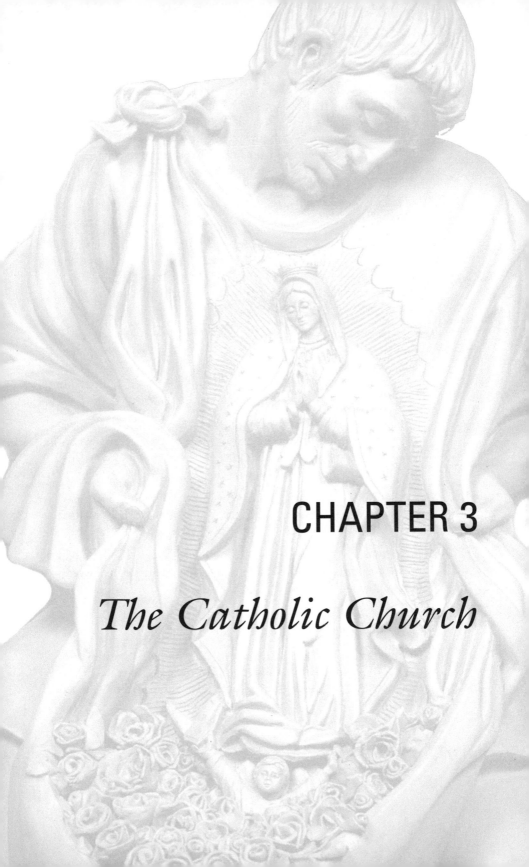

CHAPTER 3

The Catholic Church

Mystical Body

I LOVE THE CATHOLIC CHURCH! I love it especially because it's not simply an institution. It is an institution, but it's not primarily an institution. Institutions are things — and things are temporal. The Catholic Church is the unconquerable, everlasting bride of God and the spiritual mother of his people. Her mission and purpose will never change because a bride and mother are permanent. Jesus founded the Catholic Church, and just as Jesus is "the same yesterday, today, and forever" (Heb 13:8), so also is the Catholic Church! One bridegroom and one bride. "What therefore God has joined together, let no man separate" (Mt 19:6).

Unfortunately, a lot of people I meet view the Church *only* as an institution, one in which the doctrine and dogma could — and in their opinion should — change. When I became Catholic, this was one of the most difficult issues I had to deal with. I met so many people who professed to be Catholic, yet they insisted that the Church was an outdated and antiquated institution that needed to update its teachings with the times. I even heard some Catholics making statements like: Homosexuality is normal and God-given; women should be ordained as priests and bishops; abortion is a person's right; contraception is normative in marital relations. And on and on it went.

Honestly, I believe that kind of thinking comes from bad formation, a failure to understand the Church as God's everlasting bride and our spiritual mother, which is ultimately due to a lack of prayer and devotion. The truth, however, is that only the Catholic Church contains the fullness of truth, and because she was founded by Christ, her beliefs and moral teachings will never change. Let me be clear, though: I'm not condemning anyone who is not Catholic. Far be it from me to play God and judge people's interior lives. But what I am obliged to do as a Catholic priest is point out the obvious — to desire others, even cradle Catholics, to reap the *full* blessings of what Jesus came to give us — through inviting people to receive sanctifying grace by living a sacramental life as a faithful son and daughter of Mother Church.

So, for the sake of not writing a whole other book here, I want to explain a metaphor from the New Testament that helps us understand why the Catholic Church is not just an institution. Rather, similar to the permanency of a bride and a mother, the Church remains ever unchanging.

The metaphor is that the Church is the *mystical* body of Christ. This biblical metaphor comes from many passages in the letters of St. Paul (cf. 1 Cor 12:12-31; Col 1:18; 2:18-20; Eph 1:22-23; 4:12; 5:23-30). It is one of the most frequently used biblical images for what the Church is, and there is so much we can learn from it. Yet, before we delve into this metaphor, it is important to understand that the word *mystical* in the Christian tradition does not mean magical or mythical. The mystical deals with spiritual realities that draw us deeper into the mystery of God and our relationship with him. Likewise, although metaphors are generally understood to be abstract figures of speech that are used to compare two different things, the metaphor of the Church as the mystical body of Christ actually depicts a true spiritual reality.

I love the *mystical body* metaphor because it helps us understand so many Catholic doctrines. It provides a brilliant way for understanding how the Church is not primarily an institution but a living, spiritual organism that Jesus lives in and continues to work through in order to carry out his saving mission in the world. Through this metaphor, we learn that Jesus continues his saving mission on earth through incorporating — *embodying* into his *mystical body* — men and women who allow themselves to become his members and co-workers (cf. 1 Cor 3:9). When this happens, Christians are made cooperators with him in his saving work. Jesus died for us and accomplished his mission once and for all through the Paschal mystery, but it gets worked out through the centuries via his mystical body, the Catholic Church.

The mystical body metaphor shows us that there are many members of the body of Christ, and because it is the body of Christ, it is permanent. Each member of the body has a particular function to perform, and each member is unique and important. All the members are supportive of one another and work together, so that the entire body flourishes and experiences spiritual well-being. All the members of the body share the same mission, purpose, and goal, too. Each member belongs to Christ and strives to glorify God in each and every action that he does. And as in any body, whenever one member suffers, all the members suffer.

So, in the new covenant family that is the mystical body of Christ, Jesus is the "new Adam" and the head of the body. He is the origin, the leader, and the one who has the authority in this family. Yet, in order for any body to truly live, it needs a soul. Therefore, the Holy Spirit serves as the animating principle — the soul — of the mystical body because he is the "Lord and Giver of Life."

Furthermore, in the new creation — the new covenant family — Mary is the "new Eve" and mother of all the living. Everyone knows that a mother is the heart of the home. Therefore, Mary is the heart of the mystical body, the heart of God's household. As the heart in the mystical body of Christ, Mary is responsible for circulating the lifeblood of grace to all the members. Just as a heart sustains life by pumping blood to all the members of the body, Mary is the instrument through which God supplies the lifeblood of grace to all the members of the mystical body. Without her, the mystical body can't live.

This is where you and I come in. Through Baptism — and the Eucharist — we are incorporated into the mystical body. As such, each one of us has a mission and vocation and is called to cooperate with the head (Jesus), soul (Holy Spirit), and heart (Mary) in order to flourish, produce fruit, and remain a healthy functioning member of the body. We can't live without Jesus, the Holy Spirit, and Mary. Sure, like us, Mary is a member of the mystical body, but, unlike us, her role is much bigger and more vital to the functioning of the whole organism since no body can live without a heart.

And there's another way to understand Mary's essential role for the members. Many saints have noted that Mary's position in the mystical body can also be compared to that of the neck. The reason for this is because it is the neck (Mary) through which the head (Jesus) turns to the members (us). In other words, it is through the neck (Mary) that all graces flow to the members (us) from the head (Jesus). So, whether Mary is perceived as the heart or the neck of the body, all graces come to us from Jesus through Mary.

Thus, the mystical body metaphor shows us that we truly can't live without Jesus, the Holy Spirit, *and* Mary. We depend on them for life, and if we fail to fully live in union with them, we run the risk of severing ourselves from the mystery — and permanency — of the mystical body, which would be a terrible thing, indeed.

Further, there is another reason why this theological metaphor is so important for us. It gives us the awesome privilege of being able to offer up our sufferings to Christ. Saint Paul, under the inspiration of the Holy Spirit, tells us: "Now I rejoice in my sufferings for your sake, and in my flesh I complete what is lacking in Christ's afflictions for the sake of his body, that is, the church" (Col 1:24).

Obviously, on one level, there is nothing lacking in the work of salvation that Jesus has accomplished. However, because he is such a benevolent Redeemer, he desires his followers to participate and contribute their own sufferings to his, so that he can continue his saving work in and *through* us. He truly lives in his members and incorporates their sufferings and hardships into his own body. He gives those same sufferings and hardships a redemptive quality; they become co-redemptive. The abiding presence of Christ in the members of his mystical body makes the Church — and all the members in it — a living, spiritual organism that continues to carry out his saving mission!

Being a member of this spiritual organism, the mystical body of Christ, changes our view of suffering. Suffering for the Christian no longer becomes something meaningless and wasted. Through being members of the mystical body, we are given the awesome gift of being able to offer up our sufferings, pains, sorrows, disappointments, and burdens, so that Jesus can incorporate them into his saving mission and use them for good. We do not have the power to do this ourselves because we are not God. But God can turn our sufferings into great gain for the mystical body, turning them from a negative into a positive, making them fruitful and beneficial for ourselves and others. Imagine living a Christian life believing that your suffering and pain are pointless. That would be a huge bummer. It would mean that all suffering and hardship is wasted and meaningless. It would, in fact, make the cross Jesus told you to carry your enemy!

Here's something to help you understand this better: Remember the story about how Saul had his huge conversion and became St. Paul? Let me refresh your memory: "Now as he [Saul] journeyed he approached Damascus, and suddenly a light from heaven flashed about him. And he fell to the ground and heard a voice saying to him, 'Saul, Saul, why do you persecute me?' And he said, 'Who are you, Lord?' And he said, 'I am Jesus, whom you are persecuting'" (Acts 9:3-5). This is such an important event in the life of St. Paul that he recounts the episode two more times (cf. Acts 22:6-11; 26:12-18).

The important thing to note from this event is that Jesus had already risen from the dead and gone to be with his heavenly Father. So the question is: How was Saul persecuting Jesus who was in heaven? The answer is: Saul had been attacking the Church and persecuting it — even consenting to the killing of a member (cf. Acts 7:58). The lesson is this: When you persecute a member of the body of Christ, the Church, in essence you are persecuting Jesus Christ, because Jesus lives in the members of his mystical body. That's the lesson that St. Paul learned, and it became the foundation for his theology of understanding the Church as the mystical body of Christ. This profound theology helps us to understand the intimate union between Jesus and his Church, and the greatness of the mystery that we've been incorporated into. It gives meaning to both our lives and our suffering.

Sadly, however, the theology of the mystical body, with both its Marian and co-redemptive aspects, is something that many Christians have forgotten, or outright abandoned. It seems nobody wants to be a victim with Christ today. Don't get me wrong, though, nobody likes pain, not even Jesus and Mary — and Christians are not called to be masochists. But this doesn't mean Christians should run from suffering either. A truly holy soul understands the great benefit that comes from suffering in union with Christ. Such a soul knows that he only has one life to suffer for God, so he imitates Mary and the saints. He does not flee from pain, but he offers it up to Jesus so that the Lord may use it for good.

We are all going to suffer, whether we like it or not, and all of us are most certainly going to die. But the Catholic Church's understanding of co-redemptive suffering means that suffering and even death itself can be transformed if we "use our head" (Jesus), letting him transform our pain and use it for the good of souls. What the mystical body metaphor offers us is the awesome privilege of realizing our suffering is not wasted. God can use our suffering for a good purpose and make us saints in the process. Jesus himself said, "Greater love has no man than this, that a man lay down his life for his friends" (Jn 15:13).

Jesus invites his followers to have a share in his Cross and to be co-victims with him. But only those who pray and grasp the significance of the mystical body metaphor will understand this great gift. The Cross that Jesus invites each one of his disciples to carry becomes both life-giving and life-changing because a disciple — a member of the body of Christ— carries it in union with Christ, his head.

Mary, *par excellence*, is the one who shows us how to do this. Nobody suffered — was a co-victim with Christ — and loved more than she did. She was present when her divine Son was crucified. She saw him spit upon, mocked, and jeered at as he hung upon the Cross. But as the heart of the mystical body, she never stopped beating, and she never died. As a matter of fact, it was the desire of the head (Jesus) that the heart (Mary), animated and sustained by the Holy Spirit, keep the members of the body (you and me) alive while he experienced death *for our sake*. This makes Mary the very heart of hope — she is our life, our sweetness, and our hope.

In essence, Mary was interiorly crucified with Jesus, having her maternal heart torn apart. But she offered it all to God and underwent her own torturous agony in union with Christ, so that souls could have life. And because of this, God made her the ultimate model for the co-suffering, co-redeeming Church. She is the Co-Redemptrix who, though not God, is perfectly united *with* and *under* Christ and fully offers herself in union with him *for our good*. She is the first member of the mystical body who gives to Jesus all of her suffering and pain, hoping against hope, and keeping the members of the body alive as our head (Jesus) conquers death. And because of her role as the new Eve and mother of all the living, God uses all of her suffering to bring about the birth of the co-redeeming Church.

Everyone knows that children learn how to do things from their mother. As our spiritual mother, Mary shows us how to give all of our pain and sorrow to Jesus, so it can be used for good. At the foot of the Cross, the Mother of Sorrows completely trusted because she knew there was meaning and purpose to Jesus' suffering. Because of his *meaningful* suffering, there was meaning and purpose to her suffering. The Church shows us how to do this today. On Calvary, God wasn't rolling dice and hoping everything would turn out well. And he isn't rolling dice today either when both the Church and her members are being attacked and persecuted. He has a saving plan, an unchanging plan. The sufferings of Jesus *and* Mary *and* the members of his mystical body, the Church, are part of his saving plan. In fact, you have been invited to participate in this everlasting mystery. You have been invited to become a member of the mystical body of Christ!

☆☆☆ Marian Gems

☆ Everything said about the ecclesia in the Bible is true of her [Mary], and vice versa: the Church learns concretely what she is and is meant to be by looking at Mary. Mary is her mirror, the pure measure of her being, because Mary is wholly within the measure of Christ and of God. *Pope Benedict XVI*

☆ In the inspired Scriptures, what is said in a universal sense of the virgin mother, the Church, is understood in an individual sense of the Virgin Mary, and what is said in a particular sense of the virgin mother Mary is rightly understood in a general sense of the virgin mother, the Church. When either is spoken of, the meaning can be understood of both, almost without qualification. *Blessed Isaac of Stella*

☆ The Church is comparable to Mary; the Church is also virgin and mother, a fruitful virginity bringing forth the faithful members of Christ's Mystical Body. *St. Augustine of Hippo*

☆ May she throw about the Church today, as in times gone by, the mantle of her protection and obtain from God that now at least the Church and all mankind may enjoy more peaceful days. *Venerable Pope Pius XII*

☆ She [Mary] holds all the great Truths of Christianity together, as a piece of wood holds a kite. Children wrap the string of a kite around a stick and release the string as the kite climbs to the heavens. Mary is like that piece of wood. Around her we wrap all the precious strings of the great Truths of our holy Faith — for example, the Incarnation, the Eucharist, the Church. No matter how far we get above the earth, as the kite may, we always have need of Mary to hold the doctrines of the Creed together. If we threw away the stick, we would no longer have the kite; if we threw away Mary, we would never have Our Lord. He would be lost in the Heavens, like our runaway kite, and that would be terrible, indeed, for us on earth. *Venerable Fulton J. Sheen*

☆ Mary is like the neck of the Mystical Body of the Church, whose head is Christ, for in Christ we are all one body. The neck is located above all the lower members of the body and is immediately joined to the head. The neck causes the head to bend. Through Mary God bends down to us in mercy. *St. Lawrence of Brindisi*

☆ She [Mary] is the neck of Our Head, by which he communicates to his mystical body all spiritual gifts. *St. Bernardine of Siena*

☆ Unless one looks to the Mother of God, it is impossible to understand the mystery of the Church. *St. John Paul II*

☆ Mary is not only the treasure, but the very heart of the Church. *St. John Eudes*

☆ Just as in the creation of the world, every creature was brought together in man (so he is called a microcosm, that is, a small world), so in the restoration of the world, the entire church and the perfection of saints were brought together in the Virgin; hence she may be called a microcosm of the church. *St. Thomas of Villanova*

☆ We call the Church by the name of Mary, for she deserves a double name. *St. Ephrem the Syrian*

☆ If the Church gives birth to the members of Christ, then the Church greatly resembles Mary. *St. Augustine of Hippo*

☆ Mary is the heart of the Church. This is why all works of charity spring from her. It is well known that the heart has two movements: systole and diastole. Thus Mary is always performing these two movements: absorbing grace from her Most Holy Son, and pouring it forth on sinners. *St. Anthony Mary Claret*

☆ All favors, graces, and heavenly inspirations come from Christ as from the Head. All then descend to the body through Mary, since — just as in the human body — it is by the neck that the Head gives life to the limbs. *St. Robert Bellarmine*

☆ The Church is not a manufactured item: she is, rather, the living seed of God that must be allowed to grow and ripen. This is why the Church needs the Marian mystery; this is why the Church herself is a Marian mystery. *Pope Benedict XVI*

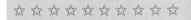

Ark of Salvation

O NE OF THE MOST AWE-INSPIRING ASPECTS OF THE MYSTICAL BODY OF CHRIST, the Catholic Church, is the papacy. When I had my radical conversion and fell in love with Jesus, Mary, and the Church, an essential part of my being set free was a deep respect for the awesome gift of the papacy. Knowing that Jesus, our head, has a visible representative on earth who speaks on his behalf so that the members of his body (you and me) can hear the voice of the Shepherd and follow him is extremely liberating. And when I learned that Jesus, not men, established the papacy, and that the word *Pope* comes from the word *Papa* (which means "father," or more affectionately, "daddy"), I just fell in love with Catholicism all the more.

Catholicism just makes sense.

Yet, on a human level, I can totally see how tempting it would be for somebody to desire such a position for himself. Appointing yourself the overseer (bishop) and spiritual father (pope) of a church, and claiming to speak on behalf of God, is very tempting *from a worldly perspective* — a man could gain quite a lot by doing that.

Being the official teacher of Christianity and starting your own church must be quite a rush. Many people have done it, and many do it today. It's appealing from a worldly perspective. After all, anyone can earn a theology degree from the back of a magazine, garner a following, and even rake in a sizable sum of money by their oratorical skill and style. It would be super easy to take the Bible and interpret it your own way, offering people the "secret" message hidden for ages but discovered by you. If it meant you had to tweak a few passages here or there, no worries, you are the official teacher of the Christian religion. Or, you could just offer your own translation of the Bible to suit *your* message.

It seems comical when put that way. But in essence, this is exactly what a person does when he "ordains" himself *the* official teacher of Christianity — *the* bridge between heaven and earth — and appoints himself to such a position. He starts his own church, takes the Bible into his own hands, and offers people his own interpretation. Essentially, this is what every non-Catholic Christian does — even if he doesn't necessarily found his own church — because every non-Catholic Christian is, in essence, a self-appointed pope. Basically, such a person is saying to people: "Listen to me. I offer the authentic interpretation of the Christian message and will tell you what Jesus meant and what the Bible means." But that's not right.

No one ordains himself or appoints himself to such an office. That's just weird. And that's not what God intended. The Bible itself tells us the following: "First of all you must understand this, that no prophecy of scripture is a matter of one's own interpretation" (2 Pet 1:20). As a matter of fact, the same Bible tells us where we need to look in order to find the true teaching and true interpretation of the Christian message of Jesus Christ. The Holy Spirit tells us very clearly that it is "the house of God, which is the church of the living God, the pillar and bulwark of the truth" (1 Tim 3:15). That's right. The Church is the pillar and bulwark of the truth!

What this means is that we have an official teacher who hands on to us the authentic Christian message; it is the Church. And not just any church, as we will soon see, but the Church that Jesus founded and established with a visible representative who has been *divinely appointed* to speak on Christ's behalf. First Timothy 3:15 shows us that the Bible is not the sole source of Divine Revelation. If that were the case, we would be in big trouble because there are tons of moral issues that are not in the Bible: for example, abortion, in-vitro fertilization, embryonic stem cell research, euthanasia, etc. Therefore, no *self-appointed* individual is responsible for determining and promulgating the authentic interpretation of what Jesus meant when he told us to eat his body and drink his blood, forgive sins, accept the gift of Mary at the Cross, etc. But there is someone with divine authority who has been *appointed by God* to teach us the Christian message and interpret the Bible, so that we don't end up with our own misguided version — that man is the Pope. If we don't have a God-appointed teacher giving us the authentic message of Christianity and an official interpretation of the Bible, everyone just does their own thing. But that's chaos. And that's not what God intended.

What God did intend is that we have the Sacred Scriptures (the Bible), Sacred Tradition (which is not man-made) (cf. 1 Cor 11:2; 2 Thess 2:15; 3:6), and the Magisterium (which means "teaching office") with the Pope as its head. In this way, we have all that we need for understanding the full message and the whole truth of what Jesus came to give us.

This is so easy to understand, and yet so many people struggle with it. For example, some people say they do not believe this because certain bishops and popes throughout history have been great sinners. But to turn away from the fullness of truth because it requires you to live with sinners is to declare Jesus unfaithful to the promises he made about the Church he founded. The fact is that in God's field, the Church, the weeds and the wheat grow up together (cf. Mt 13:30). The Church is full of sinners, and that should come as no surprise. With the exception of Jesus and Mary, everyone else who is a member of the Church, from the top down, is a sinner.

But that doesn't mean we don't trust Jesus and the Church, our spiritual mother, to lead us faithfully in matters of faith and morals. Imagine, for example, if Peter, James, and John had said to Jesus, "We really like you, Jesus, but because you allow this Judas guy to hang around with us, we're afraid that we are going to have to part ways and 'improve' things since you don't really know what you're doing. But, if you don't mind, we would still like to use your name." Nobody ever said the Pope, bishops, priests, nuns, and all the laity were not sinners. In spite of our sinfulness, God made a promise that the Church will always be "the pillar and bulwark of the truth" even if certain popes in history have committed grave sins.

I'm stating all of these things because it underscores the extreme importance of having a correct understanding of the Church *and* the papacy. Just like if you don't know Mary, you will never know the real Jesus, so it is with the Church. If you don't understand the Church *and* the role of the papacy correctly, I guarantee you are going to end up with your own version of who Jesus is and what the Church and the Christian message are all about. Even St. Paul experienced self-appointed preachers in his own day, and he became quite upset with those who chased after every preacher who offered his own version of Jesus and the Gospel message (cf. 2 Cor 11:4). Saint Paul himself, the great convert called to be a missionary to the Gentiles, made sure his own preaching and teaching were in alignment with the divinely appointed leaders of the Church, especially Peter, lest he run in vain (cf. Gal 2:2).

It is important to understand this stuff because if we don't, we are essentially making God into some kind of divine lunatic up in the heavens rolling dice with our immortal souls by sending out different preachers with different messages. But the Christian God is a God of reason and order, and he has a plan. He is not calling different people to speak on his behalf and say different things about the Bible, Christianity, the Eucharist, his mother, the Sacraments, moral issues, etc. If he hasn't established one official Church, with one official teacher who speaks on his behalf, Christianity is some kind of sick joke. But it's not.

Did you know that the word "Catholic" means *universal?* God is far from being a divine lunatic, and Christianity is far from being a sick joke. God knows what he's doing, and he wants us to know it, too.

As I alluded to earlier, there are many moral issues that a Christian has to face that are not technically in the Bible: abortion, euthanasia, in-vitro fertilization, embryonic stem cell research, and a whole host of other very important issues. So how do we authentically and with absolute certitude know what Jesus would think about such things? And how do we know exactly what he meant when he told us to eat his body and drink his blood, forgive sins, and accept the gift of Mary from the Cross? "What would Jesus do (WWJD)?" many modern people wonder.

Well, we know what Jesus would do because we know what he "thinks" and how he wants us to act since he has established a *Pontiff* between heaven and earth. The word that we use for the papacy is *pontiff* or *pontificate*, and it literally means *bridge*. Jesus has, in fact, established a bridge that infallibly links heaven to earth, so that we can know for certain what we are to believe in regards to matters of faith and morals. We don't have to make it up on our own, and Jesus has not left behind a Christianity where every Christian tries to figure out WWJD. In the Gospel of Matthew, we read about Jesus establishing the bridge that is the papacy:

> Now when Jesus came into the district of Caesarea Philippi, he asked his disciples, "Who do men say that the Son of man is?" And they said, "Some say John the Baptist, others Elijah, and others Jeremiah or one of the prophets." He said to them, "But who do you say that I am?" Simon Peter replied, "You are the Christ, the Son of the living God." And Jesus answered him, "Blessed are you, Simon Bar-Jona! For flesh and blood has not revealed this to you, but my Father who is in heaven. And I tell you, you are Peter, and on this rock I will build my church, and the powers of death shall not prevail against it. I will give you the keys of the kingdom of heaven, and whatever you bind on earth shall be bound in heaven, and whatever you loose on earth shall be loosed in heaven" (Mt 16: 13-19).

Is this awesome or what! The rock of Peter, that is, the papacy as our bridge between heaven and earth, is not man-made but God-given. All future generations would benefit from the establishment of this great teaching office. The Pope is the very Vicar of Christ and our spiritual father. When we hear him speak on matters of faith and morals, we are hearing the voice of Christ, our head — he is God's spokesman on earth. The Pope is the successor of St. Peter — appointed and given that office by Jesus Christ himself. If we truly understand what this office means and what it represents, we will not only rejoice in it, but we will honor it and defend it even with our lives. By doing so, we are showing Jesus that we treasure what he has done, and we know its importance for ourselves and future generations.

Only the biblically ignorant can make the claim that the papacy is anti-biblical, or say that Catholics worship the Pope. Anybody with a shred of common sense ought to be able to recognize that the Pope is not God. As a man, he is a sinner just like you and me. But, out of love for us, God established his office to be a *bridge* for us so that we could know the authentic teaching of Jesus Christ. Thus, we do not need to chase after the latest popular preacher. We have the assurance that the Pope can't err in matters of faith and morals, even if he himself is a great sinner. The office is built upon the promise of Christ! And Jesus Christ is not a liar.

If hearing the apostles Jesus appointed to preach in his name assures us that we hear the voice of Christ (cf. Lk 10:16), how much more can we have confidence in the one Jesus appointed as the rock of the Church? Only the Church of Peter, the Catholic Church, holds the promise that the gates of hell will not prevail against it. I don't know about you, but that's the only Church I want to belong to. The divinely established foundation of the rock of Peter cannot be moved by anyone. Thus, it is worthy of our trust and confidence, and we can build our lives upon it.

Read attentively the words of Jesus on this matter:

> Not everyone who says to me "Lord, Lord," shall enter the kingdom of heaven, but he who does the will of my Father who is in heaven. On that day many will say to me, "Lord, Lord, did we not prophesy in your name, and do many mighty works in your name?" And then will I declare to them, "I never knew you; depart from me, you evildoers." Everyone then who hears these words of mine and does them will be like a wise man who built his house upon the rock; and the rain fell, and the floods came, and the winds blew and beat upon that house, but it did not fall, because it had been founded on the rock. And every-one who hears these words of mine and does not do them will be like a foolish man who built his house upon the sand; and the rain fell, and the floods came, and the winds blew and beat against that house, and it fell; and great was the fall of it (Mt 7:21-27).

Building a house on sand is not wise; building a house on *the* rock makes you very wise. So, in order to be wise men, we need to find Jesus with *his* mother *and* build our house upon *the* rock.

Mary and the rock (Peter) are absolutely essential for understanding both authentic Christianity and the permanency of the Catholic Church. The Church cannot change or be overcome for two reasons: It was founded by Christ on the rock (Peter), having been given a divine promise of perpetual endurance; and the blueprint of the Church is the Immaculate Conception of Our Lady, the unconquerable and victorious Queen Mother!

The Church has this two-fold privilege of being both a Marian Church and a Petrine Church (the Church of Peter) because God set it up that way. Both are necessary, and both have their specific roles and functions. Only the Catholic Church has this divinely established two-fold dimension.

As a matter of fact, Mary herself leads us to Jesus through Peter. Mary knows Jesus better than anyone; she's his mother. Yet, in the early Church, she did not start her own church. She could have, but she didn't — that thought would never have even crossed her mind. In reality, she already was *the* Church perfected. Even St. Peter, the rock and foundation, would tell you that she is much holier than he; he is a sinner, she is not. It is precisely because Mary is so holy that she freely allows God to work his wonders according to his divine plan, and that plan involves establishing an office that will function as the authentic bridge between heaven and earth. Mary rejoices in this because it's the established order as given by her Son. Just as she wants us to do whatever Jesus tells us, she also shows us how to accept the treasure of the papacy from her Son and listen to the voice of his vicar, the Pope, because in listening to him, we are listening to Christ. Thus, if you truly love Mary, you will truly love the gift of the papacy. If you don't love Mary, you will not love the papacy either; they go hand in hand.

Mary, though the Mother of God, shows us how to submit to the authority of Peter, because she respects his God-given authority and loves what Jesus has established. Technically, she could have written her own Gospel account, too, but she did not because it would never have crossed her mind to do such a thing. Rather, she submitted everything to the leaders of the Church out of love for her divine Son. Yet, without a doubt, the infancy narratives in the Gospels of Matthew and Luke come from Mary. Think about it: Nobody else but St. Joseph was there when Jesus was born in Bethlehem; and it is tradition that St. Joseph had died sometime before the crucifixion. So where did the early Church get the stories of the birth of Jesus? Did they "fudge" it and just kind of make up the infancy narratives, basing them off of myths in circulation at the time? Absolutely not! Only those who don't know and love Mary propose such nonsense! The Evangelists Matthew and Luke learned about the birth of Jesus from Mary. It's a total no-brainer.

Mary shared her knowledge in submission to the hierarchy that was established by Jesus Christ, and that's what every Christian is called to do. If Mary, the greatest disciple and holiest human person who ever lived, did this, then we need to do this, too. She is so much holier than Peter, but she obeys him. She trusts her Son's divine plan in establishing the Petrine Church. She knows well that Peter is a sinner, but she obeys him out of love for her Son.

Case in point: In 2005, after Pope John Paul II had passed away, I was at a Catholic event where I overheard some of the attendees relaying their views about what the new Pope ought to be like. Some said they were praying that a liberal, "modern" Pope would be elected so that the Church could update its teachings on homosexuality, women's ordination, and contraception. No doubt they were under the impression that the Church was a male-dominated, hierarchical institution that should change.

After listening to them for awhile and feeling like I needed to spiritually vomit, I finally spoke up and said to them: "Let's pray that God does select a very progressive man to the office of Peter because you are all going to be so shocked and confused when *nothing* changes! God could elect a very sinful, deaf, dumb, and blind idiot to the office of the papacy, and still *nothing* in matters of faith and morals will change!"

I continued: "You obviously don't understand what the papacy is; it's not a man-made position that some guys in red hats elect over tea and crumpets. It's God's ongoing gift and perpetual promise to the Church that he is with us, so that we can hear his authentic teaching till the end of time." The assembled individuals, including a few religious sisters, looked at me like I was from another planet.

But the experience left me wondering how they couldn't see this. It seemed to me that they were acting like spoiled children who threw a fit when things didn't go their way, upset because they didn't get what they wanted. Instinctively, we all know that "it is a disgrace for children not to respect their mother" (Sir 3:11). But they didn't seem to care. For them, the Church was not their mother but only a mean, nasty, oppressive institution.

But the Church is our spiritual mother, and she has a right to lead us and, when necessary, to correct us. The Church, both as Marian and Petrine, is the family of God. We should never raise our voice against our spiritual mother, shouting, "Don't tell me what to do!" or "Get out of my life!" We should be mature and firm enough in the truth that we don't throw spiritual temper tantrums against our holy mother. Father will not be happy if we treat our mother with such disrespect. And that's exactly what I saw these individuals doing — it was shameful talk and behavior. After all, why would anyone shoot holes in the ship that seeks to bring them to safety?

The Catholic Church, both as Marian and Petrine, is a saving ship — *the* ark of salvation.

Remember the ark of Noah?

God told Noah to build an ark and provided him with all the dimensions and specifications. He then told Noah to get into the ark with his family and wait out the flood, because only those who were in the ark would survive the deluge (cf. Gen 7:23; Acts 27:31). This is pretty straightforward and easy to understand, right?

But did you know that Jesus spoke about Noah and the ark in relation to his own saving mission? This is what he said: "As were the days of Noah, so will be the coming of the Son of man. For as in those days before the flood they were eating and drinking, marrying and giving in marriage, until the day when Noah entered the ark, and they did not know until the flood came and swept them all away, so will be the coming of the Son of man" (Mt 24:37-40).

Due to this passage, many of the Fathers of the Church, such as St. Augustine, understood Jesus to be like a new Noah who would save his people by constructing a new ark. God promised he would never destroy the world again through a literal flood of water (cf. Gen 9:11). However, there are other types of floods. In the Book of Revelation, for example, we note that the dragon spews out a demonic flood "like a river" to destroy the woman and her child (cf. Rev 12:15). Satan has a filthy, spiritual flood that he desires to spew out to drown us all. But Jesus is our new Noah. He has been commissioned by his Father to build a more perfect ark, and he will lead his people to the shores of paradise by means of this ark (cf. Heb 11:7).

The Catholic Church, both as Marian and Petrine, is the new ark.

First, Mary is comparable to the new ark because she was made by the divine hands of the new Noah (Jesus), and his ark, this *vessel* or *ship*, can't sink. She was perfectly made; she is immaculate and unsinkable.

Mary, Sacred Tradition teaches us, is understood to be like a ship whose cargo is God — a place of refuge on the dangerous seas of the world. She alone with her divine cargo *inside her* conquers the darkness and crushes Satan's head, riding safely over the tumultuous seas of the world. Blessed Pope Pius IX, who in 1854 declared the dogma of the Immaculate Conception, wrote in that same dogmatic declaration about how Mary, as the Immaculate Conception, was like the saving ark of Noah.

What all this means is that if Mary is the new ark, we had better be inside that ark, that is, *under the mantle*. The new Noah lives in this saving ark, and so should we. If we are not there, we are going to spiritually drown. Mary can never be defeated and will never die or be overcome. She is our refuge in the storm.

Second, the Church of Peter is comparable to a new ark because Jesus himself demonstrated this when he desired to teach the crowds from Peter's boat (cf. Lk 5:3). Jesus did not do this haphazardly but on purpose and with divine intention. He could have taught from any other boat, but he intentionally taught from Peter's boat — always remember that everything Jesus does is done with a purpose so that we can learn from it.

In short, there is only one boat that was fashioned by God that gives us the fullness of the message of salvation so we don't drown, and that boat is the Catholic Church with the two-fold dimensions of being Marian and Petrine. This boat will never sink. So we don't need to panic in the tumultuous and stormy times in which we live. The Vicar of Christ is at the helm!

Jesus himself actually combines the *rock* and *flood* images in the following passage:

> Why do you call me "Lord, Lord," and not do what I tell you? Every one who comes to me and hears my words and does them, I will show you what he is like: he is like a man building a house, who dug deep, and laid a foundation upon rock; and when a flood arose, the stream broke against that house, and could not shake it, because it had been well built (Lk 6:46-48).

We need to trust and look to Our Lady, the Star of the Sea, and the bark of Peter to bring us safely to the shores of paradise. All the other boats are the inventions of men and will inevitably sink in the spiritual flood that threatens humanity. But the Catholic Church has been around for 2,000-plus years and has outlived every institution known to man. This is because the Catholic Church is not primarily an institution but our spiritual mother, the bride of Christ, the mystical body of Christ, the Church of Peter, and the saving ark of Jesus Christ!

☆ ☆ ☆ Marian Gems

☆ Just as sailors are directed to port by means of a star of the sea, so Christians are directed by means of Mary to glory. *St. Thomas Aquinas*

☆ She [Mary] is a ship of treasures, bringing to the poor the riches of heaven. *St. Ephrem the Syrian*

☆ If Peter, from the fact that, by divine revelation, he professed Christ as the true Son of God and the Messiah, merited to be called blessed and to be made Christ's vicar, the rock of the Church and the keeper of the keys, what must we say of Mary? *St. Lawrence of Brindisi*

☆ The Church must relearn her ecclesial being from Mary. *Pope Benedict XVI*

☆ All periods of the Church's history are marked with the struggles and glorious triumphs of the august Mary. Ever since the Lord put enmity between her and the serpent, she has constantly overcome the world and hell. All the heresies, the Church tells us, have been vanquished by the Blessed Virgin, and little by little she has reduced them to the silence of death. *Blessed William Joseph Chaminade*

☆ Noah's ark was a true figure of Mary; for as in it all kinds of beasts were saved, so under the mantle of Mary all sinners, who by their vices and sensuality are already like beasts, find refuge. *St. Alphonsus Ligouri*

☆ The ark saved Noah and his family from the deluge; Mary saved the human race through Jesus Christ. Noah's Ark floated on the same water in which the world was drowning; Mary was untouched by the slimy waters of concupiscence and sin. Those who took refuge in Noah's Ark were rescued from death; those who take refuge in Mary do not drown in the flood of the passions. The earth was repopulated by those who had taken refuge in the Ark; Heaven is inhabited by Mary's faithful servants. *Blessed James Alberione*

☆ When the ship of the Church casts anchor at both moorings, not only at Christ's, but also at Mary's, it will sail successfully through all storms. *Servant of God (Fr.) Joseph Kentenich*

☆ Blessed, indeed, are those Christians who bind themselves faithfully and completely to her as to a secure anchor! The violent storms of the world will not make them founder or carry away their heavenly riches. Blessed are those who enter into her as into another Noah's ark! *St. Louis de Montfort*

☆ We find ourselves in this earth as in a tempestuous sea, in a desert, in a vale of tears. Now then, Mary is the Star of the Sea, the solace of our desert, the light that guides us towards Heaven. *St. John Bosco*

☆ She [Mary] is the ark of the true Noah, to save the human race. *St. John Eudes*

☆ Consider this great mystery! The Son of God has passed whole and entire, from the heart of the Father to the womb of Mary, and from the womb of the Mother to the lap of the Church. *St. Peter Damian*

☆ She [Mary] is the ark of Noah, in which the future generation of the world was preserved. *St. Thomas of Villanova*

☆ Hail Lady, Holy Queen, Holy Mary, Mother of God, who art virgin made church, and chosen by the most Holy Father in heaven. *St. Francis of Assisi*

☆ Mary constitutes for the Church her truest image. *Pope Benedict XVI*

☆ Mary is like that single opening in Noah's ark, through which the remaining few of the human race and their offspring were preserved from the great flood. *St. Lawrence of Brindisi*

☆ At the time of the deluge even brutes were saved in Noah's Ark. Under the mantle of Mary even sinners obtain salvation. ... Let us, then enter this ark, let us take refuge under the mantle of Mary, and she most certainly will not reject us, but will secure our salvation. *St. Alphonsus Ligouri*

☆ Noah's ark was a type of Mary. As, by its means, men were preserved from the Flood, so are we all saved by Mary from the shipwreck of sin. *St. Bernard of Clairvaux*

God's Rehabilitation Center

IN *NO TURNING BACK: A WITNESS TO MERCY,* I recounted how as a teenager I was a total pothead. I started using drugs and viewing pornography when I was a pre-teen in southern California, got deported from Japan when I was 15, ended up being thrown in jail in Louisiana when I was 18, and entered two rehabilitation centers in Pennsylvania all before I was 20. But neither of the rehabilitation centers worked. Sadly, the statistics regarding the effectiveness of drug and alcohol rehab centers are discouraging. The reality is that the percentage of people who are successfully rehabilitated is very low, with relapse rates ranging as high as 90 percent.

In my opinion, most of the secular rehabs don't work because they only offer a band aid approach; that is, they fail to get to the root of the problem and eradicate it. The root of the problem is sin and the failure to conform to objective truth; entrusting your future to some ambiguous "higher power" is not the answer. So many people today are addicted to drugs, alcohol, pornography, gambling, etc., and they are in need of real help and real answers. They are crying out for healing, but they are not being offered true and lasting medicine.

The true and lasting way out of addiction and vice is the Catholic Church!

The Catholic Church has the power to turn people who have been marred by horrible addictions and sinful criminal pasts into saints. She, the Catholic Church, offers the best medicine, the best counseling, the best of everything to heal the wounded soul. And it's all free! The greatest "intervention" we can ever do is to help a person get into the rehabilitation center that is the Catholic Church. They might go kicking and screaming, as is usually the case, but I guarantee it is the only true way to heal the wounded human person.

Yet sadly, because there is a media-fueled hatred for the Catholic Church, some people don't see the Church this way. Many people think that the Church is a lunatic asylum — that only crazy people belong to the Catholic Church. There is a certain bit of truth to that, I suppose, in that we are fools for Christ (cf. 1 Cor 4:10). In the eyes of the world, Catholics seem strange and out-of-step with society. But a transformation takes place in this divine rehabilitation center that changes people from the inside out; it gets to the root of the problem. The secular world can't understand this because it's not truly interested in transforming the human person or offering them anything more than a mundane pacifier. The world is only interested in pushing its ideology of religious pluralism, secular atheism, and self-deification. Even many "professional" counselors, psychiatrists, and mental health care providers subscribe to the notion that the Church is full of nonsense and myth. They believe that it has been created by men to oppress people and lead them into an endless cycle of moral codes. And these are the people who have been "educated" at prestigious universities and are supposed to be helping others find healing and human freedom!

So let me explain how I have come to understand why it is that so many people hate the Church and abandon her today.

God is the landowner, the farmer, if you will (cf. Mt 13:24-30; 1 Cor 3:9; Jas 5:7). The Catholic Church is his field. Naturally, a farmer wants to make his field grow abundantly fruitful and produce a rich harvest. Every farmer desires this for his field. But what does a farmer put on the field to make this happen? There are many words I could use, but let's stick with *manure*. Manure stinks. It has a horrible smell, and people try and avoid it. But the farmer and the truly wise know that it's there for a reason.

Today, however, a lot of people view the Catholic Church as being the pile of manure, and they want to get as far away from it as they can. On one level, it's understandable; if you are driving down the highway and smell a farm with "fresh" manure on it, you roll up the window and speed up. However, if you want to reap the fruit of an abundant harvest, you *must* accept the manure on the field and know that underneath all the nasty stuff is something wonderful. It doesn't mean you have to like the manure, but you do have to accept it.

This is why a deep prayer life is so important for under-standing the mystery of what God is doing in his field. The Catholic Church is not the manure, but it does have a lot of manure in it. But if a person doesn't go deep in prayer, they are not going to get past the stench to understand and trust the "manure principle" of how the divine farmer produces fruit in his field. God puts manure on his field so that it can grow and, in its time, produce a rich harvest. For a while it may seem horrible, and it might be difficult at times even to breathe. But God knows what he is doing, and we have to trust him.

In my opinion, the manure in the Catholic Church today is thick and deep — at various other times throughout history, it has been very thick, too. But this doesn't mean we flee or think any less of the farmer (God) or his field (the Catholic Church). God is doing something deeply mysterious in our days, but only those who pray will stick around during the stench and reap the benefits of the field.

Anyone who gardens might see it from this perspective: If you want a beautiful rose bush, then you have to be willing to prune it and make it into something ugly and unattractive. It's the "pruning principle." You don't prune a rose bush so it remains ugly forever. If you want beautiful roses, you've got to prune it down to an ugly little shrub so that, in its time, it will become so beautiful and lovely that everyone comes and takes delight in its beautiful fragrance. It's the same thing with the Catholic Church. From a distance, to a person who doesn't have a deep prayer life, it may look like a pile of dung or an ugly, little shrub. But if you're a per-son of prayer and trust, you understand that it is God's mysterious work. Even Jesus talks about the principle of pruning with regard to how our heavenly Father makes us fruitful (cf. Jn 15:2).

So while many people believe that the Church is a pile of manure and a poison for society, it's actually the antidote — to get the stuff that is making us sick out of our systems. That sickness is our sin and vice. The Catholic Church doesn't apply a band-aid to our problems. It isn't like many of the rehabilitation centers in the world today where people gather in small groups, sit around a campfire in a circle, and share sympathy stories while making s'mores, singing "Kumbaya," and affirming each other. Such "therapy" may be "nice," but it isn't the answer to what really ails the person. It's a band-aid solution to a spiritual problem.

If you want true healing, there has to be a deeper truth involved. Sin has to be acknowledged, and the full truth about life must be offered to the human person. The truth will often seem like salt on a wound, but it will heal you. The truth will set your soul, emotions, and mind free — not just free you from an addiction and make you sober. So, for example, if you still believe that you're a monkey when you leave a rehab center, big whoop if you're sober. After all, a sober monkey is still a monkey.

We are called to greater things as the children of God. The ultimate goal in our life is holiness! Sobriety is a fruit of holiness. If you seek first the kingdom of God, you get everything else (cf. Mt 6:33). But if you seek first the things of the world, you get nothing, not even the world.

The Catholic Church invites everyone in and helps each person participate in God's rehabilitation center. In the Catholic Church, God offers divine detoxification where we literally get our heads checked out, receive a blood transfusion, and undergo a heart transplant. We are truly transformed in this hospital because the Divine Physician is Jesus and the heavenly nurse is Mary. But we have to be willing to submit to Jesus and trust his plan. It's much the same process as going to a medical doctor, where you need to have the humility to let the doctor guide you.

Of course, as the Divine Physician, God knows everything that's wrong with us. But we've got to tell him what we've done as an act of humility so that the Divine Physician (who is not going to do things against our will) is given permission to operate on us and work his wonders in our souls. Divine detox is the only way to get the poison of the world out of our systems.

Unlike the prescriptions of the world, where they go up in price, are always changing, and do not heal the soul, the prescription of Jesus never changes. Jesus is both our physician and our prescription (medication), and he is the same yesterday, today, and forever (cf. Heb 13:8). He offers us himself: "Unless you eat the flesh of the Son of man and drink his blood, you have no life in you" (Jn 6:53). Both Jesus and his sacred teachings are offered to us through the Catholic Church, and they set us free. Catholicism gets the poison out of us.

The bottom line is that the Catholic Church is the answer for what ails the world and mankind. It's the spiritual hospital that God established for a fallen world. By surrendering our lives to Jesus and allowing him — with the aid of his heavenly nurse, Our Lady — to help us, we can recover and become like a fruitful, bountiful field or a rose bush in full bloom. We can become like spring emerging after the dead of winter. You can never have a spring without a winter or a dawn without a night.

That's what is happening in our souls when we trust the Church and her rehabilitation process. We have to look beyond the stench and the stinkers, the painful pruning, and the darkness of night. We know that the transformation comes through the purifying fire and healing medicine, which is the teaching of the Church and her Sacraments. The Sacraments and the teaching of the Catholic Church are the best medicine we could ever have, and it's free! You literally can go every day to get a daily dose of this life-giving medicine at Holy Mass.

As we will see in the next chapter, the hospital of God is so very blessed to have Our Lady as its heavenly nurse, who works with the Divine Doctor as a physician's assistant. Every doctor has one. The nurse assists the doctor and sees the patient before and after the doctor works his wonders. Our Lady is that heavenly nurse. She is the one who takes our vital signs and prepares us for the operation. She is the one who holds our hand and caresses our arm and looks into our eyes, telling us that we are going to be okay as we go under the knife. Mary is the one that brings us comfort in a difficult time and assists the doctor during our surgery. She gives the doctor the instruments through which he is able to save us. And the instrument of our salvation is the flesh of Jesus Christ. Mary gave God that instrument — that flesh. Mary and the Catholic Church give us the antidote to sin and the saving remedy that gets the poison out of us.

☆ ☆ ☆ Marian Gems

☆ After Christ, Mary is the greatest of God's blessings sent to the Church, the gift of gifts beyond our comprehension, because she can do all things for us with God. *St. Lawrence of Brindisi*

☆ Let us then, whoever we may be, bless forever the divine goodness which gave us Mary as our Mother, our spiritual nurse, and our mediatrix. *Blessed William Joseph Chaminade*

☆ Mary places herself between her Son and mankind in the reality of their wants, needs and sufferings. She puts herself "in the middle," that is to say she acts as a mediatrix not as an outsider. *St. John Paul II*

☆ Oh, what great sorrow it must have been for the Mother, after Jesus was born, to think that they had to then crucify him! What pangs she must have always had in her heart! How many sighs she must have made, and how many times she must have wept! Yet she never complained. *St. Gemma Galgani*

☆ As one cannot go to a statue of a mother holding a child and cut away the mother without destroying the child, so neither can one have Jesus without his Mother. Could you claim as a friend one who, every time he came into your home, refused to speak to your mother or treated her with cold indifference? Jesus cannot feel pleased with those who never give recognition to or show respect for his Mother. Coldness to his Mother is certainly not the best way to keep warm a friendship with him. The unkindest cut of all would be to say that she who is the Mother of our Lord is unworthy of being our Mother. *Venerable Fulton J. Sheen*

☆ Take away the sun that illumines the world, and the day is gone. Take away Mary, the Star of the Sea of the great, wide ocean: What then is left, but deepest darkness, the shadows of death, and impenetrable midnight? *St. Bernard of Clairvaux*

☆ It appears to be of tremendous importance to the living God, the One Who rules and guides world history, that his Mother be glorified. By using instruments that are childlike and humble, courageous and trusting, he wants to have Mary's triumphal chariot drawn onto the battlefield of today's crisis-filled era, and in that way regain peace for the world. That is why God never tires of repeating, through the lips of the Popes, the last will and testament of our Savior — *Ecce Mater tua. Servant of God (Fr.) Joseph Kentenich*

☆ Blessed are those who nourish a deep devotion to Mary. Though she is mother of all, she harbors a special love for those who turn to her with heartfelt devotion. *St. Lawrence of Brindisi*

☆ We cannot enter a house without first speaking to the porter. Similarly, we cannot enter heaven without calling upon the aid of the Blessed Virgin Mary who is the Portress of Heaven. *St. John Vianney*

☆ A tender devotion towards the Immaculate Mother of God is one of the most powerful means of counteracting within us the effects of the virus emanating from the fatal tree of the terrestrial paradise. *Blessed Ildefonso Schuster*

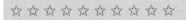

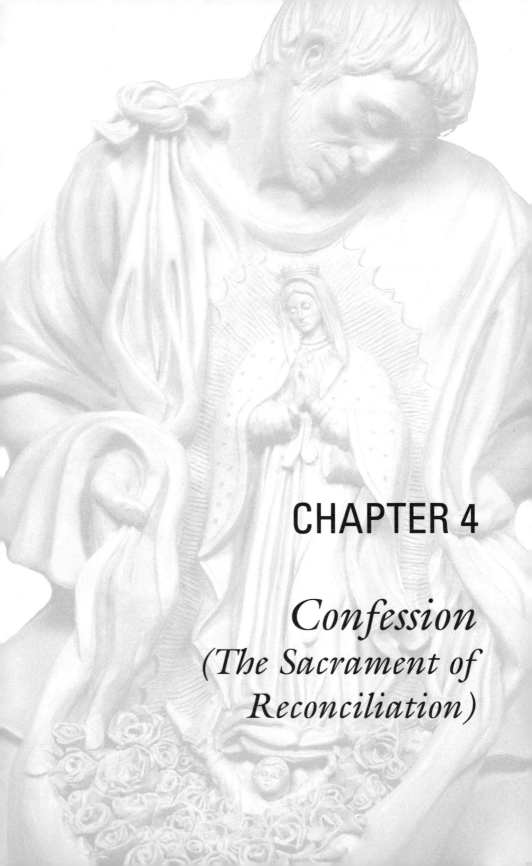

CHAPTER 4

Confession
(The Sacrament of
Reconciliation)

The Curtain of Mercy

W HO AMONG US HASN'T BEEN TO A HOSPITAL? I know
I've definitely logged in my hours behind a hospital curtain! I've been admitted to the hospital so many times it's ridicu-
lous. I've had emergency gall bladder surgery in California, been
in a motorcycle accident that broke my shoulder in West
Virginia, cracked my head open while surfing in Mexico, and
over the years received so many stitches all over my body that I've
gotten used to just taking out the stitches myself. And by far, the
most painful of all my hospital visits were the five occasions (so far)
that I've been plagued with wicked kidney stones. The pain and
bodily torture I go through from kidney stones just about kills
me. I'm literally on the floor in absolute agony, moaning like a
dying man. Having kidney stones is one of the worst pains imaginable — even worse, I'm told, than childbirth.

I am extremely grateful, therefore, that hospitals and doctors
are around. Without them, I could quite possibly be dead right
now. I simply can't deny all the good and all the healing they have
given to me over the years.

In looking back on all my visits to the hospital, I've noticed
that there has always been a certain protocol of how things were
done, with certain persons and things always being present.
Obviously, there has always been a physician; he's the one who is
primarily responsible for helping those who come to him. But I've
also noticed that, in addition to the physician, there are always
two other things present: a nurse and a curtain.

I never paid much attention to these before, but being a
Catholic has changed my outlook on everything. And in light of
this, I think that both the presence of the nurse and the curtain take
the analogy of the Church as a hospital to an even deeper level,
especially when it comes to understanding what truly happens in
the Sacrament of Reconciliation.

Here's a personal example of how this all became very clear to me: One year, during my studies as a seminarian, I noticed a growth on my right side just above my hip. I had no idea what it was, or why it was there. It just seemed to appear out of nowhere. At first, I didn't give much thought to it. But as the months went by, it really started to bother me, because it definitely was growing. So I finally went to the hospital to get it checked out.

After having my vitals taken by the nurse and being examined by the physician, I was relieved when the doctor said that my skin growth didn't seem to be anything other than fatty tissue. I guess I had been eating too many Big Macs or something. But I wasn't totally off the hook because he also informed me that although it wasn't a problem now, the X-rays showed that it could become a problem later in life.

As it turned out, it became a problem sooner rather than later. Within a year and a half, it had doubled in size and was really worrying me. Every time I took a shower I had thoughts of cancer running through my head. So I went back to the doctor, and he recommended that I have the growth surgically removed.

I went in for elective surgery several weeks later, but instead of a general anesthesia, I only received a local anesthetic. This surprised me because the surgeon was going to remove a sizable chunk of flesh from my body, but I trusted his judgment. Other than that, the pre-op experience proceeded as had always been done during all of my previous hospital visits. Namely, the nurse prepped me for surgery, led me to the physician in the operating room, drew a curtain around the operating table, and assisted both the doctor and me during the operation.

This protocol and routine I was very familiar with, but I had never really paid much attention to it before. But now, as a seminarian, I was seeing something that totally paralleled what God does with our souls in Confession.

First of all, I know I can't heal myself. I don't have the ability to do such a thing. That's why we go to a doctor. Certain people have been entrusted with a vocation that helps others get physically better — they are called physicians — and I think we are all grateful that they are around. Furthermore, the physician normally conducts his practice in a hospital and in the presence of the patient. Sure, we can all call a physician and get advice, but no surgery happens from a distance. It's up close and personal and not done, for example, over the phone.

Secondly, I observed that the nurse was the one who I always saw first. She prepped me for the surgery, took my vitals, made sure I was ready, then led me to the operating room and drew a curtain around me so the whole procedure was done in private. And not only that, but the nurse remained by my side throughout the entire operation, assisting the doctor, and even caressing my arm during the surgery, telling me that everything was going to be fine.

Thirdly, the curtain seemed to serve as a shield from the world; it made the operation personal and private. After all, I was naked on that table. Behind that curtain is where my healing was going to take place, my insides revealed, and where the miracle of medicine would be performed on my body so that I could get better. Amazing things would happen behind that curtain, things beyond my understanding; things I could not do myself. It was a curtain of mercy.

In fact, during this particular surgery, the nurse was so comforting and consoling that I was almost oblivious to what the surgeon was doing behind the curtain. The nurse served as a mediatrix between the doctor and me. In no way did she interfere with what the doctor was doing, but the doctor himself relied upon her for assistance. I could not even see the doctor from where I was lying due to the cloths that were draped between the physician and me, but I would have been a fool to deny his presence. I could hear his voice and see the nurse handing him tools and conversing with him, but I couldn't see him.

And the presence of the nurse gave me such a sense of peace as I looked into her reassuring eyes all throughout the surgery. The nurse mediated between me and the doctor, and it all felt so rightly ordered and human. It felt right because as a human person, each of us has an anthropological need to be in communication with someone who is in direct contact with the physician who is operating on us *because we can't see him*. So when the operation was over, I thanked the nurse for being there and for making it a peaceful experience by relaying to me what the doctor had done.

The Sacrament of Reconciliation (Confession) greatly parallels all of this experience of surgery. We have a physician, a nurse, and a curtain of mercy. In Confession, we are spiritually operated on, given new life, and healed of the filthy ailment that plagues our souls: sin.

It's obvious that Jesus is the Divine Physician. He alone has the power to heal our souls and bring us back into the life of grace. Without him, we can't live. But he does not walk this earth like he did 2,000 years ago. We do not see him with our eyes. But that doesn't mean he is not with us. On the contrary, he loves us so much and is such a humble and good doctor that he continues to do his saving work through others, without us even seeing him. Much like I didn't need to see the surgeon who operated on my body that day in the hospital, when a person goes to Confession, he does not see Jesus sitting on the other side of the curtain. But the person does hear his representative and knows that this means Jesus is there.

Jesus has entrusted the vocation of being spiritual doctors to his priests. The priest speaks on Jesus' behalf when the words of absolution are said: "I absolve you from your sins in the name of the Father, and of the Son, and of the Holy Spirit." At that moment, you know that you have been healed and restored to spiritual health — your sins are forgiven. It's a merciful act, an extremely deep, personal encounter with the Divine Physician who heals you through the mediation of his representative. And that's really what the Sacrament of Reconciliation is; it's an entering into an amazing healing experience of Divine Mercy.

And Our Lady and the Church are so important in all of this. They both serve as mediators and as heavenly nurses. They welcome us, prep us, lead us to the Divine Physician (and his representative, the priest), draw the curtain of mercy, assist him with the surgery, and comfort us. And in a certain sense, they hold our hand as we go under the spiritual knife. Just as we go to a doctor through the nurse, so we go to Jesus through Our Lady and the Church. This is natural, normal, and how things work. God has not established a different system for how he heals us than what we are familiar with regarding how we are treated in a hospital. The supernatural greatly parallels the natural.

In retrospect, I had already had an insight into this hospital-like aspect of the Church during a mystical experience I had while attending my first Catholic Mass. After that Mass was over, I had bumped into a door in the back of the Church with a curtain hanging next to it, with a sign above it that read, "Confession." In an instant, I knew that whatever happened behind that curtain had to be something amazing, something wonderful. I had simply been in too many hospitals not to recognize the sign of a surgical curtain. I would learn more in-depth about this great mystery of the Sacrament of Reconciliation as I was becoming a Catholic, especially later as I was preparing to hear confessions as a newly ordained priest. But the mere fact that I saw a curtain shouted out to my soul that there was healing behind that curtain.

Jesus loves us so much that he established this great Sacrament because he knows we are going to need it. And it's right in the Bible!

Recall what Jesus told his apostles after he had risen from the dead: "If you forgive the sins of any, they are forgiven; if you retain the sins of any, they are retained" (Jn 20:23). I love this passage! Jesus gave his apostles, the first priests, the power to absolve sin. This means that Confession wasn't invented by men or an institution. It is of divine origin. All the details of how this Sacrament would be performed would be provided by the Holy Spirit, who guides the Church into all truth (cf. Jn 16:13), but the fact remains that Jesus Christ himself established this Sacrament. The Church, which is "the pillar and bulwark of the truth" (1 Tim 3:15), provides the Sacrament with its ritual form, but it did not create it. This is such a beautiful gift from our Savior and is one of the greatest treasures that the Catholic Church offers. Those who do not accept this are seriously depriving themselves of the full message of Jesus Christ and the true human freedom that Confession offers.

As our Creator, God fully knows our human needs. He knows that as wounded, fallen human persons, we are anthropologically messed up. When we sin, we don't just sin in our souls; we sin in our bodies, emotions, passions, etc. Thus, as human persons, we need to audibly hear that God's mercy has been spoken to us personally. And that was not only 2,000 years ago, but it is now, today, to me personally. Just as Jesus intended his Eucharistic Presence to be received by all future generations and not just at the historical Last Supper, so is the case also with the distribution of his mercy in Confession.

Remember how I noted that it's awesome that the apostles were blessed to be able to consume the flesh of Jesus at the Last Supper, but it does us no good if we can't receive it, too? Well, it's the same reality with God's mercy. Jesus established Confession not just so that his apostles could forgive sins in his name 2,000 years ago, but he did it so that all souls in the future could encounter the mercy of God through this great Sacrament. Thus, he gave the distribution of his mercy to his apostolic priests and sent them out to the ends of the earth to set up hospitals (Catholic churches) so that all can come and receive his mercy. Just as we need to go to a surgeon for him to operate on us, we also need to go to *the* place of healing that God himself established so that we can be operated on in our spiritual lives and receive healing in our souls. That place is the Catholic Church.

And all of this happens through the mediated sacramental system God established.

Mediation, by the way, is quite natural and normal in life — on many different levels. God set up a natural order of how things are done, and that order involves mediation. Mediation does not downplay God's part, either. In actuality, it glorifies God's goodness because it displays his generosity in allowing creatures the ability to act as cooperators and mediators of his graces and mercies. God is so good that he wants and delights in our participation and cooperation.

You could think of a million examples in life where people mediate for one another and ask each other for help: prayer, making someone dinner, teaching a child to read, helping an elderly person cross the street, letting someone open a door for you, etc. There are just tons of ways we mediate for one another in daily life. Even anyone who goes to a doctor is receiving the mediated healing of God through the physician who operates on you. If you don't go to the doctor, you are not going to get better. And this principle of mediation is how things are done in the spiritual life, too.

Yet, sadly, there are some who claim that this is not true. But to claim this goes against our experience of being human. Claiming that you can go directly to Jesus and do not need the help of others turns Christianity into a privatized religion, and that's not what Christianity is about. Such thinking degrades the beauty of the human and familial dimension of Christianity; it calls the biblical Jesus who told his apostles to baptize, forgive sins, and celebrate the Eucharist a liar. Seeking to bypass the human foundations of Christianity turns Christianity into a magical religion.

Such thinking breaks down what Jesus came to do: namely, to bring us into a familial relationship with his heavenly Father by offering us an elevated, yet truly anthropological and fully personal, relationship with the Father *through* Jesus, his Son, *and* the Church, our mother. Jesus set up this method of being reconciled because we are not angels, robots, or monkeys. Reconciliation restores relationships and brings the family back together. And no family is a true family without mediation.

At its core, Christianity teaches us that to become truly free and holy human persons, we must allow God to mediate his graces and mercies to us through others.

Think about this: technically, God didn't need to become man to save us. He could have just uttered a mighty word of forgiveness from the heavens, and we would have all been immediately saved. But he didn't do it that way. To do it that way would have been to treat us as something other than human. Additionally, he didn't technically need to tell his apostles that "he whose sins you forgive are forgiven." But the fact remains that he did. And he did it for a reason.

The reason is because we are human persons and have been invited into God's family as human persons; and as human persons, we have emotions and psychological needs that must be met. Christianity is about healing and elevating the whole human person, not just our souls. Thus, due to our human anthropological necessities, we need to be personally told that we are forgiven. We need to experience this through a personal encounter with the God of mercy. This happens in Confession.

In Confession, we do not see God with our eyes or hear him with our ears, but we do mystically see and hear him when we trust the sacramental system that he has set up to heal our fallen human condition. God uses his representative to speak to us, and the power of God's words, spoken through his representative, makes for a real change in our human condition.

Recall that in Latin the word "*sacramentum*" means *oath*. This is extremely important because it tells us that God has sworn an oath to us regarding his fatherly love for us. He has promised to be faithful to it even if the priest who hears your confession is struggling with his own issues and is flawed. If we trust God and his Sacrament of Reconciliation, we know for certain on both a human and spiritual level that God is saying to us through his flawed representative, "I promise you — *I swear to you* — that I forgive you." That's what Jesus established when he said to his priests, "If you forgive the sins of any, they are forgiven" (Jn 20:23).

Jesus knew his apostles were flawed, but that didn't stop him from establishing the Sacrament. Similarly, God knows that young, immature men and women who conceive a child in a night of lust are flawed, too, but that doesn't stop God from bringing a new life into the world because he is madly in love with life.

If we fail to think that we need the human element of Confession, we are either very proud, lacking an understanding of what Christianity and human nature are all about, or think of ourselves as above a mediated love. Only the person who understands what it means to be a human person knows the power of Confession.

Confession is not magic any more than the practice of medicine is magic; both are a gift from the Heart of a merciful Father, one for the healing of our souls (interior life), the other for the healing of our bodies. Thus, even the Old Testament informs us, "Do not be afraid to confess your sins" (Sir 4:26). No one should be afraid to go to Confession and enter behind the curtain of mercy. What have you to fear? God knows everything already, but because you are not a robot or a monkey, Father God wants to hear you acknowledge your sins to him through his representative, the priest. You have to be humble to treasure the Sacrament of Reconciliation. Arrogant people do not go to Confession.

Confession heals the whole person, mind, body, and soul. I can't tell you the number of times that I've felt like skipping and dancing down the aisle after leaving the confessional. Through the mediation of the Church and the priest, I have tasted the freedom of my heavenly Father given to me behind that curtain of mercy. And I love my Father God so much because he treats me as a son, a family member. He fulfills his oath of mercy to me every single time I humble myself and go to Confession.

Dad is happy, Mom is happy, and I'm happy! And I have emotional and psychological peace because I have absolute certainty, on a human and spiritual level, that I have been unburdened of all that pressure and pain that was on my soul — all weighing me down and putting me in a torturous funk. Anyone who has known the freedom of being relieved of the pain and torture of kidney stones knows that there is a moment when you feel that instant relief, and the pain is totally gone. It's the same with absolution in Confession. In an instant, you are free!

☆ ☆ ☆ Marian Gems

☆ Through her [Mary], the long warfare waged with the Creator has been ended. Through her, the reconciliation between us and him was ratified. Grace and peace were granted us, so that men and angels are united in the same choir, and we, who had been deserving of disdain, have become sons of God. From her we have harvested the grape of life; from her we have cultivated the seed of immortality. For our sake she became Mediatrix of all blessings; in her God became man, and man became God. *St. John Damascene*

☆ She is the sanctuary, she is the mercy seat, she is the ark of the covenant, she is the urn containing the endlessly sweet manna from heaven. *St. Thomas of Villanova*

☆ Whoever consistently looks at God and themselves through this attractive mirror [Mary], will sooner or later turn into another Mary. *Servant of God (Fr.) Joseph Kentenich*

☆ Those who have great devotion to Mary not only will be saved but also will, through her intercession, become great saints. *St. Vincent Pallotti*

☆ No one is saved except through you, O All-Holy. No one is delivered from evils except through you, O All-Chaste. No one obtains the grace of mercy except through you, O All-Honorable. *St. Germanus of Constantinople*

☆ If Christ, the God-man, is the supreme and omnipotent Mediator by nature, Mary, the Mother of God, is Mediatrix by grace, as by grace she is omnipotent: her prayer is most efficacious and her mediation infallible. *St. Luigi Orione*

☆ Mary is our Coredemptrix with Jesus. She gave Jesus his body and suffered with him at the foot of the Cross. *St. Teresa of Calcutta*

☆ The apostle Paul exhorts those who want to obtain grace that they should approach the throne of grace; in other words, the glorious Virgin. *St. Bonaventure*

☆ While remaining the mother of our Judge, Mary is a mother to us, full of mercy. She constitutes our protection. She keeps us close to Christ, and she faithfully takes the matter of our salvation into her charge. *St. Peter Canisius*

Spiritual Diaper Change

AN AMAZING ASPECT ABOUT CONFESSION IS THAT IT DOESN'T COST A DIME — it never has and never will. After all, what father would charge for a diaper change?

That's right, a diaper change.

The analogy of Confession being like a spiritual diaper change came to me one day during prayer. It has helped me ever since to better understand just how loved we are and why we should frequent this great Sacrament.

Let me explain: In the spiritual life, we are always going to be like children in God's eyes. It doesn't matter if we are 2 months old, 35 years old, or 82. And in this fallen world, the reality is that until we reach perfect maturity in Christ and enter paradise, we are going to make a mess of things — a lot. This is a valley of tears. Even the Bible states that the just man sins seven times a day (cf. Prov 24:16). This is why comparing Confession to a spiritual diaper change can help us understand just how great our heavenly Father's love is for us and why Jesus set things up the way he did.

We all know that babies soil themselves — a lot. A stinky baby gets the attention of everybody in the room, too. It's one of the worst smells known to man; it's nasty and most times downright disgusting. And a baby is going to do this thousands of times as he grows up.

It is up to the parents to clean their child. The baby is incapable of cleaning himself and has to completely rely on his parents. Without them, the stench will never go away, becoming worse and eventually even visibly noticeable. No parent waits for that to happen — no good parent, anyway.

Parents need to have great patience with the child, too. They have to be willing to clean up the child every single time he soils himself. There is no "once cleaned, always cleaned" situation when it comes to taking care of a child. No parent would ever say to a child, "What's this? I cleaned you yesterday! No more cleaning for you!" It doesn't mean the parent has to like the stinky mess or the fact that the child is soiling himself, but the child totally depends on the parent for the diaper change.

In our spiritual lives, all of this is quite analogous. Throughout our lives, as we grow into full maturity in Christ, we are going to spiritually soil ourselves a lot, becoming stinky and filthy. And sin does stink. It really does. Certain saints have even noted that they can "smell" the stench of sin on souls. And the more you walk around with it on you, the worse it gets, and the more socially noticeable it becomes.

Just like a child, we are unable to get rid of the stink on our souls. We totally depend on our parents to cleanse us. And if we truly have loving and caring parents, they are going to be willing to put up with us and cleanse us every single time we soil ourselves. We, thus, can have the greatest confidence in our parent's love for us and the humility to go to them every single time. That's why this Sacrament — going to Confession — can be viewed as getting your spiritual diaper changed.

And here's *the* key component to how all this happens. It has been divinely planned into the program of our becoming fully mature in Christ and members of God's family: Just as a diaper change generally happens from the hand of the mother (for the father is usually the one supplying the diapers), this is how it happens in God's family, too. Father God supplies the diapers, and our spiritual mother cleans us up. Mary and the Church serve as our spiritual mother, and there is no other place where we can go to receive the complete cleansing of our sin than to Holy Mother Church. She alone has the diapers. Father God has entrusted them to her, and he gives her an endless supply because he knows his sinful children will need them — a lot.

Did you know that the root meaning of the word salvation (*salve*) means "clean" or "health?" That's what salvation means — a healing or cleansing. The ultimate cleanliness is eternal salvation, where our souls are made clean and we enter into everlasting life with God. God wants this for us. Thus, he instituted the Sacrament of Reconciliation, so we can know his endless love and mercy and experience it. And because we are members of his family, he supplies the diapers as our most loving and provident Father. Then, just as in most any family, it is the mother who cleans the child up. Sure, God could do it all himself, but because we are members of his family, he shares the responsibility with his bride, our mother.

In light of this, we should never be afraid to approach our Father and our mother, the Church. It shows we have humility when we, like a little child, come to Confession and echo in childlike terms: "Uh oh, I did it again! I'm messy again." Then, Dad *and* Mom clean us up every single time.

No father and mother want to see their children dirty and stinking. No mother, for example, would ever say to her child, "Carry on with your stinky self." A mother wants her child to be clean and fresh. This is why devotion to Mary and frequent Confession go hand in hand. Ask anyone who frequently goes to Confession if they have a devotion to Our Lady, and I almost guarantee you that the answer will be yes. A child who loves his mother wants to make her happy. A child who loves his father and mother is not afraid to run to them when he needs cleansing.

On the other hand, ask someone who almost never goes to Confession if he has a devotion to Mary, and I can almost guarantee you that the answer will be no. When a person fails to see the role of Mary in his spiritual life, he turns away from the spiritual diaper change — Confession. If you think you don't have a spiritual mother in Mary and the Church, you will eventually think you no longer need to have your diaper changed (your sins forgiven) through Confession.

This analogy relates to why the Church honors Mary every Saturday. Catholics know that the reason we honor Mary in a special way on Saturday is because after Good Friday, when Jesus was crucified, it was Mary who was the heart of hope. When God was crucified and buried in a tomb for three days, Mary held it all together, believing and completely trusting that what he had said was true. She is our hope. We can have total confidence to go to her with all of our needs, all of our brokenness, and all of our wounds. That includes helping us make a good Confession, so we can grow in humility and prepare ourselves for the worthy reception of Holy Communion on Sunday.

Every Saturday is *Mother's Day* in the Catholic Church. And thus, there are times for Confession in almost every Catholic church around the world on that day. All good mothers want their children to be physically clean for Sunday, the Lord's Day. So just like all good mothers have their children dress up and wear their Sunday best for Jesus, Mother Mary wants us to be spiritually clean so that we can go to church on the Lord's Day with our Sunday best in our souls, ready to receive Jesus worthily in Holy Communion.

Don't mistake what I'm saying, though. Saturday is not the only day we can go to Confession. Most parishes also offer Confession by appointment, and priests are more than willing to do that. I have been to parishes where they have Confession on, for example, a Wednesday as well as a Saturday. And tons of people go. Whenever a priest makes himself available to hear confessions, people will come because people spiritually soil themselves — a lot.

There is simply no limit to God's mercy in this awesome Sacrament! We can go to Confession an endless number of times, because this Sacrament is born out of a Father's love for his wayward children. And Our Lady helps us to understand this. In fact, just as every parish has scheduled times for Confession on Saturday, it's also a distinguishing characteristic of every Marian shrine that it has many scheduled times for Confession, even every single day.

So, for example, if you go to the Shrine of Our Lady of Knock in Ireland, or the Shrine of Our Lady of Fatima in Portugal, or the Shrine of Our Lady of Lourdes in France, or even the Basilica of the National Shrine of the Immaculate Conception in Washington, D.C., you will find that there are confessions heard every day. I experienced this firsthand when I lived in Washington, D.C., as a seminarian. I used to go to Confession at the Basilica all the time because it was right on my doorstep.

In fact, I don't know what I'd do without this amazing fountain of mercy. As part of the spirituality of my Marian religious community, we are encouraged to go to Confession at least every two weeks. I love that and need it. I'm a sinner, and I make a mess of things — a lot. And I'm so extremely grateful that my heavenly Father is always willing to forgive me, cleanse me through Mother Church, and reassure me of his love.

I was amazed when someone once told me that St. John Paul II went to Confession every week — and sometimes every day. We all know that he was seriously holy. So what the heck was he doing that he went to Confession so much? I now understand that it's because the closer you get to God, the more you are cognizant of the little things that get in the way, and the more you desire God, the more you want even those little things to be consumed by the fire of his love and mercy.

I also once heard that St. Damien of Molokai — the holy priest who volunteered to work with the lepers on the Hawaiian Island of Molokai and eventually died of leprosy himself — had to confess his sins out loud by yelling them to a fellow priest who was on a boat anchored just offshore. The priest in the boat did not want to come ashore out of a fear of contracting leprosy. Yet St. Damien knew the power of the Sacrament and was willing to be so humbled as to shout out his sins in order to receive the cleansing of his heavenly Father. So we shouldn't be afraid when we go behind the curtain of mercy, where we have total privacy.

Nor should we be afraid to reveal the full extent of our sinful behavior. When you go to Confession, you don't want to hide anything or leave anything out. If you go to Confession, you go to get the whole package. You want to have everything cleansed. That's why it's wise to make preparations — to think about your sins before you go in, or maybe even write them down so you can get everything out. A person would be weird who went for a spiritual diaper change and thought to himself, "I don't mind if I have a little stink left in my pants."

Know, too, that God holds this Sacrament in such high regard that he has put a sacred seal on it. This means whatever you say in Confession, stays in Confession. No parents change their baby's diaper on the counter at a restaurant! It's a private thing. Likewise, by analogy, a priest is forbidden to tell anybody what transpires in Confession. This is such a blessing, as you can then have the confidence to go in and get all the stinky stuff out. Priests don't even talk amongst themselves about what they've heard, because they are forbidden to. It's not as though back at the rectory, Fr. Smith and Fr. O'Malley crack open a few cold ones and swap stories about the sins of their penitents that day. They would experience major penalties for revealing what was said in Confession, even having their faculties (ability) to hear confessions taken away or, worse, losing the ability to function as a priest all together. The seal of Confession is sacred.

Last, but certainly not least, it's important to recognize that Confession does not provide a person with a license to sin. As we grow and mature in Christ, we should be growing in virtue and grower farther and farther away from sin. A person would be committing the sin of presumption to plan out and commit a sin, thinking that they could just go to Confession later. God knows that we are going to make mistakes, but we should not be planning them out.

Ultimately, Confession leads us to a preparation for the worthy reception of Holy Communion. We should never go to receive Jesus in Holy Communion if we know that we are in a state of mortal sin. That would be a sacrilege. We would be compounding our sins — adding more stink to our already foul souls. Even St. Paul talks about this in his first letter to the Corinthians (cf. 1 Cor 11:27). But when our soul is free of mortal sin by having gone to Confession, our reception of Holy Communion is like a wedding day. We go with joy in our hearts and smiles on our faces to receive Jesus, the lover of our souls. Both Father and Mother look on in joy and are so very pleased.

☆ ☆ ☆ Marian Gems

☆ All true children of God have God for their father and Mary for their mother; anyone who does not have Mary for his mother, does not have God for his father. *St. Louis de Montfort*

☆ Many not understanding you, Mary, don't know how to love you. They think there should be no one between them and God. They don't realize that your sole interest lies in bringing us closer to God. *Servant of God (Fr.) Patrick J. Peyton*

☆ There never was, nor is, nor ever will be a grace given by God in any other way than by Mary's mediation. *Blessed Michael Sopocko*

☆ To no one is mercy granted except through you [Mary]. *St. Germanus of Constantinople*

☆ God has willed that we should have nothing that would not pass through the hands of Mary. *St. Bernard of Clairvaux*

☆ No grace comes from heaven to earth but what passes through Mary's hands. *St. Bernardine of Siena*

☆ On Mary's motherly face Christians recognize a most particular expression of the merciful love of God, who with the mediation of a maternal presence has us better understand the Father's own care and goodness. Mary appears as the one who attracts sinners and reveals to them, with her sympathy and her indulgence, the divine offer of reconciliation. *St. John Paul II*

☆ A genuine child avoids everything that causes his mother sadness and sorrow. The greatest sorrow we can cause our Mother Thrice Admirable is sin, for it was sin that murdered her divine Son, that pierced her heart with a sevenfold sword. We show we are children of our Mother Thrice Admirable, therefore, when we foster a deep hatred of sin, and as soon as we are torn away by passion and fall into sin, to find our way to holy confession. *Servant of God (Fr.) Joseph Kentenich*

☆ In your hands [Mary] are laid the treasures of God's mercy. *St. Peter Damian*

☆ Through the Mother we have access to the Son, and through the Son to the Father. With such guides to lead us, let us have no fear at all of being refused reconciliation. *St. Albert the Great*

☆ There is no fruit of grace in the history of salvation that does not have as its necessary instrument the mediation of Our Lady. *Pope Benedict XVI*

Ongoing Conversion

EVEN THOUGH I'VE BEEN A CATHOLIC FOR OVER 20 YEARS now and a priest for 10, I'm still in need of a lot of conversion. Sometimes I realize how selfish I am, and it makes me sick. I realize that I'm far from being holy and the disciple I should be. The radical conversion experience that led me to Catholicism happened once, and it was awesome and unforgettable. I was dunked in the ocean of God's mercy and love. But the honeymoon is long since over, and now I have to go through the daily process of an ongoing conversion. I think this is partly why Jesus desired that Our Lady stay with the early Church after he had ascended to his heavenly Father and why he desires us to have her in our lives today. Jesus knows we need her. Mary's presence in our lives helps us persevere in our efforts to be more fully conformed to and mature in Christ.

When I go and speak at churches and conferences, I always ask people to pray for me and offer up their Rosaries for me so that I can, as St. Paul says, finish the race and remain faithful (cf. 2 Tim 4:7). Sometimes people look at me like I'm joking, and they at times laugh. But I'm not joking. I'm begging them to keep me in their prayers, because priests are sinners just like everybody else. And we are hunted men. Satan — not to mention much of society — does not like priests. We need a lot of prayer and spiritual protection — and that's one of the reasons why I wear a scapular.

Mary helps us to recognize that Christianity is not just about having a one-time conversion experience that you assign a specific date to. Nobody who is living today was saved once and for all, with no possibility for messing it all up, on a particular date in their past — as if there were no further need for personal conversion. We are all capable of messing it up even after we've had a radical conversion experience.

Don't get me wrong; having a conversion experience is incredible. But because Christianity is a relationship with God, it has to be ongoing. It must be a daily conversion of heart, a daily conversion of turning away from sin, vice, evil, and darkness while at the same time embracing truth, beauty, and goodness. That's why Christianity is a relationship — a falling in love with Jesus Christ and persevering in that love until the end.

Again, this is why I personally need the Sacrament of Reconciliation. If this Sacrament did not exist, I'd be in big trouble. Even now, sometimes I go and confess the same stupid things that I've been confessing for years. Then, I think to myself, "Why do I keep confessing the same stupid things over and over again?" But Mother Mary keeps reminding me of what Jesus said: "The spirit is willing, but the flesh is weak" (Mt 26:41).

Sometimes healing happens instantly, but most times it happens over a period of time and not instantaneously. My initial conversion to the truth of Catholicism, for example, was quick, and I did receive major areas of healing that were instantaneous. But there are many other things that continue to need to be healed in me, and Our Lady has shown me that I am still under the spiritual knife. The Divine Physician is still performing heart surgery on me. Yet Mary is at my side comforting me, and I desire the surgery to continue so that, on some glorious day, I can be totally free of sin.

This is why Jesus established Confession and why there is an endless fountain of mercy in this Sacrament. Certain Sacraments you can only experience once. For example, you can only be baptized once; you can only be confirmed once. But with this Sacrament, you can go endlessly. That's why I'm in awe of this Sacrament and the Father's love for his children.

Recall that in the Gospel of Matthew, Peter has this conversation with Jesus: "'Lord, how often shall my brother sin against me, and I forgive him? As many as seven times?' Jesus said to him, 'I do not say to you seven times, but seventy times seven'" (Mt 18:21-22). Basically, Jesus is saying that there should be no limit to how often we are willing to forgive. And God himself practices the principle he promotes. This means that as long as we are truly sorry and seek to amend our lives and try to do better, God will forgive us every single time.

As I noted earlier, the healing of the human person is not just in our souls, it's in our emotions, passions, and in the psychological aspects of what it means to be a human person. No sin occurs in a vacuum or an isolated part of our being. There is also a social dimension to sin; it affects everything and everyone around us.

As a priest, I've heard some amazing confessions. Obviously, I can't get into specifics, but I have literally seen people break down and cry uncontrollably because they are getting stuff off of their chest that is so weighty they lose it and break down in the confessional. This is why Confession rooms often have tissue boxes. If you have serious stuff on your heart, when you get rid of it, your emotions are inevitably going to come out. I have heard confessions in which people have cried to the point that they could hardly breathe. I've also been so blessed to have heard the confessions of people who had been away from the Church and from the Sacrament of Reconciliation and Holy Communion for more than 50 years! What an amazing feeling to know that God has worked through me, a flawed man, to heal a soul and bring such a person back to the family of God.

In fact, there have been times when Confession is over that I just remain there for a few extra minutes in awe of what just happened — in awe of the amazing mercy that God just showered on a soul with serious, shameful wounds. Sometimes, I want to cry myself when I see the great humility that the penitent displays when he is confessing his sins and reaching out for mercy. It's powerful stuff! Sometimes, I think there should be a tissue box on the priest's side of the confessional, too. It's like a homecoming, and I can only imagine the joy and delight Father God and Mother Mary experience at that moment.

When we sin, we are making our Father, God, our brother, Jesus, and our mother, Mary, cry. And no child wants to see his father or his mother cry. That's all the more reason why we should have the confidence to run to Confession and dry their tears — expressing our love for them and our sorrow and contrition for hurting them through our sin. That's what brings joy to their hearts. They know we are weak and wounded and make mistakes. But the longer we stay away the more they cry. When we come to them with contrite humility, we experience the touch of mercy and the healing that takes place in our relationship. All is forgotten, all is forgiven.

As I already noted, I try and go to Confession every two weeks, if not more. I guess going to Confession is kind of like going to the hospital to see the doctor periodically. It's a super good idea to do that so serious health issues can be taken care of early on. Or perhaps you could say frequent Confession is like routine, ongoing maintenance for the soul. Just like you take care of your car by getting a periodic tune-up or an oil change, it's the same thing with our souls. We have to go for periodic check-ups and make sure we are running smoothly. Everything runs a lot better if we have a tune-up periodically. This is why the Church encourages us to go to Confession — frequently. After all, there's nothing like starting up a car and listening to the engine purr like a kitten. It's the same thing with our souls.

Another benefit of going to frequent Confession is that it helps you to not want to sin anymore. Knowing that you want to receive Jesus worthily in Holy Communion, a love for the Eucharist will give you a desire to stop sinning. Thus, a great love for Confession should increase your love for Holy Communion. And a love for the Eucharist will help you want to be so pure and so good that, over time, you should see some decrease in the gravity of your sins. In that way, having a love for Confession will actually help you grow in the life of avoiding sin. It will help you develop a greater appreciation of Jesus in the Blessed Sacrament. After all, full maturity in Christ means complete separation from sin. And in heaven, where there is no longer any need for Confession or conversion, you will be perfectly united in an eternal communion of love with Jesus Christ.

I know that some people struggle with going to Confession. It's not easy to go sometimes if you've got serious sins to reveal. I am reminded of this whenever a visiting priest is in town doing a mission at a parish. It's almost comical that his Confession line is always the longest! People want to confess to him because he's going back to India, or Africa, or the Philippines. It's kind of funny, but I understand it. Sometimes, people think it's too hard to go to Confession to their own pastor because he will recognize their voice. Then he will never look at them the same way again. But don't worry. We priests have heard everything. There is nothing that will shock us — trust me.

Get rid of the stink. Our Lady will help you.

☆ ☆ ☆ Marian Gems

☆ For so great is her dignity, so great her favor before God, that whosoever in his need will not have recourse to her is trying to fly without wings. *Pope Leo XIII*

☆ When I sinned against the Son, I distressed the Mother; nor could I have offended the Mother without injuring the Son. *St. Anselm of Canterbury*

☆ Where Mary is present, grace abounds and people are healed both in body and soul. *St. John Paul II*

☆ Day after day, our life and action is assimilated anew to the altera Maria; and more and more, in spite of all hindrances, we become an apparition of Mary, at least in miniature. *Servant of God (Fr.) Joseph Kentenich*

☆ One cannot contemplate Mary without being attracted by Christ, and one cannot look at Christ without immediately perceiving the presence of Mary. *Pope Benedict XVI*

☆ When we recall the virtues with which the Virgin Mary crushed the head of the dragon from hell, we fill all of hell with fear. By imitating and practicing these virtues, the faithful cannot stray from the path to salvation for they receive deliverance and help from their Lady. *Venerable Casimir Wyszynski*

☆ As a Marian vestment, the sacred scapular is certainly a sign and guarantee of the protection of the Mother of God. *Venerable Pope Pius XII*

☆ The greatest saints, those richest in grace and virtue, will be the most assiduous in praying to the most Blessed Virgin, looking up to her as the perfect model to imitate and as a powerful helper to assist them. *St. Louis de Montfort*

☆ We must renew our devotion to the Blessed Virgin if we wish to obtain the Holy Spirit and be sincere followers of Christ Jesus. *Blessed Pope Paul VI*

☆ There is no sinner in the world, however much at enmity with God, who cannot recover God's grace by recourse to Mary, and by asking her assistance. *St. Bridget of Sweden*

☆ Every grace by which Jesus raises us to a supernatural life passes through the hands of Mary. *Blessed Ildefonso Schuster*

☆ She [Mary] is the woman long ago promised by God to crush the head of the old serpent with the foot of her strength. The serpent has been lying in ambush, employing every sort of stratagem to attack her heel, but to no avail. Alone she has crushed all heretical crookedness. *St. Bernard of Clairvaux*

☆ Satan fears Mary as a frightened dog fears the rod with which he has been beaten. *St. John Eudes*

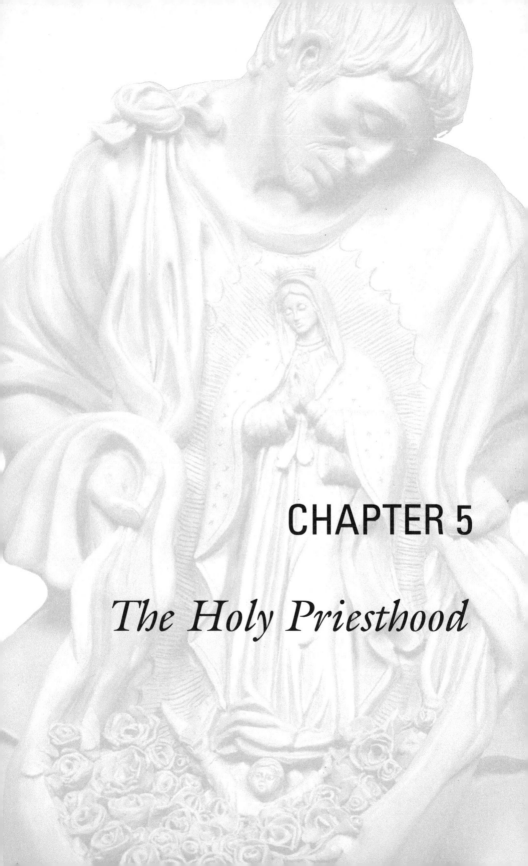

CHAPTER 5

The Holy Priesthood

Knights of the Holy Queen

WHEN I WAS AN UNDERGRADUATE STUDENT, I was privileged to be able to study at one of the best Catholic universities in the world, Franciscan University of Steubenville (FUS), in Ohio. During my time there, I got to know a bunch of guys who were in a household called the Knights of the Holy Queen — households at FUS are basically holy and truth-seeking fraternities or sororities. Since I was already in vows in my religious community, I was not able to fully commit to the household. Nonetheless, they accepted me as an honorary member. And when a man becomes a member of that household, he undergoes a knighting ceremony and takes the name of a saint or blessed, with the intention that he will strive to pray to that saint and imitate his virtues. I took the name Sir Stanislaus Papczynski, in honor of the founder of my religious community.

What I loved most about my being an honorary knight was the group's sense of manly chivalry, brotherhood, and love for Our Lady. They were not afraid to be self-emptying in the service of others, have accountability with one another, and come together in prayer. The way they prayed the Rosary gave such an example of dedicated, manly love for Our Lady that it has stuck with me to this day. I even remember shedding tears whenever they would sing their household song at the end of the Rosary. The song is a battle cry in honor of Our Lady, and I've never heard a song like it before. It stirs up manly courage and even now, whenever I hear it, I'm overwhelmed with emotion and feel like conquering the world for my Queen.

That kind of knightly spirituality gets me all fired up. It makes me want to man up to the challenge of becoming a better and more noble man, a gentleman, and a heroic man. Even as a kid, I was drawn to movies where the good guys fought against the bad guys. Sitting in dark theaters with my friends, we were mesmerized by the take-no-prisoners approach of Chuck Norris, William Wallace, and John Rambo, who sought to protect those who could not protect themselves. When beauty and brotherhood were threatened and attacked, they rose up and risked their owns lives to do what was right. Skill, strength, and manly courage were essential, as was perseverance in the face of any foe, hardship, or suffering.

One of my favorite paintings that depicts this knightly dimension of manhood is Edmund Leighton's "The Accolade." It's a painting of a man being knighted with a sword by a beautiful queen. Technically, the image doesn't feature a priest or the Blessed Virgin Mary, but for me it is easy to see how it works as an analogy for what a priest really is. The painting depicts a knight in chain mail, kneeling before his queen and being knighted with a sword. The knight is wearing distinctive knightly garb — armor with a red and black crest on his back. The King is not visible in the painting, but it is obvious that he is there, just off to the side. What man would not want to be knighted by such a beautiful princess? What man would not want to wear armor and be given a sword to conquer all that threatens such beauty? What man would not want to lay down his life for the honor of his King and Queen?

I love the Catholic symbolism in this painting. And it kind of reminds me of the Catholic symbolism we find in the game of chess, too.

Let me explain: When I was a seminarian, I would often play the game of chess with some of my seminarian brothers. Playing this game taught me a lot about the necessity of serving the King through being a servant of the Queen.

As you probably know, in chess, the object is to checkmate your opponent's king. The whole game centers around the king and he is the most important piece on the board; the game wouldn't exist without him. Yet the queen is the one who plays the key role in winning the game, and anyone who tells you differently doesn't know what they are talking about. She can move any number of squares in any direction. And everybody knows if you lose the queen, you've lost the game.

Interestingly, the game of chess, as it is played today, comes out of a Catholic culture. The king, the queen, the bishops, and the knights all give evidence of this. There is no grey on the board, either; only black and white. And when a bishop works with his queen, they can conquer the enemy in as few as three moves.

To fight for the queen is to fight for the king.

Thus, chess makes for a strong analogy in understanding the necessary role and place of Mary in the lives of Christians. Christianity is all about Jesus Christ — the King. Yet the King himself has placed an indispensable piece at the center of his victorious campaign, the piece *through* which he conquers the enemy.

No wonder, then, that great Marian saints like St. Maximilian Kolbe and St. John Paul II often played the game of chess. The knight knows how to fight for his Queen, and he is even willing to die for her or take a bullet for her. The knight knows that to defend the Queen is to the honor, glory, and delight of his King. Even a Doctor of the Church, St. Teresa of Avila, talks about the game of chess in her book *The Way of Perfection*.

The chess analogy actually also helps us to understand why it is that Satan hates the Virgin Mary so much. She is the person through whom the enemy is conquered and the King is victorious. Think about it: As God has set up the bookends of human history (from Genesis to Revelation), both the beginning and the end of human history have the theme of the woman doing battle with the enemy, and *the* woman *with* her divine Child crushing the darkness.

In the first book of the Bible (cf. Gen 3:15), God promises that it is the woman who will crush the serpent's head. And in the Book of Revelation (Chapter 12), we read that Satan remains enraged at the woman and her offspring and wages war against them. The bookends of human history feature the woman conquering the enemy. God set it up that way, and Jesus the divine King carries it out that way. If Mary is the individual God uses to bring himself into the world to defeat darkness and overcome evil, no wonder Satan has such a violent hatred for her. God lives in her and crushes evil through her. Make no mistake: It's God who does it, as Mary doesn't have the power to do it herself because she is a creature. But just as in chess, the victory is won *through* the Queen.

Some might think too much attention is given to the Queen, while the King is hardly even noticed — remember "The Accolade" painting. But this is the will of the King. The humble God-King uses her delicate, tender, dainty feminine heel to crush Satan's filthy, stinking head. Mary puts Satan and all darkness in checkmate. Game over!

This explains why Satan hates the Catholic Church and the priesthood, too, and why he would want to mock, ridicule, and destroy them, especially by highlighting the sins of the clergy. Satan desires to laugh and wag his finger and say to the modern man: "How can you be a member of this Church — this man-made, archaic, oppressive, intolerant, male-dominated, outdated hierarchical institution that doesn't update with the times? Look at those perverted priests and what they have done! How can you be so foolish as to stay in this Church?"

Don't get me wrong, though. Sadly, in our times, some priests have committed heinous crimes and sins against others, even children. Such sins are an abomination, break the heart of the King and Queen, and cry out for justice. But there is no doubt that Satan has a hold on the media, and he takes advantage of every opportunity to snap at the heels of the woman and snatch souls from under her mantle.

But the truly wise and discerning know that even in spite of such scandals, we should still listen to and love the Catholic Church because she is the one founded by Jesus Christ and promised victory over Satan. Some of her members may be corrupt and commit scandalous activities, but scandals have always been present in the Church. So that should not make a person turn away from the saving ark. The ark of Noah itself was full of manure, as is the Church today. You might occasionally step in it, but if you jump ship, you're going to drown.

Satan is just waiting for you to jump ship. Just as in chess, we have an enemy, and our enemy is a fallen angel — Lucifer. Lucifer, by the way, means "Bearer of Light." He's not dumb. He's just extremely devious, and he uses his angelic intelligence to trick us into turning away from the light just as he did. The devil hates both the King *and* the Queen. Because Satan hates them, he also hates the Catholic Church and the priesthood. For this reason, Satan takes great delight when a priest falls. It is an opportunity to parade the fallen priest through the streets (the media) and make a laughing stock of all he represents as a servant of the King and Queen.

This is why the priesthood is not for the faint of heart. As priests, men are going to be called upon to do battle with dragons — demons. If a guy is not prepared for this role, he is going to get his butt kicked by Satan. That's why a priest's work isn't primarily an office job, where he pushes papers around all day. Sure, there are times when a priest has tons of desk work, but the fact is that once he is ordained, he is on the front lines of the battlefield and must always be ready for spiritual warfare. And like his honorable knightly brothers, he should strive to defend the weak and defenseless and rid the world of darkness by laying down his life.

It might seem odd to compare a priest to a knight, or Rambo, or Braveheart, but it really isn't if you think about it. Did you know that military chaplains — soldier-priests — are considered "force multipliers" during a time of war? The military not only expects its chaplains to meet the spiritual needs of troops and serve as a moral compass in life-and-death circumstances; they are also expected to rally the troops and remind them they are fighting for what is worthy of their manly sacrifice — what is good, true, and beautiful. Priests give men courage to go into battle and defend what is being threatened.

For this reason, a seminary (or a novitiate in a religious community) is really a kind of spiritual boot camp or basic training. Boot camp is designed to prepare military recruits for all elements of service: physical, mental, emotional, etc. It's a tough process, but a rewarding one — one that helps form lasting bonds of true brotherhood. Seminary is much the same way. It's where the *seminal* seeds — seminary — of sanctity are to be nourished. It is meant to be a saint-making machine, where the Church cranks out new ranks of dedicated knights and soldiers every year, all fighting the good fight and conquering the world for Christ.

Thus, how sad it is when effeminacy and softness enter into a seminary. Seminarians are there to be trained to become spiritual warriors. They *will* have to combat the enemy and, therefore, must be tough. They may not be required to have the demeanor of John Wayne or Patton, but there is no place for pansies and wimps in the army of God. God's warriors are not called to be soft and delicate, but they are called to be gentle — gentlemen soldiers.

What men fight for is what is soft, delicate, and beautiful — their mothers, their brides, and their children. Men do not go to war to die for trivial things. No man during the heat of battle, being in a foxhole with bullets flying over his head, reaches into his wallet and pulls out a picture of a shopping mall! He reaches into his wallet and pulls out a picture of his beauty, kisses it, and rushes into the fray willing to die *as a man*.

In fact, the foundation of the priesthood is manhood. It's why women cannot be and never will be ordained priests in the Catholic Church. And I emphatically state that women will *never* be ordained priests in the Catholic Church. Why? Because it's an old boys' club and thinks little of women? Please! Everybody, especially the Catholic Church, knows that women both act and, in a certain sense, are almost always more consistently moral than men. Women are more compassionate, kind, faithful, magnanimous, merciful, loyal, etc. After all, the majority of disciples at the foot of the Cross were not men but women. And the greatest *human person* who ever lived, and will ever live, was not a man but a woman. Her name is Mary. She is the very Mother of God, and God Himself obeyed her. But she was not a priest, nor was she called to be a priest, nor did she have the desire to be one.

Women are not called to be ordained priests any more than I am called to be a mother. Such vocations are not rights but gifts to which one is called. So, for example, if I begin parading around, moaning and groaning that it's an injustice that I can't have a baby, I've got issues — theological *and* anthropological issues. If I don't like the body I've been given, I don't have issues that need to be taken up with men. I've got issues that need to be taken up with God — and that's not going to go well. So likewise, women who think it is an injustice that they can't be priests don't have an issue with the hierarchy of the Church. They have an issue with God.

Priests are soldiers, knights, and warriors. They share in the *manly* mission of Jesus Christ the bridegroom. Jesus is the bridegroom of the Church. Souls are spiritually espoused to him, and those souls are under attack. The role of a priest of Jesus Christ is to man up. In the proverbial sense, it means to take up the weapons of war, put on armor, and go face-to-face with the enemy. Jesus will provide for all that the priest needs to fulfill his mission: the weapons, the armor, and the unconquerable battle Queen. Jesus himself is *the* warrior-King, and he knows what is needed to conquer the enemy.

In the Old Testament, we read, "The Lord is a man of war; the Lord is his name" (Ex 15:3). The weapon of choice for the God-man-warrior is the Cross, and he shares this choice heavenly weapon with his warrior brothers. In life, every young boy wants a powerful weapon, one that intimidates the enemy and makes them flee. By comparison, in the spiritual life, the greatest weapon to conquer the infernal enemy is the Cross. That's why a priest must carry it faithfully and never lay it down. As soon as he lays it down, the enemy will go after his throat *and* his flock.

This helps explain why saintly priests carry and pray the Rosary. They literally carry the cross, in miniature, on their person when they carry the Rosary. The Rosary, as many saints have noted, is the weapon to whip the daylights out of the forces of darkness. A priest without a Rosary is like a knight without a sword. The Rosary is more powerful than a machine gun, and nations can be conquered with only this tiny little weapon, those tiny little beads.

The armor, too, is provided by Jesus. Consider how many vocations there are that require the wearing of a uniform — especially those that involve serving, protecting, and saving human lives. If police officers, firemen, or doctors didn't wear uniforms, how would people know who they are? A uniform is a visible reminder to both the one who serves and the ones served that the uniformed agent is available and ready to help.

Thus, a priest who for no good reason chooses not to wear his clerical attire in public makes himself unavailable to his flock. Not wearing it means that he does not desire to be seen or noticed. Some may say that he doesn't wear it so that he doesn't appear to be "higher" than the people, but that is nonsense — even a fool can wear a uniform. A priest wears it because it's a public sign that both serves to protect him and the people he serves. For example, women probably are not going to hit on or flirt with a man who wears a Roman collar (although, I have to say, some women today are so aggressive that they do it anyway). And when a soul is in mortal sin and desperately needs to see a priest for Confession, the Roman collar makes him stand out for the service of absolution.

In a certain sense, a priestly collar is kind of like a wedding ring. A wedding ring shows you are in a committed relationship and unable to indulge in certain things (courtship, dating, etc). So for example, if a married man goes out one evening to a bar with his buddies to knock back a few beers, but before going into the bar pauses to take off his wedding ring, it shows he's a player. He's open to seeing what other options might come *his* way and doesn't want to be publicly responsible for who he is as a married man. It's the same thing if a priest were to remove his collar to see what options might come his way. Then he, too, would act like a player, and it would be a sign that he has identity issues. Now, that doesn't mean a priest can't enjoy downtime and go out without it on from time to time. But if he doesn't wear it most times when he is in public, there's something wrong. Soldiers who take off their uniform in battle are known to be defectors.

And this is where the importance of the Queen comes in. A priest who loves Our Lady will want to wear his uniform, because the whole reason he is a priest is to make every soul love Jesus like Mary does and to be an *altera Maria* — another Mary for Jesus. If he doesn't publicly express this love, even by the way he dresses, how will people have confidence that he himself is serious about his own commitment or knows what he's doing? Would you trust a doctor who sought to operate on you wearing shorts and a polo shirt? It doesn't mean, technically, he can't do it, but something is suspect.

In fact, this helps us understand why Mary's role in the life of a priest is so *vitally* important. When Jesus entrusted his mother to the Church from the Cross, he entrusted her in a particular way to John, his beloved disciple *and* priest. The priest gives Mary his heart and soul and loves her with a devoted love. And the way he loves Mary will be the way he loves souls. If he doesn't love Mary, he will love souls little.

All priests are called to be Marian priests. It doesn't matter if they are Dominicans, Benedictines, Carmelites, Franciscans, or diocesan priests. All priests are called to be Knights of the Holy Queen!

And a priest's love for his Queen must be public, as any real love is. The entire parish, and every parishioner, should be able to see the love that their pastor — their priest — has for his Lady. This should be normal priestly behavior. For example, if you saw me walking down the street with a woman named Linda and heard me telling her that I wanted to be with her night and day, sing songs to her, pour flowers at her feet, conquer nations for her, and spend every waking hour by her side, that would be a problem. I am already married, so to speak, and in a committed relationship and vocation. A priest is a man who is already in love with the perfect woman — or at least he should be. Thus, you shouldn't expect to hear a priest singing the loveliness of a "Linda," but you should hear him talking *and preaching* about his great love for Our Lady. She is his princess.

In Genesis, God says, "It is not good for man to be alone" (2:18). God created the beautiful complementarity of the masculine and the feminine. Thus, he knows that every man needs an *other* — a woman — in order to be complete and fulfill his vocation. This applies to celibate priests, too. Though most priests in the Catholic Church do not marry — not because it's forced upon them but because they are already in love — it doesn't mean that they do not require the anthropological completeness of having a woman in their lives. Jesus did.

That's right, even Jesus needed a woman in his life. Not as a wife, obviously, but as the *other* who provided fulfillment and meaning to his manly, priestly sacrifice. He is not an angel or a robot. He is the God-man who saves the world in a manly way and shares his priesthood with *men*.

The following may sound like heresy, but it's not: Jesus didn't fulfill his manly, priestly sacrifice for an abstract beauty. No. He sacrificed himself for *the* woman, Mary — *and* by association the Church, our souls. This is why all his references to Mary during his public ministry refer to her as *woman* (cf. Jn 2:4; 19:26). She is the pattern of the Church, his bride, and what we must all conform to in order to experience his salvation.

Sadly, it's our sex-crazed world that thinks the only way a person can love is by having sexual intercourse. I guess heaven would be hell for a lot of people, then, because there are no sexual relations in heaven (cf. Mt 22:30). But there is everlasting love and spiritual marriage — I will elaborate more on this in the next chapter.

In short, every man is entrusted with a beauty to defend, honor, serve, and die for — just as Jesus was entrusted with a manly mission to sacrifice himself for his bride, the Marian Church. By becoming man, Jesus placed himself under the anthropological demands that he himself created. In a sense, he needed the *feminine* in order to accomplish his saving work. And paradoxically, it is the very mystery of the feminine that helped him accomplish it! All men live and die for beauty.

So if, in a sense, Mary is necessary for Jesus to fulfill his mission, Mary is also necessary for priests to fulfill their mission. A priest needs her by his side. Ordination does not do away with the dictates of human nature. All men need a woman to talk to, share their heart with, and be emotionally and psychologically close to. And because of the great demands placed upon priests — spiritual, emotional, anthropological, etc. — Jesus knows that his brother priests are going to need the best woman of all. Without her, they will not be able to carry out their mission.

Jesus does not send his priests onto the battlefield unequipped in any way. So he shares the gift of the Immaculata with his priests. They belong to her, and her to them, in a unique and special way. Mary is their life, their sweetness, their hope, their joy, their delight, their *everything*. She is their Queen, their princess, their beauty, their *spiritual* mother, and the perfect complement to their great manly sacrifice of celibacy.

And trust me, celibacy is not easy — especially in the overly sexualized world we live in today. Men called to the priesthood will often feel the anthropological sting of not having a wife. It is a great sacrifice. But it is worth the sacrifice because the salvation of souls is at stake. A temporary good is sacrificed in light of an eternal good. Even Jesus and St. Paul praise the great blessing of being celibate for the kingdom of heaven (cf. Mt 19:10-12; 1 Cor 7:7-8).

Being celibate doesn't make a man any less of a man, either, as some are accustomed to think. It's ludicrous to think that a man becomes a priest because he can't get a woman. Are you kidding me! Most women would jump at the chance to have a man as dedicated and faithful as a priest! And a man doesn't become a priest because he doesn't know how to love, either. Give me a break! He becomes a priest because he is a lover! He is madly in love with Jesus, Mary, and souls! He is a soldier on a battlefield, making a great sacrifice *for you*, so that the enemy is conquered, beauty defended, and the King glorified.

☆ ☆ ☆ Marian Gems

☆ Providence ordinarily uses the initiative and activity of men to realize its designs. It follows that the Immaculate Virgin stood in need of soldiers ready to fight the battles of the Lord under her auspices. Providence must call forth such apostles; it must inspire them from on high; it must enroll them under her banner as her ministers and soldiers. *Blessed William Joseph Chaminade*

☆ Be her soldier so that others may become ever more perfectly hers, like you yourself, and even more than you; so that all those who live and will live all over the world may work together with her in her struggle against the infernal serpent. *St. Maximilian Kolbe*

☆ Imperial maiden and mistress, Queen, sovereign lady, take me under thy protection, guard me lest Satan, the author of destruction, rise up against me, lest the accursed enemy triumph over me. *St. Ephrem the Syrian*

☆ By her intercession she [Mary] leads from heaven the army of apostles. *Servant of God (Fr.) Joseph Kentenich*

☆ For her part, Mary is the living Church. It is upon her that the Holy Spirit descends, thereby making her the new Temple. Joseph, the just man, is appointed to be the steward of the mysteries of God, the paterfamilias and guardian of the sanctuary, which is Mary the bride and the Logos in her. He [Joseph] thus becomes the icon of the bishop, to whom the bride is betrothed; she is not at his disposal but under his protection. *Pope Benedict XVI*

☆ As the pseudo-reform of Luther and his accomplices was met by an order justly renowned, assuming the name and standard of Jesus, so too Providence will now assign to its militia the name and standard of Mary, enabling the knights of the new crusade to hasten to and fro at the beck of their Queen, to diffuse her devotion and, by the fact, to extend the Kingdom of God in souls. *Blessed William Joseph Chaminade*

☆ We are on the offensive, defending religion is too little for us; rather we are leaving the fortress and, confident in our Leader, going among the enemies and hunting for hearts in order to vanquish them for the Immaculate. ... Every heart which beats upon the earth and which shall beat, until the end of the world, must be prey for the Immaculate: this is our purpose. *St. Maximilian Kolbe*

☆ The knight fights in dependence upon, by the wish and command, and for the honor of his Queen. In this case he fights for the spreading of her love and devotion with the stated intention so that the world, through you transformed, will pay due homage to your Son. This means the restoration of the world in Christ through Mary. *Servant of God (Fr.) Joseph Kentenich*

☆ The priest has duties to fulfill toward this tender Mother. He ought to be second to none in the honor he renders her, the tender love that is due her. He should most zealously make her known and loved. *St. Peter Julian Eymard*

☆ O what an honor for us to do battle under this valiant captainess! *St. Francis de Sales*

☆ With good reason does Sacred Scripture call Mary the "Valiant Woman," for she is the marshal of the armies of God himself and the principal enemy of the infernal serpent. The battalions of hell fear Mary far more than a small, weak body of foot soldiers would fear a powerful mechanized enemy force in battle array. *St. John Eudes*

☆ To serve Mary and to be her courtier is the greatest honor one can possibly possess, for to serve the Queen of Heaven is already to reign there, and to live under her command is more than to govern. *St. John Damascene*

☆ My tongue preaches Mary; my favorite, most frequent, and most ardent sermon will be the Madonna. I will not miss an occasion to speak of Mary and I will try my best to introduce this subject whenever I can. *Blessed James Alberione*

☆ Love for Our Lady is the driving force of catholicity. *Pope Benedict XVI*

☆ To begin and end well, devotion to our Blessed Lady, the Mother of God, is nothing less than indispensable. *St. Philip Neri*

☆ The Immaculata must conquer the whole world for herself, and each individual soul as well, so that she can bring all back to God. This is why we must acknowledge her for what she is, and submit to her and to her reign, which is all gentleness. *St. Maximilian Kolbe*

Fishers of Men

I LOVE TO GO FISHING. I've been blessed to be able to fish all over the United States and Canada, and even in places like Japan, Australia, Alaska, Mexico, and the Caribbean. I even keep two ready-to-go fishing poles and a fully loaded tackle box in my room, so I'm prepared to go whenever the opportunity arises. Thus, I love that Jesus told his apostles — his first priests — that they would be fishers of men (cf. Mt 4:19). It makes total sense to me why he would use this imagery. There are just so many similarities between fishing for fish and fishing for men (souls), and if a priest uses this knowledge in his ministry, he is pretty much guaranteed a huge catch.

From my own experience of fishing (for fish), I know that there are many things that go into making sure you're doing it right and effectively. Good equipment, proper bait, sharp hooks, lots of line, and tons of patience are just a few of the things that are needed. After all, as a norm, fish don't just jump in the boat. You have to find them, bait them, catch them, and put up with a fight to reel them in. Fish nearly always put up a fight.

If there's one thing that's definitely guaranteed to be true about fishing, it's that it takes a lot of patience. Many people give up on fishing quickly because they lack the patience to just sit there and cast endlessly for hours. But it's an absolute necessity to have a ton of patience when fishing. Most times, it will be slow going and require many casts just to get a bite. But that's part and parcel of fishing. Even when you do get a bite, not every fish is going to stay on the line. Sometimes they get away because the hook was old, cheap, or the wrong size — or it wasn't set firmly enough in the fish's mouth. No fisherman wants to see one get away. That's why proper knowledge and equipment are key to having a successful fishing day.

For example, I once went fishing with a friend who had little knowledge of how to fish. Right before my eyes, I witnessed him fail to catch the biggest bass I've ever seen. To this day, I've never seen such a huge bass. When it hit his bait, my friend tried to immediately reel it in, but the monster bass swam away hard and fast, putting a lot of tension on the line. Then, because it was so big, it took his bait and got away. But before it disappeared for good, the bass breached super high out of the water, flashing us its shiny, fat underbelly and shaming us by revealing and show-casing its trophy size. When my buddy reeled in his line, all that remained was a tiny piece of an old rusty hook. He later told me that the hook he put on was an old one and not even sharp.

No fish is caught with a dull hook. The hook always has to be sharp and deliver a puncturing incision in order for the fish to remain hooked. And if the fish puts up a strong fight once it's on the line, you never hold the line too tight lest you snap it. Thus, you always have to bring a lot of fishing line, because you might have to let the fish "run" so that the line isn't too taut and breaks. When you don't know these things, you don't catch fish and end up frustrated.

Having the proper bait is extremely important when fishing, too. I've been on fresh water lakes and witnessed guys who fish all day and catch nothing while I'm 50 yards away reeling 'em in like mad. What made the difference? They had the wrong bait, while I had the right bait. With the wrong bait, you can fish all day in a piranha pond and catch nothing. But with the right bait, you can catch a ton of fish, and it almost seems like you're cheating.

All the things I've just mentioned are the basics required for fishing, and every good fisherman knows them. But since not every priest knows how to fish, many priests don't realize the wisdom and the similarities between fishing for fish and fishing for men. Therefore, I'd like to present three fundamental things about fishing that can help priests more effectively catch souls. They are: the hook, the bait, and the line.

We start with the hook. The hook that every priest must use to catch souls effectively is the teaching of the Catholic Church. It is extremely sharp, and there exists no other hook like it. It was made by God himself. Once this hook gets planted in souls, they will never be able to break it. It's a penetrating hook, and a priest must not be afraid to use it and plant it firmly into souls.

If a priest is afraid to set the hook deeply because he considers it too "aggressive" an approach, he is not going to catch souls. The hook of truth — the teaching of the Catholic Church — is what catches and saves souls, not a priest's popularity or academic degrees. Just as a fisherman is not worried about "harming" the fish when setting the hook, a priest cannot be worried about offending a soul with the truth. It is the truth that sets us free (cf. Jn 8:32). The hook of truth may sting for a time, but ultimately it is in being captured by truth that a soul is set free.

The teaching of the Catholic Church will offend many people — I'm quite sure I've already upset a few readers with some of the things I've written in this book. But that doesn't mean a priest should refrain from preaching it. He must preach it. If he does not, he is not fishing so as to catch fish (souls), put them in the boat (ark) of salvation — the Catholic Church — and bring them to better shores (heaven). He is playing catch-and-release.

A priest will do no good to souls if he plays catch-and-release during his homilies. If he is primarily concerned about the collection basket and tries not to offend anyone with a message that stings, the fish are not truly caught. The Church is *not* an all-inclusive, diversified, tolerant-of-everything social group. Trying to get large numbers at Mass or a big amount in the collection plate is not what it's all about. God has more riches than we can ever imagine. What he desires from his priests is a willingness to love souls to the point of death. Thus, a priest must not be afraid to preach a hard message out of fear that people will decrease their Sunday collection, stampede out, or go elsewhere. The role of the priest is to plant the hook. Leave the rest up to God.

Furthermore, the role of a priest is to fish with the hook that God gave him, not substituting it with something else. Priests must not create their own hook, thinking themselves inventors of a new method of fishing. It won't work, and there exists no "new" or "improved" method for catching souls than the truth. Nothing is more effective when fishing for souls than giving them the hook of objective truth. Priests are not the inventors of truth either. They are simply called to freely give what they have been freely given. The teaching of the Catholic Church is universally applicable, ageless, and objectively true. Just like mathematics.

Two plus two equals four. Always. If anyone says that it doesn't, he needs to get his head checked out. None of us created mathematics, so none of us has a right to seek to change it or tweak it. It's outside of you and me to change. It's the same thing with the teachings of the Catholic Church in matters of faith and morals. They are not man-made. If a person seeks to change them or tweak them, then he puts himself on a road to ruin. The teaching of the Catholic Church in matters of faith and morals is everlasting, unchanging, and objectively true. The hook remains the same for all generations. And priests are called to plant only that hook, as no other substitute will truly catch souls.

In light of this, I have often thought that if a priest "plays" catch and release with the souls that are entrusted to him, he is guilty of committing spiritual contraception. Since we are talking about souls, not fish, if a priest mounts the pulpit but fails to deliver the *seed of truth* in its totality to the bridal Church, he is putting a barrier between the bridegroom and the bride — the priest stands in the person of Christ the bridegroom. When a priest does not preach the truth as taught by the Catholic Church, he fails to impart the life-giving seed to the bride and is committing spiritual contraception. The bride — the souls of the faithful — are unable to bear fruit when he does this.

Not telling souls the truth is tantamount to telling them you don't really love them. But a man who really loves souls is willing to be crucified, even by the very people that he loves, because love conquers all things, even death. Thus, in his preaching a priest must not shy away from topics that souls may not want to hear about — controversial topics such as homosexuality, abortion, and contraception. The priest may be hated because of his sting-ing words, but in the end, it is his manly, sacrificial love that will conquer hearts. Jesus himself showed priests the effectiveness of manly, sacrificial love when he taught them that it was through his being lifted up on the Cross that he would draw all men — all souls — to himself (cf. Jn 12:32).

Secondly, there's the bait. The bait that every priest needs to use to catch souls is the Blessed Virgin Mary. She is the bait of God.

A hook is not too attractive, but the bait always is. For many souls in the world today, the teaching of the Catholic Church — the hook — is not too alluring, but the overwhelming attractiveness of the bait is what draws them in. Every fish has to be lured in.

The truthfulness of Catholic teaching can be downright shocking to souls, just as light is initially blinding to those who have been living in darkness. By analogy, everybody knows that a doctor oftentimes has to spank a newborn on the bottom in order for the child to breathe the life-sustaining air. This is also the case with souls and the light of truth. Divine truth and light can be hard to swallow initially. So souls who have been living in darkness — in the depths of a sea of sin — often require a divine 2 x 4 in order to jolt them into opening their eyes and starting to breathe. Divine truth and light are like a sharp hook, and they sting. Yet God's fatherly love sees to it that a beautiful mother always precedes the spank and that the newborn is returned to the arms of that same beautiful mother after the life-giving blow is delivered. There is a lot a priest can learn from this.

When a priest incorporates the lovely image and person of Our Lady into his teaching and preaching, the spank of truth is made more palatable and acceptable, and the sharpness and sting of the hook even appears desirable. I guarantee that a priest will have an extremely fruitful ministry if he places before the eyes and hearts of his people the beauty and loveliness of Mary. Everyone is drawn to beauty, and a priest who knows how to preach about her, and does so frequently, will have the gift of touching hearts quickly and deeply. The hook will be set firm, but it will be less shocking and painful.

Who is not captivated by a beautiful woman? Who does not take delight in a beautiful mother? All men love princesses, and all women want to be one. It's no accident that the most painted woman in the history of the world is Mary. All of the great masters — including Raphael, Leonardo da Vinci, and Michelangelo — have painted or sculpted images of Our Lady. And she is *always* portrayed as being kind, loving, approachable, and welcoming. Her image *always* draws people closer to God. The divinity and power of God can be quite intimidating to us sinful creatures, but in most paintings of Our Lady, we see her with the Infant Jesus on her lap — the Madonna and Child. In this pose, she is inviting us to come close to her Jesus and worship him. After all, who is scared of a baby? Only madmen and demons fear babies — this is the reason why they try to kill them. But for those who are in their right minds, babies offer us no threat. We love them. We treasure them.

A priest who seeks to catch souls by baiting the hook of truth with the sweetest Heart of Mary is doing exactly what the Holy Spirit wants him to do. His ministry will have power even if he is not the greatest orator or the most educated man. It is a biblically revealed truth that wherever the Holy Spirit finds Mary, he rushes in like a "mighty wind" and sets hearts on fire for Jesus (cf. Acts 2:1-4). The very patron saint of priests himself, St. John Vianney, was not the most educated man by worldly standards. But he had the one thing necessary for bringing souls to Jesus: He had Mary. A priest who has Mary in his life and apostolate will reap a great catch of souls.

Thirdly, there's the fishing line. The fishing line that every priest needs to have in order to catch souls is mercy. If a priest is going to catch men — souls — he has to have a heart of mercy. Having a heart full of patience and mercy is extremely important for a priest because he is going to witness the struggles, hardships, setbacks, and falls of the people he is ministering to. And just like a fisherman, a priest has to be willing to give souls slack, letting them go through the struggle of being captured by truth. Eventually, they will wear themselves out, and the fisherman can effortlessly reel them in. But sometimes this will go on for a very long time.

There's an old saying: A priest must be "a lion in the pulpit and a lamb in the pew." What this means is that a priest needs to be zealous and on fire when communicating the truth but also extremely compassionate when dealing with individual souls. This is why having a heart of mercy is so important in the life of a priest.

Every fish fights. Every fish runs once the hook is set. Sometimes, they go as far away from the boat as they possibly can, going deep and threatening to exhaust the fisherman's line. But the divine fishermen has lots of line — mercy. And he doesn't hold the line too tight because he knows that risks snapping the line and losing the fish. The hook has been set. Letting a fish "run" doesn't mean he has gotten away or that the fishermen isn't concerned about catching the fish. All fishermen know that when you give a fish slack, you are not letting it go: You do this so you don't lose it. The last thing you want is to hold on so tightly that the line snaps and you lose the fish.

It's the same with truth and souls. A priest has to plant the hook of truth but not hold the line too tight. He must be extremely patient and merciful to souls as they are being caught. Being merciful doesn't mean he is overlooking the truth, downplaying sin, or letting souls get off the hook. Not at all. It means he is imitating the divine fisherman who offers us an ocean of mercy. God knows we are frightened fish and will put up a fight. He knows we are fickle and stubborn creatures.

Remember in the Gospel of John when Jesus let the people walk away because they didn't believe it was possible to eat Jesus' flesh and drink his blood? He let them walk away because the truth doesn't change. He had set the hook of truth firmly in their souls. They can run, but they will never be able to escape the truth. And when they exhaust themselves pursuing things that are passing and constantly changing — the *bread of the world* — they will know where they can go to where the truth never changes: back to Jesus. He will always take them back and welcome them into the ark.

☆ ☆ ☆ Marian Gems

☆ Mary is the most sweet bait, chosen by God, to catch men. *St. Catherine of Siena*

☆ Mary becomes the "magnet" which attracts all hearts to itself, the "lure" which attracts all like fish and leads them into "God's net." *Servant of God (Fr.) Joseph Kentenich*

☆ Eternal Wisdom calls people's attention to her in order to use her as bait, as magnet, as hook for human hearts. *Servant of God (Fr.) Joseph Kentenich*

☆ My brothers, who but a total idiot could ever doubt that he would find water in the sea? So, too, when we come to Mary, can we have the least doubt that we will find grace and mercy in one who is the

Mother of Grace, the Mother of Mercy, the Mother of Kindness, the sea of goodness, the ocean of love? *St. Lawrence of Brindisi*

☆ If devotion to the Blessed Virgin is necessary for all men simply to work out their salvation, it is even more necessary for those who are called to a special perfection. I do not believe that anyone can acquire intimate union with our Lord and perfect fidelity to the Holy Spirit without a very close union with the most Blessed Virgin and an absolute dependence on her support. *St. Louis de Montfort*

☆ I am your servant [Mary], because your Son is my Lord. Therefore, you are my mistress, because you are the handmaid of my Lord. Therefore, I am the servant of the handmaid of the Lord, because you, my mistress, became the Mother of my Lord. *St. Ildelphonsus of Toledo*

☆ If the Church shows respect and veneration for everything that came in contact with the Savior's Body, the cross, the nails, the thorns, the winding sheet of his sepulcher, the swathing bands of his infancy and similar things, what honor must be due to this venerable body of the Blessed Virgin from which the Body of the Redeemer was formed! *St. John Eudes*

☆ Hail, thou fountain springing forth by God's design, whose rivers flowing over in pure and unsullied waves of orthodoxy put to flight the hosts of error. *St. Germanus of Constantinople*

☆ We hail you, O Mary Mother of God, venerable treasure of the entire world, inextinguishable lamp, crown of virginity, scepter of orthodoxy, imperishable temple, container of him who cannot be contained, Mother and Virgin. *St. Cyril of Alexandria*

☆ Where Mary is, there is the archetype of total self-giving and Christian discipleship. Where Mary is, there is the Pentecostal breath of the Holy Spirit; there is new beginning and authentic renewal. *Pope Benedict XVI*

☆ I could conquer the world if I had an army to say the Rosary. *Blessed Pope Pius IX*

☆ The world will be completely Christianized if Mary will be known, imitated and invoked throughout the world. *Blessed James Alberione*

☆ Only through associating the Madonna with your priesthood will you become efficacious in the field of grace so as to make bud forth children of God and saints in this world. *St. Padre Pio*

☆ The priest has a deep love of Mary not only in his better moments, but even in his failings. He trusts in her intercession to combat his weakness. Then especially, he looks to her for special attention, knowing that the child who falls most often is apt to get most of the mother's kisses. *Venerable Fulton J. Sheen*

Brothers in Arms

I LOVE SURFING. There's something almost supernatural about it. I even sensed this when I was a total teenage pagan. To this day, many non-religious surfers refer to their local surf break as their *church* and surfing a great barrel as the green *cathedral*. In a certain sense, I guess surfing is kind of like walking on water. It does give you a sense of having superhuman powers. The ecstatic experience of pulling into a hollow barrel and getting deeply pitted is one of the most amazing experiences ever. I mean, after all, no mortal man should be able to be totally encompassed by water and yet not be soaked and totally freaked out! And it's even better when your buddies witness your superhuman feat, and they hoot and holler as you come charging down the line like an other-worldly superhero!

I've experienced this feeling many times and consider myself super blessed to have been able to surf in places like Japan, Guam, Fiji, Hawaii, New Zealand, Mexico, Brazil, Argentina, Barbados, California, and all up and down the East Coast of the United States. I am so grateful to Jesus and Mary for these experiences. But there's one experience in particular that I'd like to share with you because it relates to the topic at hand.

A few years ago, I was invited to speak in Australia. I'd always wanted to go to Australia. But this wasn't going to be like other speaking trips I had made. This was going to be a speaking *and* surfing trip. On some of my other international speaking trips, I have been able to surf for *maybe* a morning or two, but this trip would consist of speaking and surfing every day for two straight weeks and in Australia!

The invitation came from an Australian priest I had met while we were both speaking at a Marian conference in Arizona. His invitation consisted of this: I would first fly to Perth (western Australia) where I would speak at several events and surf at world

famous places like Yallingup and Margaret River. Then, I would
fly to Sydney where he and I would speak every evening and surf
every morning at different spots as we made our way from Sydney
to Melbourne, which would include driving on parts of the Great
Ocean Road. Needless to say, I got permission from my superiors,
and signed up.

The first few days in and around Perth were awesome. Then,
after having given talks and surfed in the biggest waves and most
shark-infested waters I've ever been in, I flew to eastern Australia
and met up with my priest friend in New South Wales to begin
our journey. What an experience we had as brothers! With our
surfboards on top of the car, and our Breviaries on the dashboard,
our daily routine for two weeks consisted of surfing at a new spot
every morning until our arms felt like they were going to fall off,
then driving to the next church while praying the Rosary and
Divine Mercy Chaplet, and having real brotherly fellowship. Once
at the church, we would celebrate Mass, hear confessions, and give
our talks, then pass out from sheer exhaustion. As a surfer-priest, I
was living the dream!

We were brothers, and the blessing of being able to surf with
a brother priest made the experience even more awesome. We
prayed together, shared waves together, discussed our hardships
and struggles, encouraged each other, and drank a few cold beers
to celebrate the beauty of life! We were stoked! We were brothers
in arms.

And we rocked that place. Both at the events we spoke at
and at the beaches we surfed, we rocked that place. One episode
in particular stands out, though, and every time I think about it I
can't stop laughing because it was like something from a movie. I'm
sure there are a few guys in Australia somewhere who are talking
about it to this day, too.

It took place near the world famous Bells Beach. One
morning, my friend and I showed up eager to surf the legendary
break, but found it way overcrowded. So we decided to surf the
extension of Bells that is called Winkipop. It's usually better
than Bells, anyway. It's just that Bells is world famous for the
yearly contest that's held there. By the time we arrived at the
parking lot, all the locals were already down the rickety old

steps that hug a steep cliff and lead down to the break. So we quickly put on our wetsuits in preparation for the frigid water — beaches in and around Melbourne have really cold water during Australia's winter — and headed down the steps.

The surf session was super fun! It's a reef break, so the waves just beautifully peel, and you can carve all over the face of the wave. Since we knew this was our only chance to surf this place, we paddled after the best waves and broke many of the rules of surfing etiquette in order to catch our share, even if it meant dropping in on the locals and spraying them with our carves. We could tell the locals were not happy with us, and one even called me a derogatory name. But we just ignored them and kept surfing. As the morning progressed and a negative low tide hit — and since we had been surfing for over three hours — we scrambled back up the dilapidated wooden steps and returned to the parking lot.

Who we found waiting for us at the parking lot were many of the locals we had been dropping in on for the last three hours. By the looks on their faces — and the murmuring under their breath — they seemed pretty *aggro* (surfer slang for those with an aggressive disposition). So in silence, my friend and I strapped the boards to the top of the car, calmly slipped out of our wetsuits, and — to the amazement of the locals — changed into Roman collars. The onlookers were speechless, their jaws agape, having suddenly come to the realization that they had been out-surfed — and upstaged — by a pair of Catholic priests! Then, as we got into the car and slowly drove right by them on the road to get out of the parking lot, I turned and gave them a gesture of blessing through the passenger side window. It was classic!

I realize now that the surfers on that beach may have written us off as jerks because of our rudeness. In hindsight, we probably should have apologized. But I relate this story because the perception of priests these days is that they are somehow less than men. That mentality cracks me up. Contrary to most all of the presentations of priests in sitcoms and television shows today where priests are presented as buffoons, most all of the priests I know are real men and dedicated soldiers for Christ. Some of the men in my own religious community are hunters, backcountry skiers, skateboarders, motorcyclists, mountain bikers, hikers, and very good baseball and basketball players. All these men could have beautiful wives, massive bank accounts, fast cars, and posh houses, but they've given all that up for a greater good — the salvation of souls.

As I noted earlier, priests are knights, soldiers, and warriors. As such, they are not called to do solo missions but to work and fight as a team — as brothers. Brotherhood among priests is a great gift. It strengthens the fraternal bond of fellowship, and it gives each man the courage to fight side-by-side with and for his brothers. And since priests have a common enemy who is of (fallen) angelic intelligence, they need each other. Jesus was the priest-warrior who drove out demons and conquered the enemy, yet he delighted in sharing a deep brotherly bond with his chosen men. The first priests spent time with him and saw him lead by his manly example. They had brotherhood; they had fellowship. And men need this. All men need this.

When I was a seminarian, the movie version of *The Lord of the Rings* trilogy was released. I can't tell you how many times my fellow seminarians and I watched *The Fellowship of the Ring, The Two Towers,* and *The Return of the King.* If we had some free time on a weekend, we would pop in one of those DVD's and get pumped up. Sure, the films were entertaining, but we appreciated those movies mostly for their spiritual overtones of good-versus-evil, rescuing the beautiful, conquering ugly beasts, and fighting as brothers in arms.

My seminarian brothers and I sought to translate these manly qualities into our spiritual lives as we prepared for priestly ordination. To this day, I have great confidence that I can count on my brothers to fight by my side in the battle against darkness. As brother priests, we despise the same enemy (sin and the devil), worship the same God (the Holy Trinity), love the same mother (Mary), fight for the same beauty (Christ's bride), and believe the same creed (Catholicism). To the attack!

Yet, as glorious and noble as this is, every now and then — in those movies and in real life — the brotherly bond is threatened by discord and selfishness. Sometimes, a brother even falls through sin and does damage to the fellowship. I can't tell you how my heart breaks when a brother priest falls. For one, it scares me because I know I'm no better than my brother and am capable of doing stupid stuff, too. All men are capable of falling back into sin. When grave sins or scandalous behavior occur in the life of a brother priest, many people are hurt — and this pain does not heal easily. It also breaks my heart when a priest falls because he is made a laughing stock by the media and society. But society doesn't realize that it's not a robot or a machine who has fallen; it's my brother.

Yet such divisions must be dealt with immediately. Jesus himself had to rebuke his disciples on occasion in order to prevent waywardness and selfishness. He had to strengthen their unity and prevent division and discord. As the Second Person of the Holy Trinity, Jesus knows the power of unity; where there is unity in truth, there is power. Therefore, anything that threatens that unity must be dealt with immediately. Where there is strife and factions among brothers, there is war. Jesus, as the Commander-in-Chief of God's army, spent three years with his first priests, and those years were comparable to a boot camp experience. During those three years, he had to keep reminding them that they must not fight among themselves, act selfishly, or allow factions to creep into the brotherhood. They must remain united and work together.

As much as men would like to think they can conquer the enemy themselves — and there is a tendency for men to think they can go it alone — the reality is that the "one-man mission" is nonsense. Men need each other; they need brotherhood. Just like they need a beauty to fight for, they need brothers who have their back, so that they can have the courage to charge the enemy head-on. When priests present a united frontal attack, they can do great things in overcoming evil. And since the enemy that priests fight against is not of this world, they must not think they can overcome this enemy with a worldly weapon. Worldly weapons are no match for this infernal beast. Only a divine weapon can conquer this dragon.

In this fallen world, men are inclined to call down thunder or break out the sword and swing it wildly in order to bring about justice and defeat the enemy. Jesus had to train his first priests in this matter, too. He trained them by giving his brother priests a higher example of manhood by teaching them to sacrifice them-

selves for the good of others. He taught his brothers the wisdom of
the Cross and how to conquer the enemy by allowing themselves
to be nailed to the Cross. In this way, Jesus flipped the weapon of
the world — the sword — upside down and made it into the Cross,
the weapon of the spiritual warrior. Only this weapon can conquer the enemy. Priests can slay demons with it, and when there
is a unified effort among brother priests to do this, the gates of
hell panic and tremble. Hell fears the priesthood, especially the
brotherhood of priests.

In fact, Satan once told St. John Vianney, the patron saint of
priests, that if there were only a few more priests like him, he,
Satan, would have no power. This is why I believe Satan has been
trying so hard in our day to cause discord and division in the
priesthood. Not only is he trying to reduce the number of priests,
but he wants them to get overworked, stressed out, and fall
through human weakness. Many priests today are in charge of two
or three parishes, live in isolation, have little to no brotherhood,
and are constantly bombarded with temptations against chastity.
Satan is, indeed, working overtime trying to get priests to sin and
cause scandal, especially by turning them away from prayer and
Marian devotion.

Satan hates priests who are devoted to Mary because he knows
they have head-crushing power. Satan hates anything to do with
Our Lady, especially a priest who promotes and preaches about her.
The homily of a Marian priest can undo the vast array of snares that
the enemy has set for souls in one single homiletic blow. And all hell
trembles when priests come together as brothers in arms and pray
the Rosary. Have you ever been in a seminary or a religious house
and experienced a group of priests praying the Rosary together out
loud? It's powerful, and sounds like thunder. It is thunder. Such
men are comparable to the "special forces" in the spiritual life. They
are the militia of Jesus and Mary. A priest with a rosary in his hand
is like a Marian Marine. One Marine is tough, but if you see a whole
bunch of them together, you better just give up. They will take you
down! Same thing with Marian priests. The enemy doesn't even
stand a chance.

Unified priests are always gathered around their Queen.
Every time in the history of Christianity that truth is being
threatened and Mary's divine Son ignored and offended, the

Queen raises up a new battle breed of dedicated knights and soldiers who preach truth and foster a renewed love for Jesus Christ and his Church. These dedicated warrior priests find their unity *under the mantle* of their spiritual Mother. She brings them together and helps them form bonds of true brotherhood, so that they pray together and fight against the darkness together. Study the various eras in the history of the Church, and you will find this to be true.

I believe Our Lady is doing this again in our times. In our day, when Jesus and his Church are mocked and ignored, babies are killed in the womb, homosexual marriage is the "new normal," and all matters of morality are in question, the Holy Queen is raising up a new battle breed of warrior priests to combat the darkness. Mary will never allow the glory and honor due her divine Son to be neglected. As a 21st century priest, I am honored to be a part of this army of soldier priests, fighting by the side of the brothers in my own religious community, other religious communities, and the many valiant diocesan priests throughout the world. I even have a personal motto for my priesthood that I try and live by. When things are tough in the spiritual battle and I need to be reminded of why I do what I do and make the sacrifices that I make, I send out a spiritual battle cry to heaven: *"For God! For Brother! For Beauty!"*

☆ ☆ ☆ Marian Gems

☆ Men do not fear a powerful hostile army as the powers of hell fear the name and protection of Mary. *St. Bonaventure*

☆ If anyone does not wish to have Mary Immaculate for his Mother, he will not have Christ for his Brother. *St. Maximilian Kolbe*

☆ Every objection against devotion to Mary grows in the soil of an imperfect belief in the Son. It is a historical fact that, as the world lost the Mother, it also lost the Son. It may well be that, as the world returns to love of Mary, it will also return to a belief in the divinity of Christ. *Venerable Fulton J. Sheen*

☆ Mary is powerful against heresy. Heresy is obstinacy in error regarding matters of faith. Mary is a hammer against heresy itself, but she is salvation for separated brethren of good will. *Blessed James Alberione*

☆ Under her guidance, under her patronage, under her kindness and protection, nothing is to be feared; nothing is hopeless. Because, while bearing toward us a truly motherly affection and having in her care the work of our salvation, she is solicitous about the whole human race. And since she has been appointed by God to be the Queen of heaven and earth, and is exalted above all the choirs of angels and saints, and even stands at the right hand of her only-begotten Son, Jesus Christ our Lord, she presents our petitions in a most efficacious manner. What she asks, she obtains. Her pleas can never be unheard. *Blessed Pope Pius IX*

☆ Even if you have to fight distractions all through your whole Rosary be sure to fight well, arms in hand: that is to say, do not stop saying your Rosary even if it is hard to say and you have absolutely no sensible devotion. It is a terrible battle, I know, but one that is profitable to the faithful soul. *St. Louis de Montfort*

☆ It is mainly to expand the Kingdom of Christ that we look to the Rosary for the most effective help. *Pope Leo XIII*

☆ Never will anyone really be able to understand the marvelous riches of sanctification which are contained in the prayers and mysteries of the Holy Rosary. This meditation on the mysteries of the life and death of Our Lord and Savior Jesus Christ is the source of the most wonderful fruits for those who use it. *St. Louis de Montfort*

☆ Let us count as synonymous the expressions saint and child of Mary! *Blessed William Joseph Chaminade*

☆ I have never read of any saint who did not have a special devotion to the glorious Virgin. *St. Bonaventure*

☆ O Blessed Rosary of Mary, sweet chain which binds us to God, bond of love which unites us to the angels, tower of salvation against the assaults of hell, safe port in our universal shipwreck, we shall never abandon you. *Blessed Bartolo Longo*

☆ Love of Our Lady is proof of a good spirit, in works and in individuals. Don't trust the undertaking that lacks this characteristic. *St. Josemaria Escriva*

☆ ☆ ☆ ☆ ☆ ☆ ☆ ☆ ☆

CHAPTER 6

Prayer and Devotion(s)

Spiritual Marriage

IT HAS BEEN SAID BY MANY PEOPLE, and in many places, that love makes the world go round. I agree. As a matter of fact, love is the reason we exist at all. We were created by a God who is love itself: "God is love" (1 Jn 4:8). And the love of the three divine persons of the Holy Trinity is so self-emptying that it poured itself out into creation. The Trinity is, in fact, inviting and wooing created persons into an endless nuptial union of bliss — the inner Trinitarian life of God. Jesus himself said, "The kingdom of heaven may be compared to a king who gave a marriage feast for his son" (Mt. 22:2).

Saint Paul wrote about this spiritual marriage in his letter to the Ephesians and called it a "great mystery" (Eph 5:32). It is, indeed, a great and awesome mystery. And though spiritual marriage with God is an analogy, there are tons of theological implications that we can glean from it. These insights will help us better understand both the role of prayer and devotion in our lives, as well as the divinely intended purpose behind creation and Christianity. All we have to do is unpack the spiritual marriage analogy.

Let's unpack it from the beginning.

Creation came to be because God's Trinitarian self-emptying love overflowed and poured itself out, causing creation to come into existence. As a result, God's self-emptying put a "Trinitarian stamp" on all created things. This means that all things have been created to love, receive love, and be fruitful — just as in the inner life of the Holy Trinity. This three-fold Trinitarian stamp of inter-personal communion is essentially what is meant when we speak about souls being in spiritual nuptials, espousal, and marriage to God. *It's spiritual, not physical.*

Furthermore, as part of the uniqueness and special dignity of created persons, mankind and angels were given the great gift of free will. This gift comes with many blessings and many responsibilities: Created human persons can chose to be in communion with others, produce fruit, and act responsibly; or they can turn away from love, live in isolation, and bring hardship and pain to others. As we know, our first parents used their free will poorly and brought sin into the world. But that wasn't the end of the story. As a matter of fact, it wasn't even the beginning of the story. Though Adam and Eve were given an earthly paradise and lost it by failing to love and act responsibly, God's providential and merciful love allowed their fall to happen — though he didn't will it or desire it. The truth of the matter is that God knew it would happen, and he allowed it to happen because he had something even better in mind.

An earthly paradise is good, but it's not good enough. God knew full well that Adam and Eve would fall, but that did not thwart his original intention for creating the heavens and the earth. Created persons were made to be in nuptial union with God. We were created for a marriage feast! And as everybody knows, marriages require preparation and planning. Therefore, being omnipotent, God had already made provisions *ahead of time* for Adam and Eve's fall. He did this because the meaning and ultimate purpose of creation is not centered on the persons of Adam and Eve. Though they came first in *chronological* time, in the divine plan, spiritual marriage was in the mind of God from all eternity. The ultimate meaning and purpose for creation was only brought to light in the fullness of time by the coming of the heavenly bridegroom, Jesus Christ. This *absolute primacy of Christ* is sung about every year by the Church during the Easter Vigil in the beautiful hymn of the "Exultet":

> *What good would life have been to us,*
> *had Christ not come as our Redeemer?*
> *Father, how wonderful your care for us!*
> *How boundless your merciful love!*
> *To ransom a slave you gave away your Son.*
> *O happy fault,*
> *O necessary sin of Adam, which gained for us*
> *so great a Redeemer!*

Since Jesus Christ, the bridegroom, provides the ultimate meaning for creation, it also necessarily follows that the bride shares in his primacy because only a bride makes a marriage complete. What this means is that God did not have a "plan B" when it came to what his intentions were with creation. He doesn't make mistakes. As God, he saw things from afar and planned *ahead of time* everything that would be necessary for the marriage feast of his Son. So, when Adam and Eve fell, God did not panic and hold a Trinitarian committee meeting in order to scratch "plan A" and initiate "plan B."

God allowed Adam and Eve to fall and planned *ahead of time* that the real meaning and purpose for creation — in the fullness of time (cf. Gal 4:4) — would only be found in the spiritual marriage between the divine bridegroom and his bride. It is this bridegroom and *his bride* who provide the ultimate meaning for all that came before them and all that will come after them. They provide the blueprint for what all created persons are invited to participate in, which is the "great mystery" of heaven: the spiritual marriage between God and souls.

Furthermore, the fact that creation and Christianity are about a wedding — the "marriage supper of the Lamb" (Rev 19:9) — reveals to us that there are certain persons that must necessarily have been planned *ahead of time* in preparation for the spiritual marriage, namely, the bridegroom *and* the bride. So while it's completely obvious that Jesus has absolute primacy in creation and is the bridegroom — he even calls himself the bridegroom (cf. Mt 9:15) — it might be easy to forget that the bride must necessarily have a share in his primacy.

Let me explain: Jesus is God, and creation and Christianity cannot exist without him. Yet, since no marriage is complete without a man and a woman, the person of the bride is necessary in God's plan *from the beginning*. If creation and Christianity find their beginning, fullness, and finality in the reality that God's eternal and unchanging plan is to espouse created persons to himself in a spiritual marriage, this means that there must be a real and specific bride who makes the "great mystery" real. Then it is not simply an idea or a possibility. If there is not a real and concrete bride who was foreseen and planned from the beginning, the "great mystery" of Christianity is haphazard and willy-nilly on God's part. But reason and revelation both tell us that God does not do things in a disorderly, whimsical, or capricious manner. *All* weddings take preparation and planning. Therefore, there must have been a bride who was foreseen and planned from the beginning and who shares in the absolute primacy of the bridegroom. And there is. She is the Church.

Yet this raises a few questions for us: Is the bride of Christ, the Church, a *what* or a *who*? Has Jesus Christ spiritually espoused a *thing* or a *person*? And is it a *thing* or a *person* who shares in his primacy as bride?

Catholicism tells us that it is both/and. On one level, we know that the Church, as the bride of Christ, is both a *what* and a *who*, a *thing* and a *person*. As already noted, the Church is an institution with rules and regulations, rites and rituals. But, more importantly, the Church is first and foremost a person, an immaculate person. If there is not one concrete *personal* bride, then there is no bride and no marriage. Obviously, neither you nor I are the pattern of what it means to be in nuptial union with God. We are not immaculate persons. But there is one who is, and her name is Mary. She is the Immaculata, the Church in her essence. She is the personification of the Church. Though a member of the Church, she is also its mother, model, and heart. No other created person can claim this privilege.

Also, in order for us, the members of the Church, to attend this wedding, there is proper attire that is required (cf. Mt 22:11-12). Those who attend must be immaculate (sinless), "having washed their robes and made them white in the blood of the Lamb" (Rev 7:14; 22:14). Each person retains their individuality and unique personhood, but each individual person *must* become *another immaculate one*, "without spot or wrinkle or any such thing" (Eph 5:27) in order to enter into the eternal wedding. This is deep stuff, I know. But it's true and at the root of everything the King is doing in preparation for the marriage feast of his Son.

Therefore, since spiritual marriage is God's purpose for creation and Christianity, if Mary did not exist, we would not exist. That's a bold statement, but by using the wedding analogy, it's easy to see how it's true. There can be no wedding without the bridegroom *and* the bride. The bride was not an afterthought in

God's providential plan. She is there in his mind from the beginning. And Jesus has not espoused to himself multiple brides (religions); he is not a polygamist. There is only one bridegroom and one bride, and there exists no other pattern than the Immaculata for what it means to be in spiritual union of mind, heart, and will with Christ. We are all called to be in nuptial spiritual union with Christ and *become the Church*, but this only happens when we *become another Immaculata*.

For this reason, Mary is not simply the New Eve but the real Eve, the first woman God had in mind when he created the heavens and the earth. Similarly, Jesus is not simply the New Adam. In the mind and plan of God, he is the real Adam and the divinely planned bridegroom of creation *from the beginning*. And just as without the reality of Jesus, nothing before him or after him has any direction or finality, so it is with Mary. She is the necessary bride that makes creation and Christianity (the spiritual marriage) possible. She is not an afterthought in the mind of God; she is the first thought God had when he designed creation and Christianity in preparation for the marriage of his Son. In her, God the Father prepared a masterpiece for his Son.

Some may think this is Freudian-type talk, but that's because they think as men do and not as God does. The nuptial union between Jesus and Mary is not a physical union, but a spiritual union of persons, hearts, and wills and a preparation for the everlasting spiritual marriage of heaven that the King desires for all created persons. This nuptial union between persons also explains how men (the masculine) can be spiritually united with Christ, because it is not a union of bodies but of persons, hearts, and wills. Bodily union between men is unnatural and against natural and divine law, but a spiritual union of hearts and wills is supernatural and a preparation for heaven. Jesus himself said that in heaven the holy neither marry nor are given in marriage (cf. Mt 22:30), yet paradise is still called the marriage supper of the Lamb (cf. Rev 19:9) because it is a spiritual union of persons.

In order to validate all of this, there are many passages in the New Testament that show us that Jesus, the bridegroom, completely understood his saving mission within the context of the "great mystery." For example, Jesus initiates his public ministry at a wedding (Cana), and it is at that wedding that he begins to refer to Mary as *woman*. Did you know that in Greek, the word for *woman* that Jesus begins to use to describe Mary means *bride*? Very interesting, huh? Even St. John the Baptist, the "friend of the bridegroom" (Jn 3:29) and "best man" at the wedding of the Messiah (cf. Mt 11:11), alludes to this "great mystery" when he prophetically states that "he who has the bride is the bridegroom" (Jn 3:29). This passage might seem strange and cryptic, but it's not when you look at it from the perspective of the "great mystery."

The bridegroom, Jesus, already has his bride by his side in the person of the Immaculata. The Father gave her to him in anticipation of his Son's sacrifice on the Cross. The Immaculata is the perfect fruit of the bridegroom's anticipated sacrifice on Calvary. Therefore, the Son *must* die for her since she has already been given to him and is, in fact, the pattern for all others. In dying for her, he is dying for all who will be patterned off of her, his one true nuptial "other."

And in the complementarity of masculinity and femininity, Jesus needs Mary by his side so that *together* they can journey toward Calvary and consummate the spiritual marriage between God and mankind. This is why from the Cross Jesus refers to Mary again as the *woman*. The consummation of the spiritual marriage requires that both the bridegroom and the bride be present and that their hearts and wills are one. Without Jesus *and* Mary, none of this is possible. And this is why the Father had to give the bride to his Son *ahead of time*, because, together, they must consummate the spiritual marriage. Therefore, Jesus *and* Mary make Christianity (the spiritual marriage) real and complete. It is consummated.

This also helps us understand that Jesus' reason for establishing the Catholic Church was to make it the antechamber to the wedding feast, the Mary-maker, and the only path to true spirituality. Without Mary and the Catholic Church, our lives have no direction, finality, or consummation. If we are not members of the Church that offers persons the ability to become holy and immaculate, we have no nuptial blueprint or mold to be conformed to and are incapable of acquiring the immaculate robe necessary for the wedding.

We were born to be immaculate and live forever in an endless nuptial union with the Holy Trinity. Not to surrender to this reality is to experience an everlasting anthropological frustration (hell) in both our person and in our nature. Failure to accept the divine proposal and become immaculate is to condemn ourselves to be eternally cut off from ever attaining that for which we were brought into existence: the beatific vision. We were created and born for union with the Trinitarian God, and if it doesn't happen, we are unfulfilled and exist in an everlasting torture of being incomplete.

So what does prayer and devotion have to do with all of this? Everything!

If our relationship with Jesus is like a spiritual marriage, we must learn to be prayerful and devoted like the one model for what it means to be in nuptial spiritual union with Christ: the Immaculata.

Since the institutional Church's purpose is to assist people into becoming like the Immaculata in order to enter into a perfect union of hearts and wills with Jesus Christ, leading a life of prayer and devotion, after the example of Mary, is an absolute necessity. As the model of what it means to live in nuptial union with God, Mary gives us the greatest example of living our spiritual marriage with God. She has "pondered all these things in her heart" (Lk 2:19), and she has prepared the way for us to do the same. She is the lover of the Trinity and the holiest human person to ever live precisely because she is the most prayerful and devoted of all God's creatures. Her person, heart, mind, and will are in complete union with the bridegroom. She is madly in love with God and is willing to do anything that he asks, even to undergoing a torturous spiritual, emotional, and mystical crucifixion at the foot of the Cross. And through her, it becomes possible for us to do the will of God and become mothers, brothers, sisters, and even spiritually espoused, to Jesus Christ (cf. Mt 12:50; Lk 11:27-28).

The true Christian is a Marian Christian. To pray is to be Marian. To be devoted is to be like the Immaculata. She shows us that prayer is the heart-to-heart relationship and spiritual intimacy that makes union, faithfulness, and fruitfulness with God possible. To pray and be devoted to Christ, therefore, is to become Marian. There really is no other way.

As in any relationship, it goes without saying that knowledge and love of the "other" will not grow in an environment where the persons do not communicate and share a heart-to-heart intimacy. No marriage begins or endures without communication. Thus, how will a person ever fall in love with God and want to be close to him if they do not talk to him and share their heart with him like Mary? Without a solid prayer life, no one can grow in a sincere and lasting love for God. Over the years, I've met many people who experience a weekend of spiritual romance with God during a retreat or a conference. But within a very short period of time, the relationship dies because there was a failure to keep in touch with the beloved. Persevering in prayer is absolutely key to growing in holiness and faithfulness to the beloved. Mary is the great teacher of prayer and devotion. Contrary to a gospel of wealth, health, and prosperity, Mary shows us how to persevere in love for God even when it costs us everything. *And it will cost us everything.*

There will be many times in the spiritual marriage with God when it will not "feel" joyful. There will be many times in the journey when we are more sorrowful than ecstatic, moments when everything is not crystal clear. But by pondering everything in prayer and devotion like Mary, we learn trust and perseverance (cf. Lk 2:50). And because our spiritual life is like a marriage, there needs to be sacrifice and commitment. Nobody ever becomes a saint without having a devoted prayer life because, at its core, prayer rekindles the heart with flames of love for God and keeps the fire of the romance alive and burning.

Prayer itself teaches us sacrificial love because we have to make time for it and do it whether it feels good or not. Sacrifice is part of the commitment of being in love. Where there is no love, there is no sacrifice. Here on earth, union with God is not always joyful and ecstatic — actually, most times it's not. Good feelings in prayer come and go, but spousal love and commitment is meant to endure forever. A person who tries to live a devout Christian life without prayer and devotion will inevitably experience a loss of the original fervor and zeal for the relationship. Then he will go off in search of other more comfortable "lovers." If the fire of love is not stoked and maintained through prayer and devotion, it will burn out and die. And if a person only prays when it feels good, they will not last long in following Christ, because Christ himself desires to lead a soul to greater holiness through teaching him how to trust like Mary and persevere in prayer even when all seems lost. Thus, what is needed for the long-term relationship and faithfulness to the covenant of spiritual marriage with God is devotion.

I have mentioned the word *devotion* many times already, but it is important to understand what it means. The word *devotion* comes from the Latin phrase *de votio* that means "of the will." Love is not magic or a feeling, and it will not endure without communication and a deliberate choice to remain faithful even when it doesn't "feel" pleasant. This is one of the major problems people face today in trying to live a marriage, and it is also one of the major problems people face today in trying to live a faithful Christian life. Many people lack the *will* to persevere because they do not get the good "feelings" they want. But love is not primarily about the senses but of the heart and the will. In our spiritual marriage with God, we must remain steadfast and faithful just as Mary did, both in the joy of Bethlehem and in the torturous agony of Calvary. Only prayer and devotion make this possible. Honeymoons don't last forever. Once the honeymoon is over, great sacrifices are required, because love grows and proves itself through responsibility and commitment.

☆ ☆ ☆ Marian Gems

☆ Every gift, every grace, every good that we have and that we receive continually, we receive through Mary. If Mary did not exist, neither would we, nor would the world. *St. Lawrence of Brindisi*

☆ We have all that we have through Mary, and in her, after God, we live and move and are. *St. Stanislaus Papczynski*

☆ She [Mary] is the cause of what came before her, the champion of what came after her and the agent of things eternal. She is the substance of the prophets, the principles of the apostles, the firm foundation of the martyrs and the premise of the teachers of the Church. She is the glory of those upon earth, the joy of celestial beings, the adornment of all creation. She is the beginning and the source and the root of unutterable good things; she is the summit and the consummation of everything holy. *St. Gregory Palamas*

☆ The term "Woman" indicated a wider relationship to all humanity than "Mother." It meant that she [Mary] was to be not only his mother, but that she was also to be the mother of all men, as he was the Savior of all men. She was now to have many children — not according to the flesh, but according to the spirit. Jesus was her firstborn in the flesh in joy; John was her second-born of the spirit in sorrow; and we her millionth and millionth born. *Venerable Fulton J. Sheen*

☆ She [Mary] alone is your [Jesus'] mother, but she is your sister, with everyone else. She was your mother, she was your sister, she was your bride, too, along with all chaste souls. *St. Ephrem the Syrian*

☆ Let us fear and worship the undivided Trinity as we sing the praise of the ever-Virgin Mary, the holy temple of God, and of God himself, her Son and spotless Bridegroom. *St. Cyril of Alexandria*

☆ The Blessed Virgin was the object of my earliest affections; I loved her even before I knew her. *St. John Vianney*

☆ Our Blessed Lady is my Mother, my Patroness, my Mistress, my Directress, and — after Jesus — my All! *St. Anthony Mary Claret*

☆ God is called Lord, and he wishes Mary to be called Lady. He is universal Lord of all things, and he wills her to be sovereign Lady of the universe. He is "King of kings and Lord of lords," and she is the queen of queens and sovereign of sovereigns. *St. John Eudes*

☆ What is sweeter than the Mother of my God? She has taken my mind captive; she has taken possession of my tongue; she is on my mind day and night. *St. John Damascene*

☆ O my Lady, my ruler, you who rule me, Mother of my Lord, Handmaid of your Son, Mother of the world's Maker, I pray you, I beg you, I beseech you, that I may have the spirit of my Redeemer, that I may truly and worthily know you, that I may speak truly and worthily about you, that I may say whatever true and worthy thing needs to be said about you. *St. Ildephonsus of Toledo*

☆ Dearest Mother, how happy was my soul those heavenly moments when I gazed upon you. How I love to remember those sweet moments spent in your presence, your eyes filled with kindness and mercy for us! *St. Bernadette Soubirous*

☆ Heaven and earth praise her unceasingly, and are nevertheless unable to praise her as she deserves. *Pope St. Gregory VII*

☆ When an artist has completed his masterpiece, he can do no more than to reproduce it in all its forms; when a genius has spoken the final word of his wisdom, nothing remains for him but to develop and explain it. When a soul has pronounced the unsurpassable word of love, she can do nothing more than repeat it in all its tones and with all the accents of that sovereign word. Similarly, after God wrought the supreme marvel of the Incarnation, he does nothing more in the world of grace than reproduce it, although it may be with faint and imperfect imitations of the masterpiece of his omnipotence and his love. The best likeness of Jesus' grace of union is Mary's motherhood. On account of this extraordinary grace, Mary is above every other creature, touching, as she does, the order of the hypostatic union. *Servant of God Archbishop Luis M. Martinez*

☆ We shall never be able to love Mary as her Son loves her. For this reason, we can love her and desire to love her without measure, knowing that we shall never love her enough. *Servant of God Mother Auxilia de la Cruz*

☆ By asking the beloved disciple to treat Mary as his mother, Jesus founded Marian devotion. *St. John Paul II*

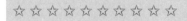

After the Honeymoon

YOU MAY RECALL THAT THE FIRST FEW YEARS OF THE 21st CENTURY were a tumultuous time in the Church in the United States. Scandals were regularly in the news, and most of them were initially emanating from Massachusetts, where I was ordained a priest in 2003.

Five months after I was ordained a priest, I was sitting in Boston's Logan International Airport waiting for a flight when a little boy who was playing on the floor near my chair used my knee to push himself up. I was wearing my Roman collar, as I almost always do when in public. To my great surprise, the child's mother reacted hysterically by standing up in front of everyone at the gate and yelling at me: "Get away from him! Don't touch my son!" Everyone within earshot turned to me and made me feel like I was some kind of pervert. Observers were giving me disapproving looks, and I got the impression that if a few of them could have, they would have spit on me. I was so shocked that I didn't even know what to say. I felt like bowing my head and crawling away. In an instant, the cross was thrust on my shoulders. It weighed me down, and I was crushed. It brought home the point to me that the honeymoon in my spiritual marriage with God was definitively over. Now was the time for sacrifice and perseverance.

Up until that event at the airport, I was comfy in my spiritual marriage with God. Most of my experiences in prayer were like a lollipop — pleasant, sweet, and delicious. But now I had to walk the walk, and not just talk the talk. Basically, the lesson I learned that day was that if I only walk in the land of lollipops, I end up a sucker!

So what do we do when the honeymoon is over? How do we persevere in the spiritual marriage when things are not pleasant?

We must stay close to the immaculate model, imitate her, sacrifice ourselves, and will to love.

Yes, God will bless us at various times in our spiritual life with little mini-honeymoon experiences, but when he wants us to really grow in the spiritual life, he will definitely begin to take the pleasant aspects of our journey away because in order to bear abundant fruit, we must be pruned. Fruitfulness requires sacrifice. And this is why having a committed life of prayer and devotion, like Mary, is so important.

In our spiritual marriage with God, we are going to have many moments of joy and many moments of spiritual aridity and dryness. Anyone who thinks that spiritual marriage to God is all joy and happiness is fooling himself. Not having good feelings in prayer doesn't mean we do not love God or that he does not love us. What it means is that we are in the post-honeymoon phase and must choose to daily live a faithful commitment to the demands of the marriage. The spiritual espousal with God must be lived out in good times and in bad, in health and in sickness, in riches and in poverty.

Clinging to Mary and imitating her helps us stay committed because, sadly, a person can spiritually divorce himself from God even after the initial grace of a tremendous conversion. The temptations of the world and our own weaknesses can lead us to turn away from Jesus even after years of living a good life. Trust me, temptations are always close at hand. I have to admit that I've been very tempted when the spiritual dryness is intense and long lasting. It's only by the grace of God, staying close to Mary, and choosing a life of prayer and devotion that I don't fall back into sin and forget that I'm already in a committed relationship and "married" to divine love. It would be super easy to "cheat" on my beloved and chase after others, but it would leave me with a divided heart, cause me to fall away from the pattern (Mary), and leave me in a wounded relationship with my beloved.

Conversion is a lifelong process, and in the covenant of spiritual marriage between a soul and God, we must allow our will to be totally devoted to him. We must constantly will to love. How sad it would be if we were to hear Jesus say to us, like he said to the Church in Ephesus: "I know you are enduring patiently and bearing up for my name's sake, and you have not grown weary. But I have this against you, that you have abandoned the love you had at first" (Rev 2:3-4). Personally, I do not want to have him say that to me. I want to persevere in fervent love till the end.

Everybody knows that Satan is wreaking havoc on marriages today through divorce, prenuptial agreements, cohabitation, adultery, pornography, contraception, homosexuality, etc. Similarly, the devil is also trying to get people to fall away from their commitment to Jesus and become lukewarm and give up when things are not convenient and pleasant. Being lukewarm is a very scary thing in the spiritual life. It might even be one of the worst things that we could allow to happen to us. Jesus himself says that he prefers us to be hot or cold. But if we are in the middle — lukewarm — he will spit us out of his mouth (cf. Rev 3:16). That's strong language and a very frightening prospect. When God says that it's easier for tax collectors and harlots to enter the kingdom of God than it is for those who are indifferent and lukewarm (cf. Mt 21:31-32), we need to make sure indifference and apathy do not creep into our spiritual marriage.

Being lukewarm does not mean not having good feelings in prayer or experiencing dryness in our relationship with God. It is a choice. It means we have lost the fire of love. For example, a person can be in spiritual dryness for years and yet be madly in love with God and totally on fire with love for him, because the person has willed to remain with him in good times and in bad. It is through the dryness we experience that our love is tested, and we are forged through sacrificial love into becoming saints. Nobody who is lukewarm ever becomes holy. The holy are those who are always seeking to be on fire with love of God and neighbor, even when they go through great trials in life and spiritual aridity in prayer.

I'm reminded of the story of St. Bernadette Soubirous, best known for the Marian apparitions at Lourdes, France. Many people assume that because she was a visionary, she must have experienced a lot of consolation in life. But in fact, she lived a very difficult existence. By the time of the famous apparitions, her family's financial and social status had deteriorated to the point where they had no choice but to live in a relative's one-room basement. And after she become a nun, her life did not get any easier. Our Lady actually appeared to her on one occasion and informed her, "I cannot promise you happiness in this life, but only in the next." During her life, she suffered from cholera and severe asthma, and before she died at the age of 35, she suffered from an extremely painful case of tuberculosis. She experienced many unpleasant things, but she remained faithful. That faithfulness made her a saint. She willed to love God through it all. She was far from being lukewarm. She was an *altera Maria*.

Such saintly examples of suffering teach us the fact that if we are going to persevere in our love for Christ, we are going to be invited to suffer with him. Sometimes, we may even undergo what feels like spiritual abandonment — with the honeymoon being a distant memory and our cry being, "My God, my God, why have you forsaken me?" (Mt 27:46). Yet we must remember that the honeymoon is just a tiny fraction of the time spent together in a marriage. Perseverance in prayer and devotion are the crucible of committed spiritual love. Willingness to love in difficult times is what produces abundant fruitfulness in our spiritual marriage with God. Nobody knows this better than Mary. She remained faithful all the way to the Cross. She experienced tortures of the heart that we cannot even imagine, but she always remained faithful. And it was because of her faithfulness in good times and in bad that God made her the most fruitful of all creatures. Through Mary, Jesus wants to teach us that it is at the Cross that we experience the consummation of the spiritual marriage.

I was reminded of this one time when I was traveling through Croatia. While in the beautiful city of Dubrovnik I witnessed a wedding where a couple exchanged their wedding vows while holding a crucifix. I thought this exemplified the spirituality of marriage perfectly! It was so insightful because as glorious as that wedding day was for the bridegroom and bride and as wonderful as the honeymoon was going to be *for a few days*, the reality is that the lifelong commitment of marriage was going to require devotion and sacrificial love. No longer were the man and woman living for themselves; they were now committed to living for the welfare of the other, and sacrifice would be essential.

It's much the same in our spiritual marriage with God. Great sacrifice is required. I'll be the first to attest to the fact that living a devout spiritual life after the honeymoon is not easy. It most definitely requires discipline and making torturous sacrifices, but one must go through this aspect of Christian spirituality in order for it to be real and patterned after the sacrificial love of Jesus and Mary. If you are not carrying a cross, you are not a Christian. If a person is not dying to self so as to please the beloved, the person is in it only for the good feelings and the honeymoon moments. If the person doesn't get what he wants and what feels good, he will most likely jump ship. But God doesn't want that kind of lover. He wants lovers who will love him at all times and stay in the ark. Only such souls inhabit heaven.

The world and the devil do not want people to remain faithful to the mystery of the Cross. If Satan tempted Jesus our bridegroom, offering him many marvelous and glorious things (cf. Mt 4:11), can we be so presumptuous as to believe that we are not going to undergo similar trials? But sadly, when some people taste the discomforts of the "Mary-maker" (Catholicism), they seek to enter into an easier commitment by finding a different preacher or an altogether different "deity," one who doesn't require sacrifice. Yet the example of Mary and the saints show us something entirely different.

One of the holiest persons in modern times, St. Teresa of Calcutta, experienced great aridity and dryness in the spiritual life. Most of us were totally unaware of this until after she died. Thanks to her writings and the posthumous process of investigating her life, we now know that for most of her life, she found very little consolation in prayer. I think most of us just assumed she was in constant ecstatic spiritual bliss because she always seemed so radiant and holy. However, we now know why she was so holy; she willed to love even when she was experiencing spiritual aridity and little to no consolation. Her example of persevering through aridity, remaining incredibly devoted to God, and serving the poorest of the poor offer such a testimony to bearing abundant fruit through sacrifice and committed love! Indeed, she was on fire with love, and the whole world knew this. She was an *altera Maria*.

Tragically, our society — and this generation in particular — has grown up with a poor aptitude for persevering. As soon as things don't go our way, we tend to jump ship and look for other options. I think this explains why we have such a high divorce rate in the United States today, with almost half of all marriages ending in divorce. As soon as there is some inconvenience or a burden, there is a tendency to try and "break free" of the responsibility of that relationship and go on to someone else who is more gratifying and pleasant. Spiritually speaking, it's very tempting for Christians to fall into this mentality, too.

Since love comes from the will, God wants us to prove our love for him through acts of devotion. We do this first and foremost when we are faithful to attending Holy Mass. Nothing will ever be greater than the prayer of Holy Mass where our person is united with the beloved. But in addition to Holy Mass and the other Sacraments of the Church, God desires us to spend time with him every day in personal prayer and devotional practices. And God's holy Church offers us so many ways to express and show our devotion. These devotions are extremely important for keeping the spiritual romance with God alive. They are like little spiritual rendezvouses with God that anyone can do.

Here are just a few examples:

Spend time with Jesus in the Blessed Sacrament either through Eucharistic Adoration or by simply visiting his presence in the tabernacle. This is a very powerful devotion; almost everyone lives near a Catholic church and can do it. This devotion is so powerful that the famous author J.R.R. Tolkien once wrote a letter to his son and told him that spending time before the Blessed Sacrament always offers a soul romance and fidelity. Likewise, the Venerable Fulton J. Sheen publicly and very frequently acknowledged that all his power in speaking, preaching, and writing came through the daily holy hour he spent before the Blessed Sacrament.

Spending an hour a day before Jesus in the tabernacle is an extremely powerful way to keep the flame of love burning brightly. But, even if your job and family life will not allow you to spend an hour a day before the Blessed Sacrament, it is still very possible for almost everyone to stop in at a Catholic Church and visit the Blessed Sacrament, if just for a few minutes. How pleasing to Jesus is the person who frequently visits him in the Blessed Sacrament and simply says, "Jesus, I love you!" After all, he is a prisoner of love in every tabernacle in every Catholic church throughout the world and waits for people to visit him. The least we can do is bow our heads or make the Sign of the Cross when we drive by a Catholic church as a sign of our love.

Reading the Bible is another great form of devotion. People often think they know the Bible, but I guarantee that many of them don't. Reading the Bible is so incredible that sometimes once I start reading it, it's hard to put it down because I want to read more. Every time I pick up the Bible, I'm amazed at what God does to my heart and soul. I often counsel people to begin reading the Bible by first reading the Gospel of John. The Gospel of John will rock your world! You will fall in love with Jesus all over again. Take me up on that challenge. I dare you.

Some people might be intimidated by being asked to read the Bible, but the Church has a great method that allows us to both read and pray the Bible at the same time. It's called the Liturgy of the Hours, and it's for everyone. Priests are required to pray it, but the Church encourages everyone to pray it. After the Mass, this is the most sanctioned prayer of the Church because it is the prayer of the Church. Through the Liturgy of the Hours, the Bible becomes a great prayer. The Psalms, in particular, come alive and help us express the joys and sorrows of life through the Word of God. Mary is Mother of the Word, and she knows the power of God's Word better than anyone.

And since Mary is the prototype of nuptial union with God, devotion to her is absolutely necessary in order to truly love God as he wants to be loved. God desires all his children to have devotion to her. We have devotion to her when we talk to her in prayer, sharing with her our joys, sorrows, wants, and needs. She is our spiritual mother, after all.

There are many different devotions we can have to Our Lady, but one of the greatest ways is through praying the Rosary. This biblical prayer transforms us and helps us keep the spiritual romance with God alive because we are meditating on the sacred mysteries of our faith as seen through the eyes of Mary. After the Mass and the Liturgy of the Hours, the Rosary is the preferred method of the saints for overcoming temptations and persevering in love. The Rosary has the power to bring peace, joy, and healing. Trust me; I know. In times when I'm freaking out over some matter, I pray the Rosary, and my soul regains its peace. In times when I'm sad and bummed out over a particular situation, I pray the Rosary, and everything is put in perspective. And at times when I'm incredibly tempted to sin, I pray the Rosary and am victorious over the darkness.

The Rosary is like a weapon in the spiritual life. I almost guarantee that a person who prays it every day will grow quickly in the spiritual life and be given the grace to overcome vice and stay committed to the marriage. In my experience, temptations against chastity usually last about 20 minutes in their intensity. I find it very interesting that the Holy Rosary takes about 20 minutes to pray and thus serves as a heavenly remedy and lifeline for defeating temptations of the flesh. I've also met married couples who have told me that there has never been any difficulty in their marriage that they could not overcome and get through if they prayed the Rosary together. For this reason, I constantly encourage couples to commit to praying a Rosary each evening *together* so that they grow in humility. If a couple does this, its problems will seem silly and trivial in the light of God's mercy and love. I dare you to try this devotion. Once you do, you will understand why the saints love this prayer and why the Church sanctions it so much.

Another Marian devotion is the scapular — two small but mighty pieces of cloth connected by a string that is worn around the neck. It's like a holy life vest thrown to us from heaven by our spiritual mother. By wearing this devotional, we are placing ourselves *under the mantle* of Our Lady's protection. Any mother who sees that her child is in danger will most definitely seek to help, right? This is what the scapular is. It's not magic or a good luck charm. It's a sign of our heavenly mother's love for us. And when her children show their love for her by wearing it and kissing it frequently throughout the day as a reminder of their love for her, Jesus is very pleased. In essence, by wearing it, we are saying to Mary: "I know that you want me to be with Jesus in heaven, and I love him so much that I am not going to do anything to turn away from him or offend him, because I wear this scapular as a sign of my devotion to you and Jesus. Thank you, Mary, for protecting me!"

Think about this: In a storm such as a hurricane or a tornado, people seek protection under something for safety. In the spiritual life, it is the same. In the storms of life, God has a place of refuge for us, and he wants us to seek protection there. It is *under the mantle* of Our Lady where we find safety and protection. A devotion such as the scapular symbolizes this aspect of being *under the mantle* of Our Lady. Just as any good mother would cover her child if he wanted to play outside in the cold — because all good mothers do this — so in the spiritual life, Mother Mary knows it is dangerous in this fallen world. Therefore, she seeks to give us her motherly protection by cloaking us with the scapular. In wearing a scapular, we are reminded of God's desire to "clothe us with a robe of salvation, and wrap us in a mantle of justice" (cf. Is 61:10).

Making pilgrimages to holy Catholic sites and Catholic shrines is another great way of keeping the fire alive. There are so many holy Catholic sites and shrines to visit, and many of them are dedicated to Our Lady because she desires all of her spiritual children to come close to God. For example, there are so many Church-approved apparitions with shrines attached to them that it's amazing! If you do not know about these places, you seriously need to do some research. Such places as Fatima, Lourdes, Guadalupe, and La Salette are the more popular ones, but there are literally tons. And it's a fact that people are renewed in their faith by visiting such places. In addition, make a pilgrimage to the Holy Land or Rome, and I'm sure it will rekindle the flame of love in your heart for Jesus and his Church.

There is also the practice of having devotion to the saints. Like Our Lady, the saints are worthy of our love and admiration. They teach us how to become immaculate. When we seek to imitate them and pray to them for assistance, God delights in this because they are our holy brothers and sisters. They are great examples of having lived a devoted life. They were completely committed to loving God while they walked this earth. Their lives teach us how to pray, persevere in prayer, make time for prayer, and let nothing get in the way of prayer. The saints have trod this path before us, and they know that spiritual espousal to God takes lifelong devotion and sacrifice. They willed to love in good times and in bad.

Saint Peter was crucified upside down out of love for Jesus. Saint Maximilian Kolbe was murdered in the concentration camp of Auschwitz. Saint Maria Goretti preferred death rather than let a man sin through raping her. Saint John Paul II took a bullet out of love for Jesus and Mary. Saint Padre Pio bore the wounds of Christ on his body and suffered greatly out of love for God, and the list of heroic and incredible saints goes on and on. Having friends in heaven is a very powerful way of staying focused and devoted to God. Personally, I don't know where I'd be without the friendship and miraculous interventions of saints like St. Philomena, St. Michael the Archangel, and my Guardian Angel. They have helped me tremendously, and there are tons of saints waiting and wanting to help you, too.

Also, inside almost every Catholic church in the entire world, you will find the Stations of the Cross. Meditating on the Lord's Passion is extremely powerful. It reminds us of the love that our beloved has for us and how much he suffered for us. We see how much we should be willing to carry our crosses out of love for him. When we meditate on the *Via Dolorosa* (Way of Suffering), we are given strength to carry our own crosses and undergo the hardships of life. The suffering of Jesus makes our suffering seem like nothing, and when we realize how much our beloved Lord has suffered for us, we become more willing to suffer for him, just like Mary did.

And we can't forget about one of the newest forms of devotion given to the Church for our times: the Divine Mercy message and devotion. A key element of this relatively new devotion is the Divine Mercy Chaplet. It is prayed on the same set of beads as the Rosary, and it only takes about five to seven minutes to pray. Yet it is a spiritual weapon packing a wallop of a spiritual punch. There are many things associated with this particular devotion, and they are all awesome. We will get into these more deeply in the next chapter.

In short, the forms of devotion offered to us by the Church are many and varied. Whether it's the devotion of the Miraculous Medal, the Infant Jesus, various novenas, the Holy Shroud, relics of the saints, devotion to the Holy Souls in Purgatory, First Friday or Saturday devotions, spiritual reading, or whatever particular devotion we favor, we simply must allow some form of devotion into our life if we are going to stay committed to God and will to love through the tough times. We must keep the romance alive! Spiritual aridity and dryness *will* come our way. Living a devoted life makes us ever more cognizant that God is at work in us and that our lives are bearing fruit for the kingdom.

☆ ☆ ☆ Marian Gems

☆ When will souls breathe Mary as the body breathes air? *St. Louis de Montfort*

☆ Take shelter under Our Lady's mantle, and do not fear. She will give you all you need. She is very rich, and besides is very generous with her children. She loves giving. *St. Raphaela Maria*

☆ The knot of Eve's disobedience was untied by Mary's obedience. What Eve bound through her unbelief, Mary loosed by her faith. *St. Irenaeus of Lyons*

☆ For the faithful can do nothing more fruitful and salutary than to win for themselves the most powerful patronage of the Immaculate Virgin, so that by this most sweet Mother, there may be opened to them all the treasures of the divine Redemption, and so they may have life, and have it more abundantly. Did not the Lord will that we have everything through Mary? *St. Pope John XXIII*

☆ The Rosary belongs among the finest and most praiseworthy traditions of Christian contemplation. *St. John Paul II*

☆ Love Mary! … She is loveable, faithful, constant. She will never let herself be outdone in love. *St. Gabriel Possenti*

☆ When we have handled something fragrant, our hands perfume whatever we touch; let but our prayers pass through the hands of the Blessed Virgin, and she will give them fragrance. *St. John Vianney*

☆ I love Our Lord with all my heart. But he wants me to love Our Lady in a special way and to go to him with my hand in Mary's. *Venerable Teresa of Jesus Quevedo*

☆ As an exercise of Christian devotion among the faithful of the Latin Rite who constitute a notable portion of the Catholic family, the Rosary ranks after Holy Mass and the Breviary for ecclesiastics [priests], and for the laity after participation in the sacraments. It is a devout form of union with God and lifts souls to a high supernatural plane. *St. Pope John XXIII*

☆ Most holy Virgin, obtain for me from your Son this grace: That I may love you more and more, trust you ever more firmly, and treasure more dearly your glorious protection. *Blessed George Matulaitis*

☆ Love the Immaculate One with all your being, will, and heart, but should you sense a time of aridity coming upon you and cannot awaken sentiments of love, do not worry much, for it does not belong to the essence of love. As long as your will desires only her will, then be at peace, for truly, then, do you love her, and through her, you love Jesus and the Father. *St. Maximilian Kolbe*

☆ The Mother of God is the Ladder of Heaven. God came down by this ladder that men might, by Mary, climb up to him in heaven. *St. Fulgentius*

☆ Heaven and earth will pass away before Mary would abandon a soul. *Blessed Henry Suso*

The Cross (The Wedding Ring)

Since Jesus is the bridegroom, the sign of his love and fidelity is the Cross. In a certain sense, the Cross is a spiritual wedding ring that Christ wears himself and gives to his bride. The Cross is really one of the best gifts that Jesus gives to his bride, because it is the sign of his committed and sacrificial love for her. By wearing this wedding band — carrying the Cross — the nuptial union between a soul and Christ is manifested to the world. And just as Jesus cannot be separated from his Cross because he is a faithful spouse and never abandons his wedding ring, so it is that no faithful Christian should desire to take off his wedding ring either. Once a person takes off the wedding ring of the Cross, there are going to be problems. Those who do not embrace the Cross (wear the ring) do not belong to Christ. Those who intentionally take it off are headed for spiritual adultery.

The Cross is the ultimate "bling" in the spiritual life. What bride doesn't want a huge rock on her finger? It shows the world that she is loved and is someone special. It should be the same with Christians. What kind of bride doesn't want to wear a wedding ring? An unfaithful one. But Jesus, the divine bridegroom, invites his disciples — you and me — to wear this ring and follow him faithfully along the *Via Crucis* (the Way of the Cross): "If any man would come after me, let him deny himself and take up his cross daily and follow me" (Lk 9:23). Those who truly love Christ want to wear the ring — the Cross — every day. If we truly love Christ, then we should be willing to deny ourselves and suffer for him.

The fallen angels hate mankind with an envious hatred because of our ability to carry a cross and suffer out of love for God. Suffering — carrying a cross — is a great gift God has given human persons. Angels can't suffer. They chose to serve God or disobey him by one act. As a result of that one act, they are either holy or fallen for all of eternity. The fallen angels hate the flesh, because they are perpetually reminded that God took on flesh in order to carry the Cross and be able to suffer and bleed for fallen mankind. Jesus was born to bleed. And every time a new human life comes into the world, and every time a person is willing to suffer for God in his flesh, the fallen angels are perpetually reminded of their decision not to serve God.

Remember: It is the flesh of the God-man that is the instrument of our salvation. Satan hates the Body of Christ and wants to destroy all flesh. And he figures the sooner he can do it the better, so he desires to prevent flesh from even being conceived (contraception). Then, if a child has been conceived, he seeks to have the baby slaughtered (infanticide). It was true at the birth of Christ when Herod ordered the slaughtering of the innocents, and it is true today when an innocent child is murdered in the womb. If Satan had his way, he would abort humanity out of existence. He hates the Cross because it necessarily involves the flesh and perpetually reminds him that God took on flesh in order to suffer for fallen mortals.

The holy angels, on the other hand, would be more than willing to suffer for God and carry a cross, but they, too, are incapable of doing this since they do not have flesh and blood and the ability to suffer. Yet, unlike the fallen angels, they do not envy mankind over this great gift. Rather, they seek to aid us in our mission of carrying the Cross and suffering out of love for God and others. I personally think that every time a human person throws their suffering away, an angel somehow spiritually weeps because they would give anything to be given the great honor of suffering for God. They would do anything to wear this most heavenly of wedding rings.

To seek to separate Christ from his Cross is basically to rip off his wedding ring. Peter tried to do that once, and Jesus had to rebuke him and call him Satan (cf. Mt 16:23). To desire Jesus to take his wedding ring off is to not understand his nuptial mission. He is the bridegroom Messiah who has come to wed his bride and give her his name — Christian — and prove his love for her by faithfully loving her unto death. Mary, as the perfect disciple, understood this. Thus, she never stood between Jesus and his

Cross. He wore it for her, and she knew that. As a matter of fact, in the mystery of her perfect femininity, she helped him carry it by her co-suffering and denying herself her legitimate concerns as his mother so that he could fulfill his mission and be sacrificed for the life of the world. No other human person ever had a cross as heavy and intense as Mary's. And for her faithful participation and cooperation in the saving mystery of the Cross, God made her the Co-Redemptrix.

Christianity without the Cross is not Christianity, and a person without a cross is not a Christian. If Christ was crucified before the nations out of love for his bride, the Church must undergo a crucifixion with him in order for the marriage to be consummated. It may not be a physical crucifixion, but it will definitely be a spiritual and mystical one. But many today want nothing to do with the Cross. And this only goes to show they are not that committed to the marriage. They only want the risen, glorious, triumphant element of Christianity. Disdaining thoughts of having to undergo hardship and suffering for the truth of the Gospel, they only want health, wealth, and prosperity. But that mentality only goes to show that they love God little. Something comparable to a spiritual prenuptial agreement has been planned, and the thoughts of their hearts speak in words comparable to these: "If this relationship begins to cause me hardship, I'm out." But only desiring the pleasant things God offers is to act like the only reason you responded to the offer of divine love was for the sake of the honeymoon. So once suffering comes along, divorce and/or adultery are in order.

In this fallen world, every marriage is constantly being threatened by the temptations of the world, selfish desires, and the evil one. Much like the parable of the seeds thrown on all kinds of soil (cf. Mk 4:2-20), we show what kind of "soil" we are by our desire to stick it out and persevere through temptations and trials. And the mystery of the Cross is so great that the greater a person's love, the deeper the seed will be planted and the heavier the Cross will be. But saintly souls, like Mary's, do not mind sacrifice because sacrifice increases love and fruitfulness with the beloved. The more you love, the more you are willing to suffer because Jesus, the beloved, is worth suffering for.

What made Mary and the saints so holy is that they actually looked for — and longed for — the Cross. No cross, no glory. No wedding ring, no marriage feast. Mary and the saints teach us that the more a person loves, the more that person wants to suffer for love. The holy know the true benefits of carrying the Cross, suffering, and persevering in devotion. Only the prayerful, saintly person can penetrate the mystery of the Cross and its power. As St. Paul says, the Cross is the power and the wisdom of God (cf. 1 Cor 1:18-19), and this great mystery is only revealed to those who pray and persevere through devotion.

Mary is the ultimate model for how to pray, remain devoted, and carry the Cross (wear the wedding ring) of suffering. She is Our Lady of Sorrows, and all who desire to become holy must learn how to love, pray, and suffer like her. This is why Christ himself desires devotion to Mary — only those who stick it out with Christ can truly be said to imitate Mary and enter into the deepest intimacy with Christ.

Consider the story of St. Ignatius of Antioch. He was sentenced to die for his love of Jesus Christ. En route to the Roman Colosseum (where he would be eaten by lions), his friends tried to intervene and stop him. But he adamantly urged them not to intervene, so that he could become food for the lions and be privileged to undergo such suffering for Jesus and the Gospel.

Sadly, the example of St. Ignatius is an enigma to people today. Even many Christians in our times have been duped by New Age movements that offer them a sense of peace and tranquility if they but participate in their "exercise" programs. Yoga, by far the most popular of them all, is presented as an innocent exercise that will free you from the burdens of the body and give you health and self-reliance. Little do those who sign up for these classes realize that the exercise mat they are provided to perform their exercise on is actually a prayer rug, and many of the postures they perform are actually ritualistic postures and gestures of worship in the Hindu religion. Even the very meaning of the word "yoga" should be a red light. It means "yoke." So what are these people yoking themselves to? It certainly isn't the bridegroom.

Most Westerners are not even aware that yoga is part of a spirituality, and by practicing it, they are yoking themselves to a belief system. The underlying belief system is that the flesh is a burden and must be overcome. The Cross is the enemy. This is why many gurus from India and certain other countries laugh at the silly Westerners who think that being "yoked" to this practice is only an exercise and has nothing to do with the religion or spirituality behind it. But if you are known by the company you keep, all a person has to do is pick up a yoga magazine and look at all the articles and ads that are there. It's all New Age, anti-Christian, and inimical to the Cross.

But our beloved Jesus invites us to have a share in his Cross when he says: "Take my yoke upon you, and learn from me; for I am gentle and lowly in heart, and you will find rest for your souls. For my yoke is easy, and my burden is light" (Mt 11: 29-30). His yoke is easy and light because it has love and truth as the foundation. Without love and truth, there is no true peace, no lasting rest. Without love and truth, there is no joy, no matter how "good" a particular practice may feel.

Yet so many Christians have been duped into thinking that such practices are legit for a Christian, and they consider those who oppose them closed-minded and radical. But practicing such spiritualities and yet claiming to be a Christian is a contradiction. It's like saying, "I'm a Christian, but I pray and act like a Hindu. I'm a Christian, but I've embraced a mindset that rejects Christ. I'm a Christian, but I refuse to wear the wedding ring of the Cross."

Thus, how appropriate it is that Catholics initiate all their prayers and devotions by making the Sign of the Cross: "In the name of the Father, and of the Son, and of the Holy Spirit." There is wisdom in the Cross, and whether our petitions in prayer are answered or not, whether we are healed or not, we trust in the power and wisdom of the Cross. A "non-suffering Christian" is an oxymoron. We are all going to have to drink the chalice of suffering as disciples of Christ (cf. Mt 20:22-23). This is not an option.

As a people who are spiritually espoused to Christ, we are called to be victims with Christ. We may not be physically crucified, but we will be invited to cooperate through our own sufferings in his saving mission. He wants our hearts to become a living sacrifice, and he wants us to love him even when it is excruciatingly difficult.

What spouse doesn't expect that from his beloved? What spouse wants the other to love him only when it's easy — and then he has to constantly worry about the other not being faithful when things don't go well? None that I know.

And that's why Mary is our pattern. She was always faithful to the spiritual marriage. She was always faithful to prayer and devotion. She carried the Cross; she wore the ring. And now she wears the crown!

☆ ☆ ☆ Marian Gems

☆ If you invoke the Blessed Virgin when you are tempted, she will come at once to your help, and Satan will leave you. *St. John Vianney*

☆ She has given us so many proofs that she cares for us like a Mother. *St. Therese of Lisieux*

☆ She [Mary] participated in the same torments, not by way of the executioners, like Jesus, but she, by way of love and sorrow, participated in all the torments, one by one. The heart of Jesus and the heart of Mary both stood united in suffering and in love, and this they offered to God the Father for all of us mortals. *St. Veronica Giuliani*

☆ From the nature of his work the Redeemer ought to have associated his Mother with his work. For this reason we invoke her under the title of Co-redemptrix. She gave us the Savior, she accompanied him in the work of redemption as far as the Cross itself, sharing with him the sorrows of the agony and of the death in which Jesus consummated the redemption of mankind. *Pope Pius XI*

☆ Am I not here, I who am your Mother? Are you not under my shadow and protection? Am I not the source of your joy? Are you not in the hollow of my mantle, in the crossing of my arms? Do you need anything more? Let nothing else worry you, or disturb you. *Our Lady's words to St. Juan Diego*

☆ To both Jesus and Mary, there are treasures in darkness – one in the darkness of a woman, the other in the darkness of a hill. Only those who walk in darkness ever see the stars. *Venerable Fulton J. Sheen*

☆ As flies are driven away by a great fire, so were the evil spirits driven away by her [Mary's] ardent love for God. *St. Bernardine of Siena*

☆ As wax melts before fire, so do the devils lose their power against those souls who remember the name of Mary and devoutly invoke it. *St. Bonaventure*

☆ Sanctity grows in the measure that we venerate Mary. *St. Peter Faber*

☆ O Most Pure, Most Holy and Immaculate Mary, above all, God made you beautiful, for he bestowed upon you the fullness of grace. I love you, I offer you my homage, and I desire to imitate you. By your Immaculate Conception please keep watch over me, and always accompany me until I die. Drive away from me Satan's temptations and snares. Obtain for me from your beloved Son the forgiveness of all my sins and temporal punishment. Supported by your love, may I be able to take delight together with you in full participation in the glory of eternal life. *Venerable Casimir Wyszynski*

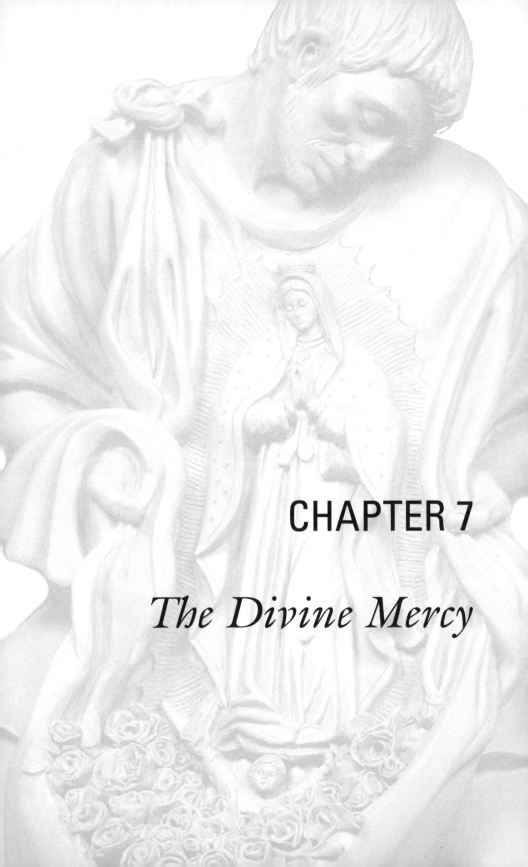

CHAPTER 7

The Divine Mercy

The Message and Devotion for Our Times

IN AN AGE IN WHICH SO MANY HAVE FALLEN AWAY FROM GOD, committed serious sins, and ditched the wedding ring of the Cross, God shows his undying love and faithfulness by reaching out to us and offering us a fresh start. He has not abandoned us. As dark as the times are, God remains our Father, and Jesus continues to be our faithful and merciful Savior. He has not ditched his wedding ring, even though we may have ditched ours. He is forever faithful. As a matter of fact, he has been trying to get our attention, to give us a new beginning, because he knows the dire situation we have put ourselves in.

It's a fact that within the last 100 years the world has experienced more reported (and approved) Marian apparitions than any other time in Church history. Indeed, God knows the seriousness of the times and how broken and wounded his children are. He wants nothing more than to shower his mercies on us and bring us back to himself. So, in addition to sending his own mother from heaven to try and get our attention, he has also given to the world a great gift for our times: the Divine Mercy message and devotion.

God has always been merciful, and his steadfast love and mercy endure forever (cf. Ps 136). There's nothing new there. Yet, God saved this very special message, with its new forms of devotion, for our times because there has never been a more messed-up time than ours. Sure, throughout human history, there have been horrible things that have happened: plagues, disease, famine, and wars. But these were usually limited to a particular geographical region or nation and were rarely on a global scale. Even "world wars" never really involved every country on earth. But today we are experiencing something different. There is something that threatens the entire world, and every individual person living today has been exposed to it: immorality and sin. And it's on a global scale.

Darkness and ungodliness have covered the earth, and everywhere people are lukewarm about faith, causing many to lose hope and abandon God and his Commandments altogether.

This is why Divine Mercy is the message and devotion for our times. It springs from the depths of a father's love. God "the Father of mercies" (2 Cor 1:3) wants us to have this great gift in our days because he knows we need it. It's a message and devotion *for you and me.* God loves us, and he has not given up on us. The entire world needs mercy now more than ever, and God knows we need an ocean of it. He has been flooding the world with this message and devotion lately, and I believe it is so crucial for our times that I would like to share with you some of the history of this message and the particular devotional forms associated with it.

In the early 20th century — specifically the 1930s — a Polish nun named Sr. Maria Faustina Kowalska began receiving heavenly messages from Jesus that focused on God's mercy. Saint Faustina began sharing these messages with her spiritual director and confessor, Fr. Michael Sopocko (now Blessed Michael Sopocko), and he instructed her to begin writing down these messages in a diary. The official version of her *Diary* that we read today is called *Diary of Saint Maria Faustina Kowalska: Divine Mercy in My Soul.* It was born in the confessional, behind the curtain of mercy, and is a theological masterpiece. Now, it is quickly becoming a classic of Catholic spirituality in the company of *The Story of a Soul* (St. Thérèse of Lisieux), *The Interior Castle* (St. Teresa of Avila), and *The Dialogue* (St. Catherine of Siena). If you do not have a copy of the *Diary*, I highly recommend that you obtain one because this message and devotion are not just intended for St. Faustina but for the entire world.

The Divine Mercy message and devotion is so crucial for our times that the devil does not want people to know about it. Most people are unaware of this, but a fallen angel actually tricked St. Faustina into burning the first version of her *Diary.* On one occasion, when her spiritual director was away on a trip, an angel appeared to her and told her that the *Diary* was not important and that she should burn it. Not knowing that the angel was a fallen angel, she obediently threw her *Diary* in the fire, only to be told afterwards by our Lord that she had been tricked by the devil. The devil does not like Divine Mercy. Satan is the accuser and wants to put souls in despair over their sins, but when people have confidence and trust in God's mercy, the evil one becomes totally powerless — Divine Mercy shuts him up. And God will not allow Satan to stop this message.

Even after St. Faustina's death (d. 1938), when her *Diary* and its contents were becoming more known, Old Stinky made a second attempt to get rid of the *Diary*. Most people don't know this either, but the *Diary* was actually banned from being published, distributed, and read for 20 years (1958-1978). The reason for this was because there was an unauthorized translation done, and it contained many theological errors. When Church officials read this version of the *Diary*, they were taken aback by the theological errors being presented by this religious sister from Poland. Therefore, believing they were protecting the people from error, the Vatican put the *Diary* on the list of banned books that was operative at the time. Yet, as recorded in the *Diary*, St. Faustina received a prophetic insight that there would come a time when it would seem that all was lost concerning this message and devotion. But God would act in a mighty way to vindicate it (cf. *Diary*, 378). And, indeed, he did act in mighty ways to authenticate its truthfulness.

As divine providence had set things up, during the time of the ban on the *Diary*, a very holy priest was serving as the cardinal archbishop of Krakow, where Sr. Faustina's body was buried. This holy priest's name was Karol Wojtyla. He was aware of Sr. Faustina's life and the messages she had received, and he decided to appoint a very learned priest to study her life and conduct an investigation into the main source of her writings, namely, the *Diary*. It took this priest 10 years to finish his work, and the result was that Sr. Faustina was considered to have practiced heroic virtue, and the *Diary* was considered to be a theological masterpiece. The issue with the faulty translation was rectified, and the *Diary* was able to be read again by the public. And you know what happened right after that, in the same year? Archbishop Karol Wojtyla was elected the new Pope, and he took the name Pope John Paul II!

From the very beginning of his pontificate, John Paul II became an ardent apostle of Divine Mercy. Everything associated with Divine Mercy was fresh on his mind due to having just closed the informative investigation into St. Faustina's life. Then, he took all this knowledge to Rome as he began his role of being the Vicar of Christ. And knowing that the Divine Mercy message and devotion was not just meant for Rome — and as a result of modern transportation — he quickly became the most traveled pontiff in Church history, and everywhere he went he began to spread the message of Divine Mercy. Not only that, his second encyclical was titled *Dives in Misericordia* (*Rich in Mercy*) and is truly one of the greatest documents ever written about God's greatest attribute: Divine Mercy.

Therefore, it was with great joy that he was able to both beatify and canonize St. Faustina at St. Peter's Basilica in Rome. Saint Faustina is, in fact, the first canonized saint of the third Christian millennium (April 30, 2000). It was at that very canonization Mass that John Paul II also established and declared that the Second Sunday of Easter would, for all future generations, be known as Divine Mercy Sunday. He was a mercy machine! It has even been noted that during the reception after the canonization Mass of St. Faustina, John Paul II was overheard to say that that day was the happiest day of his life! That's an incredible statement from a man who had seen some pretty amazing days. But it doesn't stop there.

Experiencing the happiest day of his life by canonizing St. Faustina and establishing Divine Mercy Sunday as an obligatory solemnity for the entire Church, John Paul II also noted during the canonization homily that the Divine Mercy message and devotion was a *gift for our times and the bridge to the third millennium*. When you think about it, how true this is. Did you know that the official Polish version of the *Diary* was only made available in 1981, and the official English translation followed a few years later in 1987? This means that the 20th century only had the *official* message for 19 years. Thus, the 21st century — the third Christian millennium — is being offered the great gift of Divine Mercy! We are so blessed to live in these times. Think about it: the three persons associated with being apostles of Divine Mercy and making the message and devotion known more than anyone were either beatified or canonized in the 21st century; St. Faustina was canonized in 2000; Blessed Michael Sopocko was beatified in 2008; St. John Paul II was beatified in 2011 and canonized in 2014. Amazing!

But, wait, there's more!

In 2002, John Paul II sanctioned that those who celebrate Divine Mercy Sunday may receive a plenary indulgence; a plenary indulgence takes away all temporal punishment due to sin, and if you receive one right before you die, you basically walk right into heaven. And here's the part that I love: Having been the main promoter of the Divine Mercy message and devotion and the divinely chosen instrument who made it all happen — getting the *Diary* off the banned list, beatifying and canonizing St. Faustina, establishing Divine Mercy Sunday, granting a plenary indulgence for those who celebrate Divine Mercy Sunday — John Paul II died after the vigil Mass for Divine Mercy Sunday in 2005 was celebrated at his bedside! He was also able to receive at that Mass his last Holy Communion. Do you know what this means? It means he reaped the promise of Jesus associated with this message about Divine Mercy Sunday as recorded in the *Diary*. He *most likely* also obtained the plenary indulgence granted by the Church. Then, he checked out! What a way to go! What a day to die!

And the message and devotion didn't get downgraded with the passing of John Paul II.

There might have been some who thought that Pope Benedict XVI, being a German academic, might not be as enthused about the Divine Mercy message and devotion as John Paul II had been since it originated from private revelations, but, boy, were they wrong! From the very beginning of his pontificate, Pope Benedict spoke very enthusiastically about Divine Mercy. As a matter of fact, on Divine Mercy Sunday in 2006, he even stated that *the worship of Divine Mercy is not a second-rate devotion but an integral dimension of a Christian's faith and prayer.* In addition, under the pontificate of Benedict XVI, the Church initiated ways for promoting Divine Mercy that not even John Paul II did!

Pope Benedict was such an apostle of mercy that he sanctioned and fully supported a new endeavor to make Divine Mercy known: the World Apostolic Congress on Mercy (WACOM). Traditionally, there have only been two kinds of Congresses in the Church: a Eucharistic Congress and a Marian Congress. Such events are sanctioned by the Church at the highest level, and they seek to be a source of renewal for the entire Church. People come from all over the world to participate — including bishops, priests, and groups of parishioners. They are given new vitality in their spiritual journey through the talks and activities that are celebrated. The hope is that these leaders take this new vitality back to their parishes and communities and inspire them and teach them what they have learned. Now, thanks to Pope Benedict XVI, we have a third type of Congress that seeks to bring renewal to the Church: the World Apostolic Congress on Mercy.

The first World Apostolic Congress on Mercy was held in Rome in April 2008; the second was held in Krakow, Poland, in 2011; and the third was held in Bogota, Colombia, in 2014. And more are being planned as you read these pages.

There are also regional and national events that seek to bring the message to each geographical area of the world. In 2009, for instance, I was privileged to speak at the North American Congress on Mercy that was held at the Basilica of the National Shrine of the Immaculate Conception in Washington, D.C. I also spoke at the Fiji Congress on Mercy in 2011, which brought together attendees from across the Oceania region. That was such an awesome event for me because after the Congress, I was able to go surfing at one of the best surf breaks in the world: Cloudbreak. There, I truly experienced an ocean of mercy!

Those are the basics of the history of the Divine Mercy message. Let's now switch gears and get into the particulars of the devotion.

As part of this great and awesome message, Jesus revealed to St. Faustina new forms of devotion to his mercy. He also attached to them many blessings in the form of heavenly promises. These new forms of devotion are the following: the Feast of Divine Mercy, the Image of Divine Mercy, the Chaplet of Divine Mercy, the Novena to the Divine Mercy, and the Hour of Great Mercy. Let's unpack them.

Jesus told St. Faustina that his heart wept for fallen mankind and that he wanted a new Feast of Mercy established in the Church, one that would fall on the Second Sunday of Easter and be called Divine Mercy Sunday. Jesus highlighted his desires concerning the Feast of Mercy on 14 different occasions, telling her, "On that day the very depths of My tender mercy are open. I pour out a whole ocean of graces upon those souls who approach the fount of My mercy" (*Diary*, 699). He also said that "whoever approaches the Fount of Life on this day [Divine Mercy Sunday] will be granted complete remission of sins and punishment" (*Diary*, 300). I don't know about you, but I want that!

Initially, some theologians wondered why Jesus wanted a new feast established so close to Easter. They wondered if Divine Mercy Sunday would detract from Easter. Yet, when understood in the light of sound liturgical theology, Easter and Divine Mercy Sunday actually complement one another and go hand in hand. As a matter of fact, Divine Mercy Sunday is actually the culmination of the Octave of Easter. As you may know, the Church celebrates the Easter day of Christ's rising over an eight-day period (an octave) and considers it to be one liturgical day. For this reason, Divine Mercy Sunday can be considered as the grand finale of the triumphal Easter Octave celebration of the King of Mercy!

By analogy, I often tell people to compare it with a fireworks display. For example, on July 4 in the United States, every city has an Independence Day celebration that includes a fireworks display. Fireworks displays always occur at the end of the celebration, and the display doesn't all happen at once. It's stretched out over a period of time. It slowly builds and builds until the moment of the crescendo when the sky explodes with the grand finale. During the grand finale, the heavens light up, and everyone stands in awe of the heavenly wonders that rain down upon them.

It's the same with Divine Mercy Sunday. We initiate our celebration of Christ's Resurrection at Easter, and it gradually builds and builds until the moment of crescendo when, on Divine Mercy Sunday, the King of Mercy pours out all his treasures and doesn't hold back. At that moment, the heavens open up and begin to explode with God's unfathomable mercy, and all who participate are bathed in the heavenly glory. Divine Mercy Sunday is the grand finale of the octave celebration of Easter Day!

Looking at it from this perspective helps us to more fully understand the great promise — complete remission of sin and punishment — that Jesus attached to Divine Mercy Sunday, the grand finale of Easter Day. It's simply amazing that all that's technically required for a soul to reap the promise of Jesus on Divine Mercy Sunday is receiving Holy Communion on that day in a state of grace and making an act of trust in God's mercy. (Of course, to ensure that one is in a state of grace, it's encouraged that one makes a good Confession beforehand, preferably during Lent.) That's it. It's the deal of a lifetime. And it's even easier than obtaining a plenary indulgence because there are certain conditions that have to be met for gaining such an indulgence.

So, in order to be clear, there are two distinct things that we are being offered on Divine Mercy Sunday: the promise of Jesus according to the revelations of St. Faustina and the plenary indulgence offered by the Church for those who participate in Divine Mercy celebrations. As previously noted, in order to gain the promise of Jesus (which is complete remission of sins and punishment), all a person has to do is receive Holy Communion on Divine Mercy Sunday in a state of grace and make an act of trust in God's mercy. Gaining the plenary indulgence offered by the Church, however, requires a person to do the following: Go to Confession (not necessarily on that day), receive Holy Communion, pray for the Pope's intentions, participate in some fashion in a public celebration of Divine Mercy, and be free of any attachment to sin, even venial sin.

In my opinion, why not strive to get both! I bet you that's what John Paul II did! Just like when the Blessed Virgin Mary appeared to St. Maximilian Kolbe and presented him with two crowns (one for purity and one for martyrdom), asking him which he wanted, and he replied "both," I think we should strive to obtain both the promise and the indulgence on Divine Mercy Sunday. Here's why: The promise of Jesus can only be applied to yourself, but the indulgence can be applied to a soul in purgatory. On Divine Mercy Sunday we can actually be both a recipient of Divine Mercy and an apostle of Divine Mercy if we seek to gain both the promise and the indulgence. After all, Jesus tells us: "Freely you have received, freely give" (Mt 10:8).

The Image of Divine Mercy is another very important component of the message and devotion. In 1931, Jesus spoke the following words to St. Faustina regarding this powerful image: "Paint an image according to the pattern you see, with the signature: Jesus, I trust in You" (*Diary*, 47). This now world famous image depicts rays of blood and water streaming forth from the merciful Heart of Jesus and bathing the viewer in a fountain of mercy. The image is a most powerful vessel of God's mercy and visually communicates to a person the Lord's kindness and forgiveness. Jesus once told St. Faustina the following regarding this great gift from heaven: "I am offering people a vessel with which they are to keep coming for graces to the fountain of mercy. That vessel is this image with the signature: Jesus, I trust in You" (*Diary*, 327).

The fact that Jesus wanted the inscription "Jesus, I trust in You" at the bottom of this image is of paramount importance for embracing the Divine Mercy message and devotion. So I will go deeper into a Catholic spirituality of trust later in this chapter, but let me note here the incredible promises that Jesus gives to those who venerate this holy image. He says: "I promise that the soul that will venerate this image will not perish. I also promise victory over [its] enemies already here on earth, especially at the hour of death" (*Diary*, 48). These promises are tremendous, and a person would have to be crazy not to want to reap such blessings.

Our Lady, as the one who shows us Jesus, wants everyone to venerate this image. As a matter of fact, the first time the Divine Mercy image was publicly venerated occurred in 1935 at the Shrine of Our Lady of Ostra Brama in Lithuania. *Ostra Brama* means "Dawn Gate." Mary truly is the dawn announcing the coming of the Son and his life-giving rays. Placing yourself before this image is comparable to spiritual sunbathing. The healing rays of the mercy of Jesus cleanse us and offer us hope and pardon. Today, there are many different versions of the image that are available, and I highly recommend that you obtain one for your home.

Next is the Chaplet of Divine Mercy. What I love about this devotion is that it has a tangible Marian component. Jesus personally taught St. Faustina the Chaplet of Divine Mercy — a short but powerful prayer that only takes about 5-7 minutes to pray. He instructed her that it was to be prayed on ordinary rosary beads (cf. *Diary*, 476). It is so wonderful that Jesus chose to give this great gift to the world through the Rosary since the Rosary of Our Lady always leads us closer to Jesus.

Even though the Divine Mercy Chaplet takes less time to pray than the Rosary, it gets to the heart of the Christian mystery of salvation because it flows from the theology of the Holy Mass, the greatest Christian prayer. In essence, the Chaplet of Divine

Mercy is a devotion flowing from the Cross and Holy Mass. Through it, God's people, both the clergy and the laity, offer to God the Father, in prayer, the most holy body and blood, soul and divinity of Jesus Christ. It's a cry for mercy for ourselves and those of the whole world. And the promises that Jesus gives to those who pray this chaplet are stupendous! Here are a few of them:

- Say unceasingly the chaplet that I have taught you. Whoever will recite it will receive great mercy at the hour of death. Priests will recommend it to sinners as their last hope of salvation. Even if there were a sinner most hardened, if he were to recite this chaplet only once, he would receive grace from My infinite mercy (*Diary*, 687).

- Oh, what great graces I will grant to souls who say this chaplet (*Diary*, 848).

- It pleases Me to grant everything they ask of Me by saying the chaplet. When hardened sinners say it, I will fill their souls with peace, and the hour of their death will be a happy one (*Diary*, 1541).

- At the hour of their death, I defend as My own glory every soul that will say this chaplet; or when others say it for a dying person, the indulgence is the same. When this chaplet is said by the bedside of a dying person, God's anger is placated, unfathomable mercy envelops the soul, and the very depths of My tender mercy are moved (*Diary*, 811).

I can personally attest to the power of the chaplet when prayed at the bedside of a dying person. When I was a seminarian, I was asked to visit the home of an elderly woman who was very near death. As I entered the room, the family members who were there were unsure of what to do, so I recommended that we pray the chaplet. Over the course of the next seven minutes, we all witnessed the dying woman go from having a look of fear and agony on her face to having a countenance of peace and joy. There was no doubt in anyone's mind that she was being filled with incredible graces of surrender to God's mercy. And within the hour, she died. God is so merciful!

There's also the Novena to Divine Mercy that Jesus taught St. Faustina. Though initially intended only for St. Faustina, this aspect of the Divine Mercy devotion is very pleasing to Jesus and helps us enter into the heart of the mystery of salvation and act as intercessors for others. The novena (nine days of prayer) begins on Good Friday and ends on the Saturday before Divine Mercy Sunday. Each day has a particular intention for which the chaplet is prayed. Yet, this novena can be said any time throughout the year. At the National Shrine of The Divine Mercy in Stockbridge, Massachusetts, the novena is prayed daily at the 3 o'clock hour, the Hour of Great Mercy. This is what Jesus had to say about this novena: "By this novena [of chaplets], I will grant every possible grace to souls" (*Diary*, 796).

Lastly, there's the Hour of Great Mercy. This is the hour during which Jesus died for us: the three o'clock hour. And once again, Jesus made exceptional promises associated with this most holy of hours. Here are a few:

- At three o'clock, implore My mercy, especially for sinners; and, if only for a brief moment, immerse yourself in My Passion, particularly in My abandonment at the moment of agony. This is the hour of great mercy for the whole world. In this hour, I will refuse nothing to the soul that makes a request of Me in virtue of My Passion (*Diary*, 1320).

- As often as you hear the clock strike the third hour, immerse yourself completely in My mercy, adoring and glorifying it; invoke its omnipotence for the whole world, and particularly for poor sinners; for at that moment mercy was opened wide for every soul. In this hour you can obtain everything for yourself and for others for the asking; it was the hour of grace for the whole world — mercy triumphed over justice (*Diary*, 1572).

This hour has power. I will never forget the time I was in the Philippines in a secular department store. All of a sudden, an announcement was made over the store intercom that said: "It is the three o'clock hour. Let us pause to pray a decade of the Chaplet of Divine Mercy." I couldn't believe it! What a cultural witness to God's mercy! God truly desires to shower an ocean of mercy on us. He has given us this message, with all of the heavenly promises and new forms of devotion, so that we can reap all the graces and mercies that we need for ourselves and the whole world.

☆ ☆ ☆ Marian Gems

☆ To give worthy praise to the Lord's mercy, we unite ourselves with your Immaculate Mother, for then our hymn will be more pleasing to you, because she is chosen from among men and angels. *St. Faustina Kowalska*

☆ God rules the world and distributes his mercy through secondary causes, the principal one of which is the Mother of Mercy. *Blessed Michael Sopocko*

☆ Mary is the one who has the deepest knowledge of the mystery of God's mercy. *St. John Paul II*

☆ Since this blessed Lady Mary goes as a dawn between our night and the day of Christ, between our darkness and his brightness, and lastly between the misery of our sin and the mercy of God, to whom should wretched sinners turn for help, so as to be delivered quickly from their wretchedness and come to mercy, but to this Blessed Virgin Mary? *St. John Fisher*

☆ She [Mary] is the "Administrator of Mercy" because God has endowed her with extraordinary goodness, meekness, generosity and kindness, with unparalleled power, that she may desire and be capable of helping, protecting, sustaining and comforting all the afflicted, the miserable, and those who have recourse to her in their needs and necessities. *St. John Eudes*

☆ If our strength fails us, let us cling to the Mother of Mercy, and hide, with childlike love, under the cloak which she draws round us with a motherly gesture. *Blessed Michael Sopocko*

☆ If Mary and Martha's tears compelled Christ to raise their dead brother from the tomb, what sin can be so strong, that the power of

Divine Mercy cannot extinguish it through the intercession of the Virgin Mother? *St. Anselm of Lucca*

☆ The moment of conversion is not the same for all. St. Augustine, St. Mary of Egypt and many others spent a considerable part of their lives far from God, while others were ravished by grace from the very beginning. But however we are converted, the Mother of Mercy is always the instrumental cause, for, by God's will, no grace is given to us but through the mediation of the Immaculate Heart of Mary. Let us not be too certain that we are safe now and have no need of our Mother's care. Like little children we should always remain under her mantle, to press continually to the bosom of our Mother who nurses and rears us and obtains mercy for us. *Blessed Michael Sopocko*

☆ The Heart of Mary is the court where the assizes of mercy are held. *St. Madeleine Sophie Barat*

☆ Full of kindness and mercy, he [God] has given over to her [Mary] in a certain sense the dominion over his mercy while reserving for himself the final day of judgment. *Servant of God (Fr.) Joseph Kentenich*

☆ The axis of mercy supporting the world turns on these hinges or poles, that through the Mother we have access to the Son and through the Son to the Father, so that being thus led we should have no fear that our reconciliation would be rejected. *St. Albert the Great*

☆ The nearer a thing approaches to its principle the more does it partake of the effect of that principle. But Christ is the principle of grace, and Mary is nearest to him, since he received from her his human nature. Hence she ought to receive from Christ a greater fullness of grace than anyone else. *St. Thomas Aquinas*

☆ Mary is our advocate, the mother of grace and mercy. She is not ungrateful to those who serve her; she never forgets and always rewards them. She is like a fiery chariot because she conceived within her the Word, the only-begotten Son of God. She carries and spreads the fire of love because her Son is love. *St. Catherine of Siena*

☆ Among the effects of divine mercy we must enumerate three principal realities, which in turn embody numberless effects. The first is the Incarnation of the God-man; the second, his Mystical Body, namely Holy Church; the third is the Mother of the God-man, namely the most Blessed Virgin Mary. These constitute three admirable masterpieces of divine mercy. *St. John Eudes*

☆ ☆ ☆ ☆ ☆ ☆ ☆ ☆ ☆ ☆

Vessels of Mercy

I AM EXTREMELY GRATEFUL THAT JESUS CALLED ME TO BE A PRIEST, to be a witness and vessel of mercy. I am especially grateful that he called me to the religious community that has been the official promoters of the Divine Mercy message and devotion since 1941. I am so unworthy to live and work among such good men. I can never thank Jesus and Mary enough for all the graces and mercies that they have shown to me. I truly do not know where I would be without Divine Mercy. I even tell people during my talks that I consider myself to be the poster child for God's mercy. Mercy brings people back to God. And this is why I see the Divine Mercy message and devotion as being such a big part of the New Evangelization.

Saint John Paul II initiated the New Evangelization, and Pope Benedict XVI continued it. Both of these incredible Popes were tremendous vessels of mercy in our times. Indeed, Pope Benedict XVI repeatedly told the members of the Church that they are to be witnesses of mercy. This is one of the reasons why when I was praying about a subtitle for my conversion story, I decided to title it: *No Turning Back: A Witness to Mercy.* I want people to know about God's mercy, and I truly believe that when we combine Our Lady and Divine Mercy, we have a one-two punch for the New Evangelization. Both Mary and Divine Mercy lead us to conversion and back to the teachings of the Church. Both Mary and the Divine Mercy lead us back to prayer and the Sacraments, especially Confession and the Eucharist.

As the great Pope of mercy and the initiator of the New Evangelization, St. John Paul II gave us the greatest example of how to be a vessel of mercy by teaching us how to live *under the mantle* of Our Lady. John Paul II knew better than anyone that if there is to be fruit in our efforts to help people rediscover their faith, we have to do everything through Our Lady. Mary and mercy cannot be separated. Divine Mercy lives in Mary. As we see in many images of Our Lady — for example, the pregnant image of Our Lady of Guadalupe as shown on the cover of this book — Jesus abides in her. She is pregnant with mercy. She is, in fact, the Mother of Divine Mercy.

The Divine Mercy abides *under the mantle* of Mary. She is the mother of the New Evangelization.

Jesus once told St. Faustina, "Mankind will not have peace until it turns with trust to My mercy" (*Diary*, 300). Living *under the mantle* of Mary is a school of trust. God himself entrusted his only begotten Son into her care, into her womb. And when we seek refuge in her, we learn how to trust in the mercy of God. She is the greatest recipient, witness, and vessel of God's mercy. Mary has a superabundance of God's mercy because she is the immaculate mother and perfect fruit of Jesus' sacrificial love. She is the masterpiece of mercy.

Let me explain in more depth the deep connection between Mary and mercy: Mary is not a sinner like us. God poured out all the treasures of his mercy upon her, preserving her from original sin. Part of the reason why this was done was due to her future role of being the Mother of Mercy. In other words, since she is the chosen vessel destined to bring Jesus, the Divine Mercy, into the world, she must be a totally pure and unique vessel of his mercy. And since God's plan from all eternity was to also make her our immaculate mother, God emptied all of his mercies into her, so that she could mediate God's mercies to us. Remember: A mother can't give what a mother doesn't have. Therefore, Mary received a superabundance of God's mercy in preparation for her role of being both the Mother of Divine Mercy and our spiritual mother.

In light of this, the Church teaches that Mary is saved by the merits of Jesus Christ just as we are but in a different and more perfect way. Here's a way to help you understand it better. There are two ways God saves someone from the pit of sin: 1) once a person has fallen in, God gets the person out; or 2) God saves the person beforehand by preventing him from falling into the pit in the first place. The latter is how God saved Mary. Divine Mercy not only has the power to forgive sin, but it also has the power to prevent sin.

For example, after we pray the Our Father at Holy Mass, the priest prays out loud the following beautiful prayer:

Deliver us, Lord, we pray, from every evil,
graciously grant peace in our days,
that, by the help of your mercy,
we may be always free from sin
and safe from all distress,
as we await the blessed hope
and coming of our Savior, Jesus Christ (emphasis added).

This prayer shows us that God's mercy not only forgives sin; it also prevents it. And this is precisely what Divine Mercy did for Our Lady. Thus, Mary's Immaculate Conception is a special and unique gift that God gave to Mary because of her role as mother. This singular role will also require of her a unique participation in the redemptive mission of Christ, because her maternal heart and soul will be pierced so that we can obtain mercy from the saving mystery of the Cross.

God created Mary uniquely *for our sake*. The unique privilege of her Immaculate Conception does not separate her from us, but it actually joins us to her in a profound filial bond. Our mother precedes us, prepares the way for us, and shares with us what she herself has received in its fullness: Divine Mercy and sinlessness. Divine Mercy made a mother for us, and because of her, we can drink the milk of mercy that flows from the Heart of Christ through the Church and her Sacraments.

As the Immaculate Conception, Mary is the greatest witness and vessel of God's mercy. She knows God's mercy better than anyone, and she is the greatest model for teaching us how to be vessels of mercy. She has taught the saints this for 2,000 years. This is why every age of the Church experiences Marian apparitions. They remind us to accept God's mercy in our lives and call us to be witnesses and vessels of his mercy to others. Saint Faustina herself, the great apostle of Divine Mercy, learned how to be a vessel of mercy through the example of Our Lady. The saint had a very intense and filial relationship with the Mother of Mercy. She lived *under the mantle* of Mary and daily went to Jesus through Mary.

As a matter of fact, the Solemnity of the Immaculate Conception was her favorite Marian feast, and she would sometimes prepare for it months in advance. She would even pray a novena of 9,000 Hail Marys in anticipation of December 8. That's the equivalent of praying 180 rosaries in 9 days, or 20 rosaries a day for 9 straight days! Try that sometime! That's how much she loved Our Lady. There's so much we can learn from St. Faustina's great love for Our Lady. If you want to find out more, read my book *Purest of All Lilies: The Virgin Mary in the Spirituality of St. Faustina* (Marian Press, 2008).

It is in light of the inner theological connection between Mary's Immaculate Conception and Divine Mercy that it totally makes sense that God entrusted the spread of the Divine Mercy message and devotion to my religious community, the Congregation of Marian Fathers of the Immaculate Conception. This religious community was the first religious community of men in the Church to have the privilege of bearing Mary's Immaculate Conception in their official title. Saint Stanislaus Papczynski founded the Marian Fathers in 1673, which was 181 years before the Immaculate Conception of Our Lady was even declared a dogma and long before the Divine Mercy message and devotion was given to the world. Divine Providence had set everything up *ahead of time.* And as we have seen so many times now, God delights in doing things this way.

Even Pope John Paul II, at the Marian Fathers' General Chapter in 1993, told our community that we were to *be apostles of Divine Mercy under the maternal and loving guidance of Mary.* In fact, my community incorporated this mandate of the Holy Father into our Constitutions and way of life, which means that promoting devotion to Divine Mercy is now part of our path to holiness. This may not seem like a big deal, but it is. The Constitutions of a religious community can only be changed with the approval of the Holy See.

The history of how my religious community became such a vessel of Divine Mercy is quite fascinating and miraculous, but in short, God used one of our priests, Fr. Joseph Jarzebowski, MIC, to bring the Divine Mercy message and devotion to the United States during World War II. And today the vast majority of all

Divine Mercy literature in English that is distributed throughout the world comes from Stockbridge, Massachusetts, where my community operates the Marian Helpers Center and the National Shrine of The Divine Mercy. To me, it's amazing to think that God has used my community in the United States to bring Divine Mercy to the world. For example, did you know that both of the miracles that were approved for St. Faustina's beatification and canonization came from the United States? Mary and Divine Mercy are truly the keys to renewal and new life in the Church today. And it gives me great joy as the vocation director for the Marian Fathers to inform you that we are bursting at the seams with vocations! God wants more vessels of mercy!

What we need in the world today is both a love for Our Lady and a culture of mercy. Through Our Lady and Divine Mercy, people can learn how to love and forgive. Jesus and Mary show us how. Jesus himself forgave his executioners from the Cross, and Mary had nothing but mercy for those who killed her Son before her very eyes. The saints, too, desire nothing but mercy for those who put them through trials and sometimes even torture and death. And we are called to imitate Jesus, Mary, and the saints.

In our times, what family doesn't have issues and stand in need of mercy? What married couple couldn't use a message of forgiveness and mercy? What priest would not want to be an ardent promoter and vessel of mercy for his people? We all need mercy, and God wants to give it to us in abundance. But he needs vessels to do it. We must become a vessel of mercy like Our Lady. We must receive God's mercy ourselves and bring this message to others through our words and deeds.

Jesus himself demanded from St. Faustina that she perform deeds of mercy (cf. *Diary*, 742). After all, it is important to remember that faith without works is dead (cf. Jas 2:26). So, how can we be vessels of mercy for our times? Sometimes, people think they have to have a big name, lots of money, or social and political influence, but that's not true. There are many things we can do within the context of our daily life — within our families, at our workplace, and in our social surroundings — that can make us a vessel of mercy. Specifically, a great way to begin living as a vessel of mercy is to practice the spiritual and corporal works of mercy. Just in case you don't know what they are, here's the list:

The spiritual works of mercy:

Teach the ignorant;
Pray for the living and the dead;
Correct sinners;
Counsel those in doubt;
Console the sorrowful;
Bear wrongs patiently;
Forgive wrongs willingly.

The corporal works of mercy:

Feed the hungry;
Give drink to the thirsty;
Clothe the naked;
Shelter the homeless;
Visit the prisoners;
Comfort the sick;
Bury the dead.

Practicing the spiritual and corporal works of mercy is a great way for us to become vessels of mercy, and there really is no excuse not to perform at least some of them. They show us that being a witness and vessel of mercy can be done by anyone. It doesn't require getting a doctorate, learning multiple languages, or developing the facility of being a public speaker. All that is required to be a vessel of mercy is a right intention and a heart of service. Life will definitely present us with tons of opportunities to be merciful. All we have to do to be fruitful missionaries of mercy for the New Evangelization is to receive mercy ourselves, live *under the mantle*, and be willing to perform deeds of mercy towards others.

☆☆☆ Marian Gems

☆ Mary is the one who obtained mercy in a particular and exceptional way, as no other person has. *St. John Paul II*

☆ In the conception of Mary it was as if divine mercy and divine justice were running side by side. ... Mercy outran justice and reached Mary sooner, because God by his very nature is much quicker at showing mercy than justice, especially when it concerns something in conformity with reason and common sense. *St. Lawrence of Brindisi*

☆ The heart of a mother is a marvel of mercy. When we fear to go to God, when we are overwhelmed by our unworthiness, we can go to Mary, because God has entrusted to her the realm of mercy. *Blessed Columba Marmion*

☆ She [Mary] is his mystic channel; she is his aqueduct, through which he makes his mercies flow gently and abundantly. *St. Louis de Montfort*

☆ God, who gave us Jesus Christ, wills that all graces that have been, that are, and will be dispensed to men to the end of the world through the merits of Jesus Christ, should be dispensed by the hands and through the intercession of Mary. *St. Alphonsus Liguori*

☆ You [Mary] are a vessel containing every grace, the fullness of all things good and beautiful, the tablet and living icon of every good and all uprightness, since you alone have been deemed worthy to receive the fullness of every gift of the Spirit. *St. Gregory Palamas*

☆ Divine mercy reigns so perfectly in Mary's heart that she bears the name of Queen and Mother of Mercy. And this most loving Mary has so completely won the heart of God's mercy that he has given her the key to all his treasures and made her absolute mistress of them. *St. John Eudes*

☆ She is called the Queen of Mercy because she opens the abyss and treasure of divine mercy to whom she chooses, when she chooses and as she chooses. *St. Bernard of Clairvaux*

☆ She [Mary] is the motherly principle, the apparition of God's arm of mercy which even a person with an icy heart has difficulty to resist. *Servant of God (Fr.) Joseph Kentenich*

☆ Through her, as through a pure crystal, Your mercy was passed on to us. Through her, man became pleasing to God; through her, streams of grace flowed down upon us. *St. Faustina Kowalska*

☆ Mary is the glory of creation, the delight of the angels, the model of saints, the strength of the vacillating, the consolation of the weak and the secure refuge of sinners. *Servant of God Mother Auxilia de la Cruz*

☆ In honoring Mary, in every thought of her, we do homage to the superabundant mercy and love of the Redeemer of men. *Venerable Pope Pius XII*

☆ O Mary, temple of the Trinity! O Mary, bearer of fire! Mary, minister of mercy! Mary mother of the divine fruit! Mary, redemptress of the human race because it was by your flesh suffering in the Word that the world was redeemed! *St. Catherine of Siena*

☆ Before the second coming of Christ, Mary, more than ever, must shine in mercy, might, and grace in order to bring unbelievers into the Catholic faith. The power of Mary in the latter days will be very conspicuous. Mary will extend the reign of Christ over the heathens and the Mohammedans, and it will be a time of great joy when Mary is enthroned as Mistress and Queen of Hearts. *Venerable Mary of Agreda*

Jesus, I Trust in You!

AN ESSENTIAL PART OF EMBRACING THE DIVINE MERCY MESSAGE AND DEVOTION is a desire to live a spirituality of trust. There is nothing more urgent in the life of Catholics today than that they trust in Jesus and the Church he founded. Many people today claim to love Jesus and call themselves Catholic, but they neither trust in Jesus nor in his Church. This is why I believe he wanted the specific phrase — *Jesus, I trust in you* — on the bottom of the Divine Mercy image. It could have read: "Jesus, I love you," or "Jesus, I adore you," or "Jesus, I praise you," but he was very specific about what he wants. He wants *trust*. Without trust, we really can't be devoted to him. For it is trust in Jesus that tests if our love, adoration, and praise can go the distance.

Trusting in someone means you have confidence in them. The word *confidence* when broken down means "with faith." Trusting in God, therefore, is faith (belief) in action. This is why in some of the romance languages the inscription at the bottom of the Divine Mercy image reads: *Gesu, confido in Te* (Italian); *Jesus, en Ti confio* (Spanish); *Jesus, j'ai confiance en Toi* (French). Having a living faith in Jesus means that even when things are not pleasant or convenient, you still have total confidence and trust in God's providential plan. And Catholics need this necessary dimension of faith more than ever.

We live in an age where people have been taught not to trust in Jesus and the Church he founded. Children are taught in school, for example, that many tenets of the Judeo-Christian faith are myths, that the Bible is full of errors and written by prehistoric homophobes, and that the Catholic Church is a man-made, oppressive institution that hates women. If you were to be so unfortunate as to have to take a religion class at a secular college today, you would hear this nonsense constantly, perhaps daily.

And the greatest perpetrator of instilling in society a lack of trust in Jesus and his Church is the media. Inevitably, every year around Christmas and Easter, the media gathers their "experts" and puts into question the historical veracity of Jesus Christ and the moral tenets of the Church he founded. They make a mockery of divine revelation with their revisionist history and ludicrous theories of how creation, the Bible, and the Church came about. As a matter of fact, a person learns very little factual history on the History Channel anymore. The media would rather instill a "belief" in little green men and UFOs than the Ten Commandments and common sense.

Sadly, this mentality has crept into the Church, too. Today, theologians waste their time discussing the probability of baptizing aliens and welcoming our "inter-galactic brothers and sisters." How lame is that! In my opinion, there isn't anything out there but a bunch of big rocks, and the only other-worldly being we need to be worried about is Satan. He is the one who wants to "abduct" you and instill in you a lack of trust in God and his Church by tricking you into believing the very fascinating media presentations about how celestial visitors built the pyramids, about how hell is just an invention of "organized religion," and how the Vatican holds back "secrets" from society. The subtle trickery of Satan makes people question God, divine revelation, and his Church. The smoke of Satan causes people to lose their way, become confused, and discontinue trusting in Jesus and his Church. And we were warned about this.

On June 29, 1972, Blessed Pope Paul VI, in a homily in which he was preaching about how modern man lacks trust in God and his Church, stated that *the smoke of Satan has entered the Church*. That's a huge statement coming from the Vicar of Christ! On a personal note, I have to say that his statement keeps me humble because June 29, 1972, is the day I was born. Yikes! Nevertheless, the fact that the Pope made such a huge statement is serious stuff. Obviously, Satan isn't running the Church, and the Church can never be destroyed or overcome by evil. But there is no doubt that many people today have become confused about what to believe, what to profess, and how to act. And how could they not be confused when the vast majority of seminarians over the last 40 years have been taught that the Bible is an outdated misogynist document, the Red Sea crossing in the Exodus event was a natural phenomenon (at low tide), Moses and most of the Old Testament prophets probably didn't even exist, the Gospel of Matthew wasn't written by Matthew, and many of the miracles in the New Testament — even those performed by Jesus — were "fudged" by later authors. When seminarians are forced to read books by "educated scholars" who assert that the Catholic Church has "secrets" that they don't want the public to know lest they find out about "real" Christianity and are liberated from the hierarchical structure of the Church, both priests and the laity learn to have little confidence in Jesus and his Church.

But we must remember that the confusion is only smoke. It will eventually clear. Satan can never overcome the Church. The Church is an unconquerable fighting machine! But what we are left with is an era in which people don't trust.

The insidious "wisdom" at work in the word today can be summed up in the following phrase: "Jesus, I *don't* trust in you." Many people have given up on faith, reason, and common sense today. They tend to judge things solely from experience. If their experience has been pleasant, they "love" God and his Church, but if their experience has not been pleasant, they jump ship. Yet having trust in Jesus means totally believing everything he said and relying entirely upon it, no matter what bad experiences you have.

Even figures from the Old Testament can teach us a lesson or two about trust. Take Job, for example. After having undergone — experienced — the loss of basically everything, he rouses up his confidence and boldly declares, "Although he should kill me, I will trust in him" (Job 13:15). Trust in God *will* require one to die to self. Trust is a matter of letting go and learning to live in total abandonment to divine providence. This is why the Book of Proverbs tells us the following: "Trust in the Lord with all your heart, and do not rely on your own insight" (Prov 3:5).

Interestingly, St. Faustina, being an apostle of the spirituality of trust, quotes in her *Diary* (77) the exact passage from Job mentioned above. She was willing to die rather than give in to the deceptions and confusion — the smoke — of Satan. He had tricked her once into burning the *Diary*, but she would make sure he would not trick her again. Her trust was radical, and that trust was manifested by her total willingness to give absolute priority in her life to the wisdom and guidance of the Church. She even placed the guidance of the Church above the revelations she was receiving.

To not trust Jesus is to become like Satan. That's why Jesus had to rebuke Peter on one occasion and call him Satan (cf. Mt 16:23). Though Peter knew who Jesus was and believed in him, he was acting in a distrustful, Satan-like way by seeking to have Jesus show distrust of his Father by taking off the wedding ring of the Cross. Jesus trusted his heavenly Father to the point of death, and Peter needed to learn to have this same trust in Jesus. As we know, Peter did eventually acquire a bold confidence and trust in Jesus, and he was crucified out of love for him.

This brings us to an interesting question: Is simply acknowledging who Jesus is enough to save us? Here's an example of what I mean: On several occasions in the New Testament, demons fully profess who Jesus is, crying out: "What have you to do with us, Jesus of Nazareth? Have you come to destroy us? I know who you are, the Holy One of God" (Mk 1:24; cf. Lk 4:31-34). Demons profess that he is the Holy One of God; they don't deny it. But, as we all know, they are not saved. The reason is because they lack the one thing that makes their belief alive and active: trust. They don't trust God. Trust requires allowing God to lead us in ways that we don't fully understand. Trust requires the mystery of the Cross and a willingness to die in the service of God. And Satan will have none of that.

To trust is to have more than just knowledge of Jesus. It requires an intentional surrender *from the will* to all that he is and all that he taught. And it is this lack of volitional faith (trust) in our midst today that causes many people to identify themselves as "spiritual persons" who believe in Jesus but want nothing to do with the "organized religion" of Catholicism. But we must remember that Satan is also a spiritual person who wants nothing to do with the organized religion that Jesus founded. The devil prefers his own way of thinking. If we think like him, we are no better than him. Scripture itself warns us, "He who trusts in his own mind is a fool" (Prov 28:26).

God's ways are far above our ways, and being a disciple means that we have to be willing to die to self and live for God. Therefore, if we do not have trust in Jesus, our belief in him might just be in vain. Jesus even told St. Faustina that he made himself dependent upon her trust, and that if her trust were great, his generosity would be without limit (cf. *Diary*, 548). In other words, God will not force us to receive his blessings without our consent. Knowing Jesus and acknowledging him is good, but Jesus wants more from us. He wants our trust. Trust unlocks the Heart of God. In the *Diary*, Jesus tells us the following:

- The graces of My mercy are drawn by means of one vessel only, and that is — trust. The more a soul trusts, the more it will receive (*Diary*, 1578).

- I am Love and Mercy itself. When a soul approaches Me with trust, I fill it with such an abundance of graces that it cannot contain them within itself, but radiates them to other souls (*Diary*, 1074).

- I desire to grant unimaginable graces to those souls who trust in My mercy (*Diary*, 687).

In light of this, consider Our Lady and her great trust. Nobody trusted more than she did. And nobody is more blessed than she is. She is the ultimate model of trust, and because her trust was so great, God's graces radiate through her to us. Her profound trust made her the Mediatrix of all grace. Think about it: The crucifixion happened before her very eyes — it was a horrible experience — and it made no sense to the world, but she stood firm in her trust. Her experience of the Cross told her it was madness, but she trusted not in her own understanding but in the infinite wisdom of God. She completely trusted in Jesus and knew that everything he was allowing to happen was part of the saving plan of God. She is the greatest vessel of trust the world has ever seen. At the foot of the Cross, her maternal heart was crying out: "Jesus, I trust in you!"

Where there is trust in Jesus and his Church, there is peace and harmony. But where there is no trust in Jesus and his Church, there is discord and division. This is why, in my opinion, one of the greatest tragedies to ever befall Christianity was the Protestant Reformation. It can basically be described as a radical lack of trust on the part of certain individuals, causing great discord and division. While it is true that in the 16th century the Church needed to clear away the smoke of Satan and undergo a purification and renewal, nonetheless, there occurred the great tragedy of millions of people leaving the one true Church because they didn't trust in what Jesus established. In essence, certain members of the Church freaked out over the smoke and jumped ship because they relied on their own understanding. They wanted to do things their way, outside of the hierarchical structure, sacramental system, and dogmatic foundations of the organized religion Jesus founded: Catholicism. It was a time when many "reformers" professed that they loved Jesus, but by their actions, they proved that they neither trusted him nor the Church he founded. They should have known that God's people are always in need of renewal and reform, and they could have been a part of the renewal and become saints by trusting God and enduring the manure. But they chose rebellion and disobedience, rather than the wisdom of the Cross.

With the exception of Jesus and Mary, each and every member of the Church is a sinner. This should not shock us. What we should be in awe of is that in spite of us being a bunch of stinkers and sinful people, God sustains the Catholic Church because he made a promise to do so (cf. Mt 16:18). We can totally trust this, even though many times our experience of the Church and her members is horrible. Jesus will deal with that. Our role is to trust. And this only happens when we have a living faith that has total confidence in Jesus.

It is estimated that during the distrusting rebellion of the Protestant Reformation, about 5 million people left the one true Church. And what did God do as a result? He gave the faith to a people that would trust him. It began with one little trusting soul, St. Juan Diego.

It's an historical fact that during that same exact period when so many people in Europe were manifesting a lack of trust in Jesus and his Church, God gave the miraculous image of Our Lady of Guadalupe to a little unknown nobody named Juan Diego —

causing almost 10 million people to convert to Catholicism in less than a decade. And what did God see in little Juan Diego that he didn't see in the people rebelling in Europe? Trust. Saint Juan Diego trusted enough to be willing to look like a fool and take his *tilma* filled with roses to a bishop. He had no idea what would happen once he got there. All he knew was that he loved Jesus and the Church, and Mary told him to do this. So he did it. And the result of his trust was that basically a whole people converted to Catholicism. If large portions of Europe wanted to rebel and display a lack of trust in Jesus and his Church, God planted the faith elsewhere.

Is not the same thing happening today? Has not another image been given to the world today by means of an apostle of trust? Is this not an age in which massive amounts of people have left the one true Church in favor of following their own ideas? And the irony — and the similarity to what happened in the 16th century — is that, just as many have left the Church in our times, God is filling in the gap by bringing about massive conversions to Catholicism from among Protestants! Many cradle Catholics are in rebellion against the Pope and the Magisterium (and the teachings of the Church), and they are causing discord and division. But God's response is to provide an image from heaven and bring about tons of conversions and reversions to Catholicism from among the Protestants! Where there has been a void created because of a failure to trust in Jesus and his Church, God fills in the gap. He gives the true faith to a new generation that will treasure it and trust it.

☆ ☆ ☆ Marian Gems

☆ Mary [is] the pledge of divine mercy. *St. Andrew of Crete*

☆ In Mary we see how a truly good and provident God has established for us a most suitable example of every virtue. *Pope Leo XIII*

☆ Let us run to Mary, and like little children, cast ourselves into her arms with perfect confidence. *St. Francis de Sales*

☆ A deep veneration of Mary removes the bitterness and harshness usually connected with the striving for perfection. *Servant of God (Fr.) Joseph Kentenich*

☆ The sword that Christ ran into his own heart and Mary's soul has become so blunted by the pressings that it can never wound so fiercely again. *Venerable Fulton J. Sheen*

☆ I take refuge in Our Lady, with trust, with certitude … I have carved her image so deeply in my heart that no one will be able to take it away. *Venerable Bernard Maria Clausi*

☆ We are like ivy, which cannot support itself, but which, if it twines round a tree, can grow to great heights. Our souls, which also need support, grow rapidly in perfection if they trust the Mother of Mercy. We see this in the many saints who made rapid progress by loving and honoring her. *Blessed Michael Sopocko*

☆ O happy confidence! O perfect refuge! The Mother of God is my Mother. What firm trust we should have, then, since our salvation depends on the judgment of a good brother and a tender Mother. *St. Anselm of Canterbury*

☆ From Mary we learn to surrender to God's Will in all things. From Mary we learn to trust even when all hope seems gone. *St. John Paul II*

☆ I trust you completely, Lord. Strengthen my trust. In whom else can I hope, being so poor and miserable in spirit, if not in your goodness, if not in the heart of your Beloved Son, filled with love and mercy; if not in the powerful intercession of the most Blessed Virgin Mary? *Blessed George Matulaitis*

☆ Let us trust God through the Immaculate One with a limitless trust, and make every effort to the extent of our understanding and strength, to go forward, but in serenity of spirit, placing all our confidence in the Immaculate One. *St. Maximilian Kolbe*

☆ After God, we should have a great confidence in the Blessed Mother of Jesus, who is so good. *St. John Vianney*

☆ In every situation I will trustingly adhere to the Blessed Mother and go hand in hand and heart in heart with her to our Savior and to the Father. *Servant of God (Fr.) Joseph Kentenich*

CHAPTER 8

Manhood

Like Father, Like Son

WE LIVE IN SERIOUSLY CONFUSED ANTHROPOLOGICAL TIMES. Many people no longer understand what it means to be a man or a woman anymore. Nowadays, in certain places, it can be really hard, almost impossible to differentiate between whether a person walking down the street or serving you a drink as a flight attendant is a guy or a girl. The old nursery rhyme "snakes and snails and puppy-dogs' tails; that's what boys are made out of" seems to have been forgotten. As research clearly shows (contrary to the androgynous culture that modern education and the media are trying to create), there really are traits that are objectively masculine and feminine. People intrinsically know this. It's just that everybody is trying to be politically correct and not lose their job if they call a spade a spade. Or, as is often the case, many people have a son or a daughter who is sexually "confused." So, out of a false sense of love, misplaced compassion, or for fear of losing their son or daughter, they don't want to say anything to cause any drama. State something totally obvious today, and it's considered intolerant hate speech. You could get sued, or the media brings up your own faults and sins and chastises you for judging others.

What is really scary are the people who seriously do believe that there is nothing objective about what it means to be a man or a woman. They claim that what we describe as masculine and feminine traits are merely culturally conditioned, and there is nothing objective about them at all. But the fact of the matter is that boys and girls do things differently, and the research I've read shows that it's biological.

For instance, there's a study from Texas A&M University that used eye-tracking technology on infants ages 3 to 8 months old. The research showed that the baby boys looked at trucks more than girls and that the girls looked at dolls more than trucks.

Duh! Another study from the University of Cambridge tested infants ages 12, 18, and 24 months, and guess what … same conclusion! Yet another study, this one from Uppsala University in Sweden, showed that boys and girls ages 1, 3, and 5 chose masculine and feminine toys respectively. Finally, according to research from the University of Oxford, such sex differences in toy choice could even be found in monkeys! I'm telling you, give a boy dolls to play with and they will end up going to war; give a little girl trucks to play with and she will end up playing with Mama truck, Papa truck, and Baby truck. This stuff is hard-wired into us.

So I have to insist that masculine and feminine traits are inborn. Our sex (gender), with all of its traits and qualities, is God-given, not simply a conditioned response to our culture. And if we fight against our biology or want to change it, we are fighting against our very nature and, in a sense, against God. Those who insist that there is no difference between boys and girls or men and women seemingly fight against common sense and have a nonsense agenda. Although they may have the biggest soapboxes on which to stand and shout, we don't have to listen to them, and we've got sound science on our side. Still, it can be difficult to avoid the pervasive liberal agenda.

Case in point: We live in an age where the public school system educates its children into believing that it's normal to experiment and find their sexual orientation. Children are encouraged to think positively about sex changes, homosexual activity, and transgender or bisexual lifestyles. But this is like trying to get people to think positively about eating soup with a fork. On one level, you can pretend that it's great and that it works, but that doesn't make it right or proper. In fact, it's unnatural and doesn't make sense — even a child will tell you that!

Now, ironically, where the liberal agenda will say that the differences between men and women are largely culturally conditioned and I say they're inborn, regarding other aspects of sexuality, the liberal agenda declares that they are inborn and I say they're culturally conditioned. For instance, the liberal agenda loves to say that same-sex attraction is inborn, but the evidence I've seen says it's largely culturally conditioned, just as are many other aspects of sexual identity.

For instance, I think part of the reason so many people have a confused and wrong understanding of manhood today is because the example of fatherhood given over the last few decades has been terrible. Many boys, in particular, have witnessed their father being an abuser of the feminine, which often times drives the boys to become rabid, irresponsible heterosexuals themselves. The young man goes through his teen years trying to "score" and "bag" babes with as little responsibility as possible. Like father, like son.

On the other hand, due to decades and decades of fatherless children, mothers have often been left to fill in the gap created by absent fathers, which oftentimes causes a woman to become overly protective of her son. When this happens, the boy can end up clinging too closely to his mother and hanging around girls too much. The result is that he becomes girly, soft, and effeminate, and may even end up struggling with same-sex attraction.

People can deny these things all they want, but it's the truth. Make no mistake: Both of these ways of acting — rabid, irresponsible heterosexuality and homosexuality — are not normal. If there's anything that's culturally conditioned, it's rabid hetero-sexuality and the practice of homosexuality. Rightly ordered manhood is when a man treats women with respect and dignity. He is kind, compassionate, humble, and gentle towards others — but not in the same way women are. No woman in her right mind wants to marry a man who tells her he is going to sleep around on her. And no woman wants a husband who is effeminate and dainty; men were not made to curtsy. Every woman wants a strong man whose strength she can both depend on and be gently caressed by. Deep down, notwithstanding so many wounds and anger, all women seem to want this. All of them.

This is why fatherhood is so important in the raising of boys to become true men. Manhood is within little boys by nature, but it has to be nurtured. And in this fallen world, boys must be taught how to become virtuous. This is actually what it means to be a man. In Latin, the word for "man" is *vir*, from which we get the word "virtue." In this sense, no boy becomes a true man unless he becomes a virtuous man. This means he must possess qualities such as being humble, chaste, charitable, and merciful.

During his formative years, every boy should be able to look up to his father and want to be like him. The father is essential in helping a young boy form his manly identity. A father should be a model for what it means to be virtuous. And the father needs to affirm his "little man" and give him the affirmation that he, too, will one day be a virtuous grown-up man. That's why a father instinctively lets his little man punch his hands, acting like it stings and hurts. It doesn't hurt the father, but he acts like it does so that the boy can know his strength and learn to use it for good and with restraint. He needs to learn virtue. Only a father calls his boy his "little tiger," wrestling with him on the carpet and in the dirt. All of this is done for a reason: to teach the little tiger that his strength is for a purpose and a mission — to be a provider and a protector, just like Dad.

In almost all cultures prior to modern times, a father would initiate his son into manhood through some form of a ritual passage. Whether it was going on a hunt, a sea voyage, or a fishing trip, the father took his boy out of the home, away from mom and the girls. He brought the boy through a rite of passage so that both the boy and the public knew that he was now a man. As part of this passage to manhood, the boy would oftentimes receive a new name, too. This name would designate traits of his masculine character and mission. And this experience of becoming a man was not only for the boy, but it was also for the father. It would make the father proud to see his son master the transition from boyhood to manhood, with the father saying something like, "That's my son!"

A mother can't do this for a boy; her affirmation of a boy is different. She needs to let the father and the son go through this together. She must not interfere but let it happen.

Mothers do not teach their boys to be rough and tough. A mother will always want her little boy to "play nice" and "be careful" and not do anything dangerous. She winces at the thought of him climbing to the top of a tree, picking up a snake, or jumping off a cliff. But that's not the case with the father. The father affirms the boy's adventurous and wild side, and he tells him to climb higher and jump further. Boys were born to be adventurous and do dangerous stuff. To deprive him of that is to emasculate him and turn him into a pansy. His strength must be affirmed and, through the love of a father, fine-tuned through trial and error into something virtuous (manly).

It's totally normal for a boy to want to go fishing and hunting with his dad (which means they have to kill stuff and get blood all over themselves). I remember the first time I was taken out to my grandpa's barn to watch him shoot a cow in the head, then hoist it up with a chain apparatus and slit its throat. I was terrified as I watched rivers of blood pour into buckets on the ground and witnessed my grandpa slice up the cow with a knife. Yet I knew then and there that my grandpa was awesome, and I wanted to be like him. He was a warrior.

I also remember the first time I went hunting with my uncle in West Virginia. It was beyond thrilling! I was so nervous I couldn't stop shaking long enough to aim right. When I did finally pull the trigger to shoot my first white-tail deer, I twitched and shot the deer in the wrong area — you are supposed to shoot a deer slightly above the front shoulder. But even though it wasn't a perfect shot, my uncle affirmed me with a hearty "Atta boy!" as he slapped me on my back. We both knew it wasn't the best shot, but he was proud of me for trying, and I had the sense from him that it was a good start and that he was telling me I was going to be a good hunter. That meant so much to me and gave me the courage to persevere. In fact, the icing on the cake was that, from that day on, my uncle began calling me "Mountain Man," a name that has stuck with me to this day.

What hunting with my uncle taught me was that showing someone mercy is incredibly manly. I was affirmed by my uncle even though I didn't deliver a perfect shot; he knew I would eventually perfect it through perseverance. That experience taught me that if a person makes mistakes, it's manly to be kind, compassionate, and forgiving. I also learned from some of the other father figures in my life that if you do something wrong, you ask for forgiveness. When a boy sees that humble quality in the men around him, he learns to be a true man: strong, yet humble and merciful.

This is why one of the most important lessons that needs to be taught by a father to his son is the importance of prayer. No boy ever becomes virtuous (manly) without a prayer life. Unfortunately, this is something severely lacking in father-son relationships today. Oftentimes, the reason so many boys are ashamed to pray is because their father told them it was a woman's thing to do. But if a boy only learns to pray from his mother, he will most likely consider it a girly thing and eventually stop doing it. Whereas, if a father teaches his son to pray, it will stick and last, because part of who the boy is and wants to be is an image of his father — a deeply devout man. Even Jesus, though he had the perfect mother in the Immaculate Virgin, also had the great fatherly example of St. Joseph to follow. Jesus was not only given an example of prayer in Mary, *the* woman of prayer, but also in the father that God appointed for him: St. Joseph, the just man.

"Train up a child in the way he should go, and when he is old he will not depart from it" (Prov 22:6). This is sound wisdom and applies to a lot of things in life, especially a boy's relationship with God and the Church. Therefore, if it is the father who wakes the boy up to go to church on Sunday morning, then going to church isn't just for the girls; it's an adventure and a quest. And if it is the father who brings the family to church for Confession, those formative moments will stick with the boy and greatly shape his manhood and future fatherhood. A boy learns to do what he sees his father doing. And there is no doubt that the example of a father's love for his wife, the Eucharist, the Church, the Pope, the saints, and Our Lady will have an everlasting positive impact on his son.

A father needs to tell his son that the greatest adventure in life is to become a saint. To desire to become a saint is the most noble endeavor anyone can have. Telling a boy that becoming a saint is an adventure involving a King, scary monsters, weapons, and a princess will make him want to set out on the great quest of becoming holy. One of the best ways a father can prepare his son for this great adventure is through praying the Rosary. When a father prays the Rosary himself and invites his son to pray it with him, chivalry and manly power emanate from the home.

The home becomes a castle where love, peace, and joy reign. Images of the King and Queen are seen in the house. Great heroic saints who have fought valiantly in the service of the King and Queen also are visible in the castle. And the weapons of war (the Rosary and other devotionals) are honored as they rest on the fireplace mantel and the bedposts, ready for use at a moment's notice. A father who turns his house into a stronghold of faith forges true manhood in his son and instills in him a desire to be a knight and a soldier for Jesus and Mary. He creates a desire in his son to want to be a warrior. And what boy doesn't want to be a knight and a warrior?

All boys want to be heroes, and they look to their dad to supply the weapon.

In certain cultures, a father passes down to his son a weapon or a symbol of his fatherhood and manhood. Wouldn't it be great if a father passed down to his son the Rosary he prayed on for most of his life! It is a weapon. It is a symbol of manhood. Passing such a gift on to a son is tantamount to telling him that this great treasure will help him become a true man, too. The Rosary will help him in times of temptation, giving him the strength to slay dragons and helping him become a true knight and defender of beauty.

A man will face many dangers in life, and it is during his formative years that he must learn how to "man up" and be willing to do what is right, defending and protecting what is good, true, and beautiful. Teaching a boy to pray teaches him not only about God, but it also informs him about the reality of evil and the devil. A boy must be told by his father about the reality of evil, Satan, and sin. If the mother is the only one who tells him, he won't understand that he is being invited to enter into a spiritual battle and slay dragons. He doesn't want to be like his mother; he wants to be like his father — a dragon slayer. Therefore, the father must tell him about the reality of evil. He must inform his son that someday he will have a beauty of his own to serve, honor, protect, and defend against all the threats and tactics of the enemy. The boy must be trained to become a defender of beauty, and his strength and power are to be at the service of love. He must be given the example of being willing to sacrifice and die for God and others.

This understanding of manhood is something we could use a little more of in seminaries today, too. Yes, the men need to study and learn orthodox theology, but the seminary experience isn't just all about books. It's a rite of passage, and guys are being trained to be fathers, knights, and protectors of the sacred. They will receive a new name at the end of their training. On the day of their ordination, they will be called *Father*. In my opinion, as part of the human formation required of men becoming priests, seminarians should be encouraged to go hiking, camping, canoeing, and fishing. Hunting probably wouldn't hurt either. In short, manly stuff.

Why not put a pile of wood behind the seminary and have the men take turns chopping it? It's manly, natural, and normal, and you learn to sweat like a man. Teach a seminarian how to change a tire, too, not just how to do research and write fancy papers on computers. Chances are many of the men in seminaries today did not have a virtuous fatherly role model growing up, and they don't just need classroom learning. They need human formation; they need to learn how to be fathers, warriors, and gentlemen soldiers.

And where do we learn the ultimate model for what it means to be a man? Jesus Christ. He is the God-Man who, by taking on flesh and human nature, specifically manhood, placed himself under the laws of human development and anthropology. This means that he had certain human and masculine needs that needed to be met. He made the rules of human nature, and when he became man, he abided by them. Therefore, from him, the perfect man, we learn the true meaning of what it is to be masculine.

Jesus is the Eternal Son of the Eternal Father. As his Father's Son, he needs his Father's presence, affirmation, guidance, and example. This is what it means to be a son. And Jesus knows that he is loved by his Father and that the Father is always with him when he states, "He who sent me is with me; he has not left me alone, for I always do what is pleasing to him" (Jn 8:29). Jesus always seeks to do what is pleasing to his Father because he loves his Father, delights in his affirmation, and follows his paternal example: "Truly, truly I say to you, the Son can do nothing of his own accord, but only what he sees the Father doing; for whatever he does, that the Son does likewise" (Jn 5:19). Like Father, like Son.

The Father takes great delight in his "little tiger" and publicly affirms his Son at his Baptism. During this public event, a voice from heaven is heard to say, "This is my beloved Son, with whom I am well pleased" (Mt 3:17). In his masculinity and in his sonship, Jesus would delight in this fatherly affirmation, giving him the strength to be led by his loving Father's Spirit into the desert for

40 days and 40 nights to be tested and do spiritual battle with Satan. The desert is a dangerous and wild place, and Jesus could get hurt there. But it was his Father who led him there, and the Son trusts his Father. As God, Jesus could have used his strength in the desert to turn stones into bread, but he did not use it that way because his strength was meant to serve others, not himself. He is all powerful (manly), but his power (virtue and strength) is at the service of others. So, when he emerges from the desert and begins his mission, he is not just his Father's "little tiger." He is, in fact, the "Lion of Judah."

The mother's role in all of this is very important, of course. She must let it happen. A mother must allow her little boy to become a man. This is what Mary did. She let the mysterious ways between the Father and his Son be lived out. As a creature, she did not always understand the mysterious workings between the Father and the Son, but she completely trusted and "kept all these things, pondering them in her heart" (Lk 2:19).

As a matter of fact, she not only let the mystery happen; she desired it to happen. I'm sure she both cried and rejoiced as Jesus left her home at Nazareth to go off on his saving adventure with his Father. The mysterious ways being lived out between the Father and his Son required great trust on Mary's part. What Jesus was doing was dangerous, very dangerous. She knew that, but she let it be done. She had to be willing to let her boy get hurt. And in the greatest agony any mother could ever experience, she allowed her Son to be crucified before her very eyes because it was the mysterious, saving plan designed by the Father of mercies and his eternal Son.

Mary, let it be done.

☆ ☆ ☆ **Marian Gems**

☆ Mary is the depository of all graces, but who can better induce her to open the celestial treasury than Joseph, her glorious spouse? A servant of Mary will therefore have a tender devotion to St. Joseph, and by his pious homage of respect and love, will endeavor to merit the protection of this great saint. He will beg of him the grace of dying as he himself did, with the kiss of Jesus and in the arms of Mary. *Blessed William Joseph Chaminade*

☆ The Blessed Virgin loves above all to see in her children purity, humility, and charity. *St. John Vianney*

☆ My desire is for the young people of the entire world to come closer to Mary. She is the bearer of an incredible youthfulness and beauty that never wanes. May young people have increasing confidence in her and may they entrust the life just opening before them to her. *St. John Paul II*

☆ O wonderful girl, mother of her own creator! O stupendous honor, that a woman should have a son with God, to whom she may say, as the Father said: You are my Son (Ps 2:7), and that this girl should be the mother of one whose Father is God! The Son is seated at the right hand of the Father, the Mother at the right hand of the Son, and in turn they behold their common Son in their midst with happy gaze. *St. Thomas of Villanova*

☆ She desires to form her Only-begotten in all her sons by adoption. *Blessed Guerric of Igny*

☆ She [Mary] is the woman every man marries in his ideal. *Venerable Fulton J. Sheen*

☆ In our day, Our Lady has been given to us as the best defense against the evils that afflict modern life; Marian devotion is the sure guarantee of her maternal protection and safeguard in the hour of temptation. *Pope Benedict XVI*

☆ If we love our Mother, the Blessed Virgin, we should make it both our duty and privilege to have one of her pictures or statues in our home, which from time to time will remind us of her. *St. John Vianney*

☆ Talking to Mary should be very simple. Many have found the way easily. More should try it. *Servant of God Catherine de Hueck Doherty*

☆ She [Mary] overcomes both the Heart of God and the heart of man. *Servant of God (Fr.) Joseph Kentenich*

☆ The greatest saints were the most ardent devotees of Mary. *St. Vincent Pallotti*

☆ If you wish to convert anyone to the fullness of the knowledge of our Lord and of his Mystical Body, then teach him the Rosary. One of two things will happen. Either he will stop saying the Rosary — or he will get the gift of faith. *Venerable Fulton J. Sheen*

☆ It is impossible to meditate with devotion upon the mysteries of the Rosary and live in a state of sin. *St. John Vianney*

☆ The Rosary is the most complete and easiest instruction about the Blessed Mother, and it is the source of devotion to the Divine Master. *Blessed Timothy Giaccardo*

☆ Piety towards the most holy Virgin is the mark of a truly Catholic heart. *St. Pope John XXIII*

Band of Brothers

WHEN I GREW UP AS A TEENAGER IN THE 1980s, there was a plethora of movies about men who were missing in action as a result of the Vietnam War, perhaps most memorably *Rambo* and *Missing in Action*. As a young boy, I remember being so drawn to those movies and even wanting to go search for the MIAs (Missing in Action) myself when I grew up. Seriously, I did. I was young and naive, taking the movies at face value. I felt it was my mission to bring back the boys. But why would I think this way? After all, I didn't personally know any guys missing in action in Vietnam. Why was I willing to risk my life searching through faraway jungles for men I didn't even know? I think the reason is because guys are naturally fraternal. So when a brother is taken captive, we want to do something to help. If we don't do something, part of our manhood dies. If we don't do something to help our brother, we are not really men. Every man wants to be able to depend on a brother.

I also remember the first time I heard the song "Goodnight Saigon" by Billy Joel. Oh my gosh, did that song speak to my growing awareness of brotherhood. It's basically about a band of brothers who went off to fight and die together in Vietnam. I believe I heard it for the first time when I was around 12 years old, and I actually had tears coming down my face as I listened to it. The main refrain of the song states: "And we would all go down together, we said we'd all go down together, yes, we all go down together." That line alone speaks to the masculine heart and soul. Brothers are willing to go down in battle together.

All men are born with a desire to do battle. This is because all men are born into a fallen world with an infernal enemy seeking to destroy them. There are dragons and demons that threaten men and the things they hold dear: life, liberty, mothers, children, wives, land, and brothers. Men were born to be fighters. This is not a perfect world and to deny that there is a spiritual battle going on is to live in ignorance of reality.

All men are born to slay dragons, rescue maidens, and become a hero.

Every man wants to be a hero. No man wants to be a loser.

This is why boys are instinctively drawn to play sports and war games. It's why men naturally form fraternities and even come together in their golden years to share stories about the glory days of when they were a hero.

Men are naturally drawn to movies that honor brotherhood and heroism, too. Movies like *We Were Soldiers* and *The Fellowship of the Ring*, for example. And all little boys play with toy soldiers, plastic guns, axes, and bows and arrows. That's normal. Boys love to blow things up and throw fake grenades. That's normal, too. No boy wants to lose a battle or lose at sports. Boys play to win. They live to win. Women will not always understand why boys shoot each other with paintballs, dare each other to climb higher, or spend hours throwing a pigskin around a field, but they must let it happen, just as Mary did. As the saying goes, "Boys will be boys." Mary trusted the Father's plan completely, and that meant seeing Jesus leave her home at Nazareth and go off to war with his brothers.

For their part, men instinctively know that the only way to win a game or a battle is to do it with your brothers. Men inherently know that you have to play as a team, look out for each other, cover each other's back, and if need be, "go down together." No man goes through boot camp and basic training alone. Even in religious life, it is generally frowned upon to go through the novitiate alone. It is meant to be an experience that forms a band of brothers united for a common mission, against a common enemy.

No man can conquer evil, the temptations of the flesh, and the distractions of the world unless he has brothers to help him. If you think you can, you are fooling yourself. As the Book of Proverbs states: "As iron sharpens iron, so one man sharpens another" (27:17). Men need each other for encouragement, discipline, camaraderie, and accountability. There are no solo missions.

I think this is why Satan has been attacking men so much lately. If the devil can get men isolated and separated from brotherhood, he can cause all kinds of chaos in their lives. So many men today do not have brotherhood and fellowship. They are living in isolation and separation from fraternity, and it's breeding unaccountability and sin. For example, if a man struggles with lust but has no brother to share this with, he will continuously fall and end up being his own worst enemy. Every man needs at least one good male friend to be open and honest with about his struggles — a man he can trust. Some things men should not talk about with women. Just as women understand each other, so it is with men. Even for priests, this is true.

And each man, and each group of men, needs God. Without God, real manhood is just not possible. Some of the things that a 21st century man has to go through and overcome are unconquerable without the help of God. Studies show that the vast majority of males living today who are above the age of 13 or so have been exposed to pornography. If you think I'm exaggerating, I'm not. It's absolutely everywhere, and it's more likely than not that the vast majority of the men reading this book have fallen into sin through it. Viewing pornography, and acting out as a result of it, is probably the number one sin affecting men today. Trust me, I hear a lot of confessions. Nothing else even comes close.

This is such a strong battle that not only do men need each other for accountability and brotherhood, they also need God for strength to win this battle. Although men like to try to go it alone, they're bound to fail if they forget God. In fact, the Lord supplies the antidote to get the poison of lust out of a man's heart. As I already noted, most temptations against purity last about 20 minutes. After that time, a man either gives in or moves on. But a guy will find it impossible to "move on" unless he has help from on high. It's like trying to stop an arrow already in flight; without God's help, it's not going to happen. And God has given a most effective method for fighting against sins of impurity in the heavenly gift of the Rosary. It only takes about 20 minutes to pray and is always available, anytime, anywhere.

If you want to be a real, virtuous man, pray the Rosary. If you want to overcome temptations of any kind, pray the Rosary. It was good enough for the saints, so it should be good enough for us.

Wouldn't it be great to go to Church on Sunday and walk in to find a bunch of men leading the congregation in praying the Rosary before Mass? Now, that would be a sight to behold! Women would love it. Imagine a seminary where the brothers prayed the Rosary in common in the chapel every day. At one time, this was the common practice, by the way. When it stopped and seminarians were told to stop praying the Rosary together in the chapel is when all hell broke loose in the Church, in the world, and in the hearts of men. Without Mary's presence in the lives of men, Satan causes division, isolation, and chaos.

From Mary's divine Son, Jesus Christ, there's so much we can learn about true brotherhood. He is our Savior *and* our older brother.

As God, Jesus doesn't technically need us for anything. Even in the mystery of redemption, he alone is sufficient to accomplish the mission. However, since he is the God-*man*, he did require the anthropological necessity of being in communion with others. No man is an island, not even the God-man. Therefore, he called and gathered around himself a band of brothers, brothers he would share his mission with. And in the life of Jesus, we see that he and his spiritual brothers did manly stuff together. They went fishing, hung out in the mountains, and prayed together. This is real manhood. This is real brotherhood.

Jesus even used strong, manly titles when communicating with his brothers. He gave them names that described both their personalities and their God-given mission. For example, he called Peter the *Rock*, and James and John, the *Sons of Thunder*. The three years they spent with him was their formation, their boot camp. He was the Commander-in-Chief of this militant band of brothers. Not a militia of the world but a spiritual militia, carrying a spiritual weapon, the Cross. And they were willing to die for one another and go down together.

I love being part of this brotherhood. Jesus is my King, and I desire, with my brothers, to conquer nations and hearts for his kingdom. Incidentally, it wasn't until I followed Jesus that I discovered my mission and the true meaning of my name. For most of my life, I had no mission and very much disliked my name: Donald. My name always seemed too Disney and comical.

But when I had my conversion to Catholicism, I was informed that Donald means *World Conqueror*. Now that I love! It is my mission. With my brothers, I desire to truly conquer the world for Jesus and Mary.

Modern feminists may be uncomfortable with being told that Jesus is a fighter and a warrior, but he truly is. And though he no longer walks this earth, he continues his leadership of his band of brothers through his visible representative who speaks on his behalf: the Pope. In any brotherhood, there has to be a visible leader, a commander whom the men defend, protect, and obey. If there is not a leader, there is chaos and confusion. The sacred Christian brotherhood is centered around Jesus Christ, and he leads us today through his Vicar and spokesman, the Pope. Thus, any true brotherhood among Christian men must be gathered around the Pope to defend and obey him, just as men in battle take orders from their leader and defend and obey him. Therefore, for a man to claim to be a brother of Jesus and yet go against his spokesman is comparable to a brother in a family, or a soldier in an army, going against his leader. It is scandalous and shameful behavior, and it is worthy of a dishonorable discharge.

True brothers of Jesus respect, love, and obey his spokesman, *and* they love and obey his mother. As a matter of fact, Jesus loves his brothers so much that he wants them to call Mary their mother. Just as boys who hang out at each other's homes often end up calling their friend's mother their mom — because she takes care of their needs by feeding them, housing them, and cleaning up after them — so it is with Jesus and his band of brothers.

We observe this in the life of Jesus when, on several occasions, Jesus takes his brother disciples back to his hometown (cf. Lk 4:16; Mt 13:54; Mk 6:1). Are we not to think that Jesus took his band of brothers back to Nazareth so that they could spend time getting to know Mary, learning to think of her as their own mother? Without a doubt, it delighted the Heart of Jesus to bring his brothers back to his mother's house and have them spend time with her. He loves his disciples and wants them to have the great privilege of calling Mary their mother, too. And who on earth would not consider it a privilege and an honor to call the mother of Jesus your own mother? You would have to be crazy not to desire this! Would not Jesus be offended and upset with the person who considered Mary worthy to be his (God's) mother, but not good enough for you (a creature) to call her mother? Any Catholic man would have to be arrogant and ignorant not to want to call Mary his mother. Failing to call Mary mother would result in division and discord in the brotherhood. And God's Word tells us that there are certain things that God hates, and one of them is "a man who sows discord among brothers" (Prov 6:19).

True brotherhood means sharing the same mother. And true brothers are always united around their mother: "For those whom he foreknew he also predestined to be conformed to the image of his Son, in order that he might be the firstborn among many brothers" (Rom 8:29).

☆ ☆ ☆ Marian Gems

☆ Let us venerate Mary with every fiber of our being, from the deepest part of our heart, because this is the will of him who wanted us to receive everything through Mary. *St. Bernard of Clairvaux*

☆ Mary is the mediatrix between us and Christ, as Christ is between us and God. She is the gate of heaven, for no one can enter heaven unless it be through Mary. *St. Bonaventure*

☆ A man is no true Christian if he has no devotion to the Mother of Jesus Christ. *St. John Eudes*

☆ Mary will be the happy bond to draw together, with strong yet gentle constraint, all who love Christ, no matter where they may be, to form a nation of brothers yielding obedience to the Vicar of Christ on earth, the Roman Pontiff, their common Father. *Pope Leo XIII*

☆ The serpent lifts up its head throughout the world, but at the same time the Immaculate One wipes him out with smashing victories. *St. Maximilian Kolbe*

☆ God willed that his Son come into this world by being born of the seed of Adam and of a daughter of Adam that we might have the God-man for our brother and the Mother of God for our mother. Thus we have the same father and the same mother as the Son of God himself. We are his brothers, and as he is our mediator with his Father, so his heavenly Mother is a mediatrix between himself and us. *St. John Eudes*

☆ Just as God preserved the blessed angels from sin through his Son, so you, O Beauty of Purity, will save wretched men from sin through your Son. For just as the Son of God is the happiness of the just, even so your Son, O Salvation of Fruitfulness, is the reconciliation of sinners. *St. Anselm of Canterbury*

☆ Are you afraid to approach God the Son? He is your brother and your flesh, tempted in all things except sin, that he might show you mercy. Mary gave you this brother. But perhaps you fear the divine majesty within him, because, even though he was made man, yet he remained God. Do you want to have an advocate in the Son's presence, too? Turn to Mary. *St. Bernard of Clairvaux*

☆ The Son whom she brought forth is he whom God placed as the first-born among many brethren, namely, the faithful, in whose birth and education she cooperates with a maternal love. *Vatican Council II (Lumen Gentium)*

☆ No one ever knew Christ so profoundly as she [Mary] did, and no one can ever be a more competent guide and teacher of the knowledge of Christ. *Pope St. Pius X*

☆ The more each one of us draws near to the Immaculate, the more we will draw near to one another: this unity is our strength. *St. Maximilian Kolbe*

All for Beauty

FROM WHAT YOU'VE READ SO FAR, you can probably guess that one of my favorite movies is *Braveheart.* I believe it's one of the favorite movies of all men. When the beauty in that movie is taken captive, what man watching is not thinking to himself, "Unleash the sword, bro!" In the scenes where William Wallace is taking down the bad guys, I'm glued to the television and practically throwing blows with him. What guy isn't?

As a man, I love movies that appeal to my God-given desire to fight for and rescue a beautiful maiden. I've had this desire ever since I was a little boy of about five years old. In retrospect, even many of the cartoons I watched as a kid were based around this theme: *Speed Racer* and *Underdog,* for example. The comics I read, too, always seemed to feature a beauty who was being threatened, as well as a hero who had to rescue and protect her from the villain: Superman, Spiderman, Tarzan, etc. And having spent the first nine years of my life in the backwoods of West Virginia, even the country music I grew up listening to always seemed to revolve around the theme of a battle-scarred man saving a beautiful country girl. Some soldier or cowboy was always singing about fighting for a girl, going to war for a woman, and dying for a beauty.

At the time, I was young and mentally thought girls were somewhat icky and weird. Nevertheless, in my masculine soul and in my play with other boys, it was always all about saving beauty. I might not have been able to articulate it at the time, but my friends and I played Cowboys and Indians because there was a beauty that was being threatened — someone we could save if we would man up to the challenge and take on the bad guys. And on any given day in my youth, I was always fighting for Sacajawea, Princess Leia, or some damsel in distress far, far away. It was my duty to save her.

All of this child's play just points to something God-given in the masculine heart. All men are called to be defenders of beauty. Modern feminists will decry that this mentality is indicative of male chauvinism and the patronizing of women, but if bullets were being fired at them I guarantee that more than a few of them would hide behind me and want a man to defend them. The dignity and mystery of the feminine is worthy of the sacrifice of men. Society didn't create this desire in men. It's been there from the beginning. There is no doubt that it has been seriously warped since the fall of Adam and Eve, but it has been there from the beginning.

The mystery of femininity is what motivates men to become heroes and soldiers, and in the spiritual life, it is the feminine genius that helps men become saints. Without the great mystery of woman, man would be lost, alone, and lacking in the necessary complementarity of the "other." No man becomes a true man without a woman in his life. All men are going to have battles to fight, mountains to climb, crosses to mount, and beauties to rescue.

Sadly, much of this fundamental masculine anthropology has been abandoned today. In an age in which boys are encouraged and trained to be cheerleaders, we have a problem. Men are supposed to be the ones on the battlefield, being supported and encouraged by the beauty who cheers them on. In a time of war, who is sent overseas to rally the troops by the United Service Organizations (USO)? Women! Naturally, they could do without the immodesty, but the truth of the matter remains the same. Women give men strength, courage, and the ability to conquer the enemy. Men need women to remind them why they are fighting.

For this reason, if a man does not have a desire to fight for the feminine, he is lacking an essential dimension of his manhood. And if a man does not feel a natural attraction toward the beauty and wonder of the feminine mystery, I almost guarantee that there is some traumatic experience in his past that caused his emasculation — whether it was sexual abuse, lack of a true father figure, or an overly protective mother who never let him go outside and play in the mud and get his hands dirty by doing combat for a captured princess.

Boys naturally want to impress girls. Like many of my guy friends growing up, I remember creating scenarios in my head that involved me beating up some bad guy in order to save and impress a beauty. I think almost all boys do this. For example, on any given day in my youth when I would be at a store with my buddies, I would mentally create a scenario where robbers came in and took everyone hostage — especially the beautiful girl behind the register. Then it was up to me to become Bruce Lee and unleash some round-house kicks on the bad guys. And in my mind, I did. I would be throwing punches and delivering a beating the likes of which you have never seen. I would be bouncing off walls, doing back flips, drop-kicking the bad guys, and pulling off superhuman feats of strength. And in the end, I would save her. I was the hero. Sure, it was all in my head, but in my heart and my soul, I knew that someday it *would really* happen. I just didn't know when or where, but I was prepared.

For a man not to be prepared to do battle for beauty is to lack a mission. Every man is going to be entrusted with a beauty. A beauty he is to honor, serve, protect, defend, and die for. And every woman in her feminine heart wants this kind of man — we will see this in the next chapter.

Sadly, many men don't realize that the beauty entrusted to them is threatened by a dragon and requires their protection. In a time when many deny Satan even exists, it's no wonder men are such failures in marriage. If you don't think there's any threat, you don't see any need to fight. I can't tell you how many men I've seen destroy a marriage with a dream wife — a beautiful woman who has a great heart and a fantastic personality. It was all because they don't know how to be men and fight for her. Rather than protect her and honor her, they end up abusing her and using her beauty for their own sensual gratification. And when her physical beauty is no longer as stunning as it was when she was 21, the man goes in pursuit of a younger, more physically beautiful woman. This is a huge problem today.

But part of showing your true worth as a man is sticking by the side of your beauty, even when gravity takes effect and things aren't as firm as they once were. A good man loves a woman's heart, not just her body. All bodies grow old and wrinkle, but true love is in the heart. To abandon a woman in mid-life or in her older years is shameful, and when a man does this, it gives evidence to the fact that his manhood was only self-serving, and not Christlike.

This is why contraception in a marriage is wrong. If a man doesn't love his wife enough to give himself completely to her every time there is conjugal union, then that man is a liar. He tells her with his words that he loves her, but he is really only seeking to gratify himself by using her body for his own sensual pleasure. This is not the example that Jesus gives us of true manhood. For, from the Cross, he poured himself out completely — body, blood, soul, and divinity — for the beauty who was entrusted to him.

Jesus, the God-man, was entrusted with a beauty to defend, honor, serve, and die for. His beauty is the Church (our souls). He seeks to serve, defend, protect, and die for us so that we can be as pure as the Virgin Mary, the Immaculata. He literally poured out his blood (the life-giving seed of the Church) so that we could know just how much he loves us. He holds nothing back and sacrifices everything, so that we can be happy and bear fruit.

As the perfect man, he did not abandon us when we became ugly from sin, crippled by our own faults and weaknesses. He showed his true manhood and goodness when "while we were yet sinners Christ died for us" (Rom 5:8). Imagine if while hanging on the Cross, Jesus had said: "Wait. Hold on. I can't do this. I can't give you everything. You're not worth dying for." Of course, that would never happen. The reason it could never happen is because God loves us totally and completely. He doesn't commit spiritual contraception from the Cross by not giving his bride, the Church, the fullness of his life-giving seed (his body and blood). He is the Bridegroom Messiah who pours out everything from the marriage bed of the Cross — and he continues to do this every time Catholic Mass is celebrated. This is why only those who share the full commitment of the mystical marriage with God, as faithful members of the Catholic Church, can receive Holy Communion (the Body and Blood of Christ).

In light of this, it's no wonder many men do not go to church today. A man can't give what a man doesn't have. If you are not a real man, you have nothing to give because you are only a taker and an abuser. If a man abuses his beauty at home by using contraception, the Church will make very little sense to him. Eventually, he will treat the Church just as he treats his wife — she only exists to please him, so he only seeks her out when he is in need of gratifying moments of pleasure. In the modern mind, if a man can't get any form of satisfaction from the Church, why bother attending? The contraceptive mentality not only turns men away from being virtuous husbands and protectors and defenders of beauty, it also turns them into being absent from church.

What we need today is a generation of men who seek to pattern themselves off of the example of the God-man. There are signs that many men are striving to do this in our culture today. For example, I love the fact that Men's Conferences are springing up and spreading in just about every diocese in the United States. These are good and noble endeavors. I highly encourage them and frequently speak at them. Yet, it must be remembered that renewal cannot simply consist of a weekend experience. A renewed manhood must be a life-change, involving a daily effort to be conformed to Christ. For us fallen men, this is not easy to do. But we must do it, and it must start in the home and at church.

Concretely, if a man wants to be a true man, he must be the one to take the family to church. A true man seeks to be the head of the family and considers it an honor to take his wife and children to church to receive Jesus in the Most Blessed Sacrament. He also takes them with some frequency to the Sacrament of Reconciliation. This should not be the role of his wife.

If a man wants to raise a daughter who will grow up to be a woman of God, then he has to let his daughter see him treating her mother with the same love and devotion he would have if the Virgin Mary were his wife. A man's daughter should hear him saying beautiful and lovely things about her mother. If the daughter hears her father expressing his love for her mother — how he would die for her and how she means the world to him — that little girl will grow up knowing her worth and dignity as a woman. She will grow up wanting a man who desires, and is willing, to fight for her and die for her.

On the other hand, how shameful it is when a man speaks against, mocks, or makes fun of the beauty who has been entrusted to him, whether it is his wife or his daughters. A man does a lot of damage when he does this. And a man shows how truly ungodly he is when he does this in regards to God's bride, the Church. If a man speaks badly of the Church, ridicules her, and makes fun of her in front of his children, he should not be shocked when his children grow up to disdain and hate the Church. You reap what you sow.

Boys, in particular, pay attention to every little thing the father says and imitate him. So, if a man wants to raise a boy who doesn't end up being an abuser of the feminine and a man who never attends church, he must give him a truly virtuous example of what it means to be a man. When this is done, the boy will see both the great dignity of women and the great need to attend church faithfully. From the father, a boy learns to treat both women and the Church with respect. They are both beauties worth praising, speaking highly of, serving, honoring, and dying for. A boy will want to be like his father — an honorable, kind, and faithful man — if he sees this example of manhood put forth by his dad.

Once again, this is why one of the best things a father can do with his son is to pray with him and show him that prayer is a manly thing to do. The father must show the boy that it is honorable for a man to pray. He should take him occasionally to visit the Blessed Sacrament, pray with him before a statue of the Virgin Mary in church, and let him have the experience of watching and observing his father be on his knees before beauty. The little boy will consider his father a knight if he does this.

Here is something concrete I would like every father reading this book to do with his son:

Drive to a store with your son and buy a dozen roses. When your son asks you who the roses are for, inform him that half are for your wife, his mother, and the other half are for Mary, the mother of Jesus and our spiritual mother. Then, drive to a Catholic church. Once there, walk inside with your son, genuflect before the Blessed Sacrament, and go to the statue of Mary. Kneel down with your son and give him the roses designated for Mary. Tell him that you are both going to give your lives to Mary, so that you can become good, holy men and defenders and protectors of beauty. Let him get up and lay the roses at her feet. Then, have him continue kneeling with you for a brief time of prayer. I guarantee you that this will be a memory that will last forever in the mind and heart of your son.

Next, drive home with your son and do the same thing with your wife, his mother. Kneel down before your wife and have your son give her the roses on your behalf. And in the presence of your son and while still kneeling, take your wife's hand in yours and tell her that you love her and are at her service. Tell her she is beautiful, that you consider it an honor to be married to her, and that you would die for her. Without a doubt, your little boy will want to be like you, and he will remember that day for the rest of his life.

☆ ☆ ☆ Marian Gems

☆ She [Mary] is the one whom every man loves when he loves a woman — whether he knows it or not. *Venerable Fulton J. Sheen*

☆ It is theologically and anthropologically important for women to be at the center of Christianity. Through Mary and the other holy women, the feminine element stands at the heart of the Christian religion. *Pope Benedict XVI*

☆ An infallible and unmistakable sign by which we can distinguish a heretic, a man of false doctrine, an enemy of God, from one of God's true friends is that the heretic and the hardened sinner show nothing but contempt and indifference for our Lady, and endeavor, by word and example, openly and insidiously — sometimes under specious pretexts — to belittle the love and veneration shown to her. *St. Louis de Montfort*

☆ She [Mary] is the key to paradise. In her let us place all our hope, because we can expect all things from God through her mediation. *St. Francis Anthony Fasani*

☆ Beauty is said to be a woman's honor. Physical beauty is her honor among men; spiritual beauty is her honor with God. How could anyone imagine that God would deprive Mary of her honor? *St. Lawrence of Brindisi*

☆ She is the standard of holiness, the model of virtue, the example of religion, the scourge of demons, the helper of men, and at last the summary, abridged and collected, of all brilliance and grace, in whom all the beauty and grace of angelic and human creation are ordered. *St. Thomas of Villanova*

☆ Truly she has become the Lady ruler of every creature, since she is the Mother of the Creator. *St. John Damascene*

☆ O man, run through all creation with your thought, and see if there exists anything comparable to or greater than the holy Virgin, Mother of God. Circle the whole world, explore all the oceans, survey the air, question the skies, consider all the unseen powers, and see if there exists any other similar wonder in the whole creation. *St. Proclus of Constantinople*

☆ If I call you the "beauty of God," you are worthy of the name; if I call you "mistress of the angels," you are shown to be so in all things. *St. Ambrose Autpert*

☆ Looking at Mary, how can we, her children, fail to let the aspiration to beauty, goodness and purity of heart be aroused in us? *Pope Benedict XVI*

☆ Devotion to Mary has decisively contributed to elevating the status of woman. *Blessed James Alberione*

CHAPTER 9

Femininity

Daddy's Princess

THE FEMININE MYSTERY IS THE CROWN OF CREATION. Therefore, every woman is a princess.

But, sadly, not every woman knows this.

I began the last chapter noting that many people today do not understand masculinity and, unfortunately, the same is true for femininity. While there's a lot of talk about femininity in the world today, especially in academic circles and in the media, very little of it is objectively true, resulting in very few women actually knowing what it means to be a woman. As a matter of fact, many modern women are almost completely unaware that they are the bearers of a great and awesome privilege and that God considers them to be the crown of creation. If women only knew who they are, they would stand in awe of the great gift of their femininity!

Without a doubt, there are many reasons why there is so much confusion concerning femininity today. One of the main reasons is because young girls are not treated as princesses by their fathers. Instead of being assured that they are beautiful and lovely, young girls have hearts that are wounded, leaving them searching for affirmation and identity in the wrong way — we will delve more into this in a minute.

Another reason that women are so confused about their femininity is because almost every secular university in the Western hemisphere now has a Women's Studies department that puts forth its own understanding about femininity. Year after year, new students are indoctrinated and forced to learn the feminist ideologies that are offered in the college classroom. What exactly are the students being taught in these classes? In particular, what are young women learning about what it means to be a woman? Are they learning about their "crown status" and their great dignity, worth, and potential for the tremendous gift of motherhood?

No, unfortunately, this is not what they are learning. The focus in these classes is usually centered on how birth control and abortion are women's reproductive health issues and "rights" they should be defending, promoting, and voting for. College girls are essentially being taught that being a woman is a burden, not a blessing. Unsuspecting parents are probably clueless about the fact that their daughters are being brainwashed into believing that because they were not born men, they are the bearers of a curse, victims of male-dominated societies, hierarchies, and religions — especially Christianity — that have sought to snuff out the voices of women. Young women are being "educated" to believe that men have done nothing but oppress women throughout history and that such things as the Christian Scriptures — the Old and New Testaments — were written by men to oppress women and keep them forever in a position of inferiority as the helpmates and servants of men.

As a result, what young girls are being educated and encouraged to do is break free of the old slogan that spoke of their femininity as being made of "sugar and spice and everything nice," and learn how to man up. Young women today are taught that there is nothing objective about what it means to be a woman, and if a woman wants to get anywhere in this world, she must learn how to work like a man, talk like a man, walk like a man, dress like a man, act like a man, play sports like a man, and fight like a man.

In light of this, is it any wonder that today, unlike any other time in human history, we see a global masculinization of the feminine? While radical feminists argue that this is exactly what they are against (a masculine worldview), they, ironically, have ended up promoting a masculine understanding of what it means to be feminine. As such, it should come as no surprise that we see a huge increase in lesbianism today. Radical feminism basically does nothing but destroy true femininity and breed the masculinization of women — where women end up looking like, walking like, and talking like men.

Therefore, in order to have a correct understanding of the gift of femininity, we need to go back to the foundation, back to the blueprint. For example, if you're an engineer or an architect and desire to find out how a building or a bridge was constructed so that you can better understand how it functions and is held together, and can build others like it, it's necessary to study the original design. After all, who trusts a bridge or a building constructed by an engineer or an architect who fails to provide blueprints? It's the same idea behind understanding the mystery of femininity. If you want to truly understand it, it's necessary to study the blueprint.

And there is a blueprint.

Her name is Mary.

She was made by God.

There is no other model, no other blueprint, for perfect femininity than the Blessed Virgin Mary. In her feminine person, she teaches all women what it means to be a woman. And it is this model, this blueprint of true femininity, that is not being studied in universities today. As a matter of fact, the opposite is being done. The Blessed Virgin Mary, the masterpiece of God, has been cast aside as irrelevant, unimportant, and too servant-like for the modern woman.

A new model of what it means to be a woman is being taught: the emancipated and liberated woman. The masterpiece and blueprint has been re-interpreted by radical feminists as the invention of oppressive religious men who deviously desired to set up the model of femininity, Mary, as a servant of a masculine God. As a result, Mary is considered unworthy of study at all. Or, if she is studied, she is mocked, ridiculed, and considered an antiquated and outdated model for the modern liberated woman. So it is no wonder that when a woman graduates with her degree, she enters the workforce trying to become another man, not another Mary.

Nevertheless, it remains objectively true that in the mind of God, as revealed to us through divine revelation, the feminine mystery is his masterpiece. Just as an artist only truly rests when he has put the finishing touches on his creation, so God did not fully rest with the creation of the masculine (Adam) but only with the creation of the feminine (Eve). Though she came after Adam and from Adam, she is by no means secondary or second-rate. On the contrary, God saved the best for last. Indeed, God is in love with the mystery of the feminine and has given her an elevated status in his creation. In a certain sense, she is the better half of man, and God made her the crown of his works, the very crown of creation. She is a princess.

So, how did we end up with the "girls gone wild" mentality that is in the world today? And how did we get to a culture where women are sexually aggressive, masculine in manner, and no longer know the beauty of the feminine blush?

It all starts at the beginning with the father-daughter relationship.

When a girl is very young, she must be affirmed in her feminine beauty by her father. Every little girl is beautiful and a princess, and she needs to hear this from her father because it gives her a sense of security. When a girl is not secure in her femininity, she will buy into the lies of the culture, the education system, and the media. Tragically, so many girls have not been affirmed in their formative years and have grown up to be extremely insecure.

If a young girl is not affirmed in her beauty by her father, she grows up still craving the affirmation of her feminine mystery but will seek it in the wrong way. Most likely, she will seek this affirmation through trying to get the attention of boys. Girls are meant to get the attention of boys. But if she is not secure in her femininity by having been affirmed by her father, she will seek the affirmation in the wrong way. And in a fallen world where boys' passions are disordered, many boys will charm a girl by telling her what she wants to hear (affirmation of her beauty) only to use her for their own sensual gratification. Then the boys will move on, leaving her even more insecure. I can't tell you how many women I've talked to that have lived through this cycle.

On the other side of the spectrum, if a father does not affirm his daughter but wounds her heart by making fun of her appearance or speaking harshly to her about an overweight issue, it can lead to the girl not trusting men. She grows up believing men, in general, can't be relied upon for kindness. The harsh words of her father, in fact, may lead her to think she may never be pleasing to men. And if the girl gets hurt later by a man whom she was seeking affirmation from, she might just abandon a desire for men altogether and experiment with her sexuality and become a lesbian. If men fail to treat her feminine heart tenderly and affirm her, she might just seek the affirmation she needs from other women. This is not a generalization, of course, but is sometimes the reason for why a woman becomes a homosexual.

This is why Daddy needs to affirm his little princess from the beginning. There's a deep anthropological reason a little girl jumps up on the coffee table, twirls around in a dress, and keeps yelling out: "Look, Daddy. Daddy, look. Daddy, look. Look, Daddy!" Daddy needs to look and affirm his little princess. He needs to pick her up and make her feel like the princess she is. If he doesn't do this but is emotionally distant from her, or only gives her a fleeting glance over his morning paper, I can almost guarantee he is going to have many days of heartache and pain when she becomes a teenager.

She will walk around half naked, wear super tight jeans, low-cut blouses, and be extremely immodest in just about everything she does. She is crying out for attention and affirmation. And boys will take advantage of the girl a father failed to affirm. His daughter craves masculine affirmation and will do whatever boys ask her to do in order to get it. So, when the little girl does her twirling dance, a father needs to tell her she is beautiful, telling her to twirl again for Daddy because Daddy sees her and loves her.

All little girls are beautiful. All of them. And all little girls are meant to be seen and affirmed.

How sad it is that so many girls today are not just ignored and un-affirmed, but they are sexually and emotionally abused by men. It totally breaks my heart when women tell me that their father emotionally abused them by telling them they were fat, had an imperfect nose, or constantly criticized her for not being like the "prettier" sister. This is so not what fatherhood is about. A young girl's heart is a delicate thing. Words cut deep and leave wounds that are long-lasting and hard to heal. Every girl is completely aware of her physical deficiencies; no father has to point them out to her. On the contrary, a good father treats his daughter with great love. He shows he values her true worth when he affirms his little princess no matter what she looks like. This teaches a girl that it is she as a person who really matters. She doesn't have to look like all the girls on television to be beautiful. She is beautiful just the way she is.

I've often thought that a great way for a dad to affirm his daughter and make her feel special is to take full advantage of the original intention behind Halloween. Many people are unaware of this, but Halloween is not about dressing little children up like ghosts, goblins, and witches, and watching scary movies. Our godless culture has turned something that was meant to celebrate the saints, "All Hallow's Eve" (the word *hallow* means *holy*), into something that celebrates the devil. So, once a year, most of America dresses up its sons and daughters as demons and witches and sends them out to be seen by the neighbors and get free candy.

If a father really believed in demons, he wouldn't dress his daughter up as an ugly witch and send her over to the neighbor's house to show them how ugly she is. How twisted is that! If a father really believes that there are fallen angels who disobeyed God and are now seeking to destroy his children's souls, he wouldn't celebrate it by dressing up his princess like a demon or a gargoyle. Don't get me wrong, though: There's nothing wrong with going door-to-door for candy and showing off your daughter's costume to the neighbors. But a father should want to dress up his little girl like a princess or a saint (the *hallowed*). Have her wear a costume of St. Kateri Tekakwitha, St. Faustina, or the Blessed Virgin Mary. That's what it's all about.

The Blessed Virgin Mary is, in fact, the most lovely little girl who ever existed. Yes, Our Lady was once a little, tender beautiful girl. It's strange, but sometimes I meet people who have an unintentional way of treating Mary as if she were something other than human — as if somehow because she is the Mother of God that she is above the anthropological needs of her feminine heart. But this is not true. She was a girl with a tender little heart, needing affirmation, tenderness, and affectivity. This is human. This is normal. And like any little girl, Mary needed this affirmation from her father. This affirmation is needed by all little girls, even the immaculate little girl we honor as the Mother of God.

Did she receive this affirmation? She most certainly did — and in the most perfect way. In the Word of God, we read that God the Father sent his messenger to Mary with the heavenly salutation, "Hail, full of grace, the Lord is with you!" (Lk 1:28). This particular fatherly affirmation is the greatest thing a father could ever say to his daughter. It reveals that he sees her, loves her, and considers her all lovely and beautiful. She is full of grace and has the plentitude of feminine wonder! This girl is a beautiful princess, and God delights in the delicate femininity of his daughter. For this reason, some translations render this fatherly affirmation as, "Rejoice, highly favored daughter." Though this is not a literal translation and misses the deeper theological truths, it does emphasize the anthropological dimension of what "Hail, full of grace" implies. This little princess is all beautiful.

Being told by her heavenly Father that she is all beautiful would, no doubt, delight her feminine heart. She knows that the Father loves her. He can't take his eyes off of her and wants his little princess to twirl and dance because his eyes are fixed upon her. She is his little sweetheart, his little princess, and a joy to her heavenly Father. Interestingly, certain mystics who have written about the hidden life of Mary depict little Mary, on the day she was presented in the temple, dancing on the steps out of pure joy for the Father who loves her so much. And in Christian art, there are even paintings that depict this event.

Mary's heart is secure because she is affirmed by her heavenly Father. And the heavenly Father loves his little princess so much that he will raise her up to be the Queen of heaven and earth. Father God is in love with his little princess.

Every little girl should be treated like this.

☆ ☆ ☆ Marian Gems

☆ Mary is a great Princess and a most powerful Queen; Queen of men and angels, Empress of the universe. She was Princess and Queen from the womb of her mother. *St. John Eudes*

☆ All through her life she [Mary] felt secure and sheltered in the will and heart of God. *Servant of God (Fr.) Joseph Kentenich*

☆ Woman is made for the sacred. She is heaven's instrument on earth. Mary is the proto-type, the pattern-woman who fulfills in herself the deepest aspirations of the heart of every daughter of Eve. *Venerable Fulton J. Sheen*

☆ Women who in order to please men, fall prey to the infatuations of the times, deny their true essence and their mission for our present day. In order to overcome the Eve in our time, the bride of Christ must glowingly demonstrate by her being, by her every word and deed, that Mary is the protector of woman's nobility. *Servant of God (Fr.) Joseph Kentenich*

☆ Now if grace is beauty of spirit, what must be Mary's beauty that surpasses all the beauty of the angels? *St. Lawrence of Brindisi*

☆ Holy Virgin Mary, among all the women of the world there is none like you. You are the daughter and handmaid of the most high King and Father of heaven. *St. Francis of Assisi*

☆ She [Mary] was formed in the heavens, and only the Artificer who formed her is able to comprehend her greatness. *Venerable Mary of Agreda*

☆ Mary is the most loved and loving Daughter of God the Father. *Blessed Gabriel Maria Allegra*

☆ This grand Princess [Mary] is the honor and perfection of all in the order of nature, since in her and by her the Creator of the world has united himself to man. *St. John Eudes*

☆ Behold the power of the Virgin Mother: she wounded and took captive the heart of God. *St. Bernardine of Siena*

☆ There is no more excellent way to obtain graces from God than to seek them through Mary, because her divine Son cannot refuse her anything. *St. Phillip Neri*

☆ The heart of the divine Father belongs to Mary, as the heart of the most loving of fathers to the most devoted of daughters. *St. John Eudes*

☆ *"Full of grace"* … is Mary's most beautiful name, the name God himself gave to her to indicate that she has always been and will always be the *beloved*, the elect, the one chosen to welcome the most precious gift, Jesus: "the incarnate love of God." *Pope Benedict XVI*

☆ We will never be able to go deeply enough into the stupendous fact of what God has accomplished in Mary! *Blessed Pope Paul VI*

☆ Mary was a princess of God, and God gave her the best blood of Israel. *Servant of God (Fr.) Patrick J. Peyton*

Capture Her Heart

A FEW YEARS AGO, I was blessed to help out every semester for a woman's retreat at Franciscan University of Steubenville called "Capture My Heart." During this retreat, I would expose the Blessed Sacrament for the young ladies and give them a talk on the feminine mystery and how sacred and special it is. I would tell them about how much God loves, honors, and respects the blessing of their femininity. Knowing that many of the girls who attended were longing to find a good man whom they could give their hearts to, I would tell the young women that you should only give your heart to a man who professes to love God more than he loves you. By doing this, you will avoid much heartache and pain as a wife and mother.

Sometimes, afterwards, I would talk with a few of the women, and they would all tell me that they loved being told their femininity was fascinating, dazzling, alluring, captivating, and, therefore, worth fighting for. They all seemed to know they were worth a man's sacrifice; they all seemed to know that they were royal and princesses. And they wanted a man like Jesus who was worthy of capturing their hearts. For me, as a man, to be present and witness 40 or so young women expressing their love for Jesus by singing songs to him and laying roses before the Blessed Sacrament was extremely powerful stuff. The experience as a whole convinced me more than ever that every woman deep down inside knows she is a princess and wants to be told she is beautiful and captivating. I remember thinking to myself every time I drove back to my religious house after my part in the retreat was done that it would be incredible if every college-age woman could experience something like this.

Those retreats affirmed in me, as a man, that all men deep down inside know that women are sacred, delicate, sweet, tender, captivating, and worth fighting for. In days of old, men used to express this awareness of the special status of women through acts that were public. For example, I have been told that years ago, it was common for men to stand up if a woman walked into the room. Such a public observance gave evidence to the sacredness of women, and it allowed men to publicly honor their feminine mystery. Standing up when a woman walked into the room gave evidence of the honor due to her as a woman, a bearer of life, and the crown of creation. And if the princess blushed when men rose in her honor, it was a beautiful thing. Men were men, and women were women. But, sadly, such things don't happen much anymore. Men don't stand when a woman walks in the room today. Neither do they offer a woman their seat in church if all the pews are full. Men rarely even open car doors for women today.

Yet, at the heart of every woman is the desire to be respected and fought for. Radical feminists will despise me for stating this, but every young woman wants to be courted, romanced, and even captured. Yes, captured. Of course, *not* "captured" in the sense of trapped and suppressed and *not* captured in the sense of being made the object of domestic violence. Rather, women want their *hearts* to be captured. They want to be swept off their feet and taken off into the sunset by a tall, dark, and handsome man. Every girl dreams of an officer who will take her breath away, a cowboy who will build a home for her, and a soldier who is willing to take a bullet for her captivating beauty. This is why girls love "chick flicks" like *The Notebook* and *Return To Me*, and they love to listen to songs about how a guy is willing to prove himself and win his lady's heart. Everybody knows that a girl, from her youngest years, plans out her wedding a million times — in her mind.

It is, indeed, the captivating beauty of women that helps men become noble and sacrificial. And everyone knows that behind every great man, there is always a very good woman who has helped him become the man he is. In fact, men are so captivated by the mystery of the feminine that they are willing to fight wars to protect such a mystery. Attack a man's beauty, and you are headed for trouble. Disrespect a man's mother, and fists will be raised. Honest men know that it is the captivating mystery of femininity that gives them courage and motivation. And as I've already stated in a previous chapter, no man can truly become a godly man without a woman in his life, not even a priest. This is why a priest needs the Virgin Mary in his life.

Proof of the existence of God, for man, is the existence of woman. Yet women are not divine but only sparks of the divine beauty.

But God and men are not the only ones who are aware of the power and captivating beauty of femininity. Satan knows it, too. As in all things, a great asset can also become a great liability if placed in the wrong hands. In this sense, God's created masterpiece, the beautiful feminine mystery, if tricked by Satan, is capable of becoming the cause of the downfall for the whole human race. Is this not in fact what happened at the beginning of time?

Think about it: Lucifer hates mankind and wanted to destroy God's creation from the very beginning. In order to do this, he devised a tricky plan to have mankind fall from grace and lose its earthly paradise. And because of his angelic intellect, the devil knew full well that if he was to truly destroy the human family, he had to overcome both the head (man) and the heart (woman) of the mystery of creation. Therefore, his plan was to go after the (head) man by first going after God's created masterpiece and crown of creation (woman). Adam may be the head, but woman is the crown, heart, and conscience of creation.

In light of this, the serpent intentionally went after the woman first knowing that, by doing it this way, he could deliver a fatal wound to both the head and the heart with one single blow. It was as if he deliberately had Eve stand in front of Adam so that the demonic dagger would wound them both, but it went through the heart first. The reason he did this is because the home of every man is the heart of a woman. If the heart of a man dies, the head and all the members of the man will die, too. Satan knew very well that if the woman falls, we all fall.

Satan knew what he was doing and used God's masterpiece as a liability. And to this day, there remains a great battle raging over the feminine genius. In the hands of God, feminine beauty is the gateway to true liberation because it is the feminine mystery that brings the Savior into the world. But in the hands of Satan, feminine beauty can be used as a tool to enslave mankind and bring it to ruin.

It should be made clear, however, that what I have noted above does not place the entire burden of the fall of mankind in the Garden of Eden on women's shoulders. On the contrary, man (Adam) was just as responsible for the fall as the woman (Eve), but each sinned according to their failure to love God and each other in their respective masculinity and femininity. As a man, Adam failed to fight off the demonic assault threatening his feminine beauty, failing to trust in his God by being unwilling to suffer death at the hands of the serpent-dragon out of love for his God and his beauty (cf. Heb 2:15). As a woman, Eve failed because she disobeyed God as a woman by listening to the trickery and advice of the serpent, eating the forbidden fruit, and passing on the poison to her husband. Each fell because they failed to live up to the sacrificial demands of their respective sex. Anthropologically, Adam didn't man up, and Eve didn't ponder and interiorize what was spoken to her. In other words, Eve acted wrongly, and Adam failed to act at all.

Sadly, this same scenario happens over and over again all throughout time. Specifically, men disobey God by failing to protect the beauty entrusted to them. And when men no longer defend and protect the feminine mystery, women feel they have to man up and act. Worse yet, when men become disrespectful towards women and abuse them, the slogan of woman becomes, "I am woman, hear me roar!" She will turn against man because he failed her and did not fight for her. This does not mean, by the way, that women should not be working outside of the home. What it does mean, however, is that no career should take priority over motherhood — as we will see in the next section. It is worth noting here, however, that when a woman places action (work) above being (motherhood), she begins to view the domestic as her enemy. She may even end up despising it, and all that goes with it: cooking, cleaning, and children.

Yet I firmly believe that every woman still clings to the dream of being taken and captured. She only turns away from the dream in her heart because she has been let down by men. But all women, no matter how wounded, continue to dream of being proposed to by the perfect man. All women know it is totally unnatural for a woman to propose to a man. And every woman would love to have a man tell her that she is second only to God and that he adores her.

Incidentally, in an old English (British) marriage ritual, at the time when the bridegroom professed marital vows, he would publicly declare to his bride the following: "With my body I do thee worship, and with all my worldly goods I do thee bestow." Every woman wants to be worshipped. Worshipped, not in the sense of adoration, but worshipped in the sense of honored, respected, and loved. Women know they are special. It's when men hurt women that women want real worship, as in adoration. So, when the strength and power of men have been used to harm them, they want to fight back through obtaining power as a witch, a wiccan, or a medium. With so many women having been wounded by men today, it's no wonder there's so much "goddess" talk in our times.

We live in a very pornographic age where women are both worshipped as goddesses and yet, ironically, only used and abused for their anatomy and physical beauty. At one and the same time, the media claims to fight for the rights of women, yet they also ardently promote and defend the abuse of women through the smut of pornography that is daily displayed in their sitcoms and television programs. It's schizophrenic!

This is why Satan is the great pornographer because he appears to want to liberate women, while at the same time he delights in seeing their feminine dignity abused, used, and abandoned. In reality, he hates the feminine mystery, but he knows that he can use it to his advantage. Satan can use beauty as bait to capture men in his net of sin. God, on the other hand, uses beauty to transform the hearts of men, helping them to become saints and heroes. It's no wonder, then, that in the pornographic age in which we live, there are also more reported Marian apparitions than any other time in Church history. Beauty is being fought for.

God's beautiful feminine masterpiece, indeed, has the power to transform this fallen world. And we must remember that God's masterpiece was once a young girl. She, too, had a desire to be courted, romanced, and captured. Yet her desire was solely for divine courtship, divine romance, and being captured by God. As the Immaculate Conception, she is pure and God-centered in all her desires, but that does not mean she didn't have them. She did. She is not a robot or an angel. She is a girl.

She is, in fact, courted, romanced, and captured by God. From her earliest years, her heart and soul is shared with whom she wills, but her body she saves for God and his plan. That plan is revealed at the Annunciation when she is of the age when girls dream of being taken. And she allows herself to be taken. When the angel comes to her, he arrives as a divine messenger with a divine proposal. God has courted Mary through her intense relationship with him in prayer, and the Annunciation is where God proposes to her and asks for her hand in spiritual marriage.

It is a nuptial event. Mary in her beautiful femininity, a mystery that has captivated the very Heart of God, gives herself away to the love of her life with the word every single girl longs to say to the desire of her heart. She says, "*I do!*" Mary's *fiat* is a bridal *I do*. It's a girl's heart crying out: "Yes! Take me! Sweep me away! I'm yours! I will take your name, bear your children, and love you always!" Mary is madly in love with God, and God is madly in love with her. In her feminine heart, she knows that the Song of Songs was written for her. She is the Dove of Beauty.

Mary's heart rejoices in her state of being espoused to God. And God will use her delicate feminine mystery to bring the Savior into the world, raise up his adopted children, and crush Satan's head. She will become the Mother of God, the Mother of the Church, the mother of men, and the ultimate saint-maker. All will honor her and stand up when she walks into the room. God himself captured her heart, and now he uses her beauty and femininity to capture our hearts.

☆ ☆ ☆ Marian Gems

☆ The hidden wish of every woman in history, the secret desire of every feminine heart, is fulfilled in that instant when Mary says: "Fiat" — "Be it done unto me according to thy word." *Venerable Fulton J. Sheen*

☆ Your name, O Mary, is a precious ointment, which breathes forth the odor of Divine grace. Let this ointment of salvation enter the inmost recesses of our souls. *St. Ambrose*

☆ God is captivated by your grace and beauty [Mary]. As a magnet draws iron, so your grace and beauty have drawn God down from heaven to you. As Jacob was smitten with love for Rachel, David for Bathsheba, Ahasuerus for Esther, Adam for Eve, so God has fallen in love with you. *St. Lawrence of Brindisi*

☆ In Mary God has given back woman's lost crown. In her, woman has again become queen. The one only purely created being who is allowed to enter into the most intimate imaginable union with God is a woman: the Queen of heaven and earth. In her, all the members of her sex experience the solar radiance of feminine dignity and beauty and a piece of their own God-given greatness. *Servant of God (Fr.) Joseph Kentenich*

☆ Your Creator has become your Spouse, he has loved your beauty [Mary]. *St. Amadeus of Lausanne*

☆ She [Mary] is what every woman wants to be when she looks at herself. *Venerable Fulton J. Sheen*

☆ God could create an infinity of suns, one more brilliant than the other, an infinity of worlds, one more marvelous than the other, an infinity of angels, one more holy than the other. But a creature more holy, more ravishing, more gracious than his mother he could not make; for in making her his Mother, he gave her at once, so to say, all that he could give of beauty and goodness and holiness and sanctity in the treasury of his omnipotence. *St. Leonard of Port Maurice*

☆ The Church sees in Mary the highest expression of the "feminine genius" and she finds in her a source of constant inspiration. *St. John Paul II*

☆ Four instincts deeply embedded in the human heart: affection for the beautiful; admiration for purity; reverence for a Queen; and love of a Mother. All of these come to a focus in Mary. *Venerable Fulton J. Sheen*

☆ Man beholds and experiences in Mary the shining ideal of woman-hood as it slumbers in his soul; by it he develops into a personal, radiant totality and produces an unaffected reverence toward everyone who bears Mary's countenance. *Servant of God (Fr.) Joseph Kentenich*

☆ There has never been a woman, even the most beautiful, gracious, and lovely, who has had such power over her most passionate and loving husband, as Mary did over God because of her grace and beauty. *St. Lawrence of Brindisi*

The Blessings
of Motherhood

ALL WOMEN LOVE BABIES. Even the most hardened feminist bows down before the cradle. And if a woman is unable to bear children due to physical complications, she will always have a desire in her heart for children. On occasion, I've met a few hardened women who have told me they have no desire for children. But it doesn't take long in the conversation to find out that there are fears and wounds in their feminine hearts that are at the root of their desire to remain childless. The fear or wound will manifest itself. It always does.

Every woman is made for physical and/or spiritual maternity.

Every month, a woman's body reminds her that she was designed for motherhood. A woman's body was made by God, not men. Yet, today, women are told they don't have to be under the monthly burden of their femininity. They are implicitly taught that it has been imposed on them by a mean masculine deity, and they are encouraged to take a pill that will alleviate them of their monthly cycle, reducing it to maybe three or four times a year.

But the reality is that this rebellion against nature leaves them very susceptible to having serious, even life-threatening, health issues. It's a known fact, confirmed by both the World Health Organization and the Mayo Clinic, that using contraceptive pills highly increases a woman's risk of having breast cancer and other serious health issues. And it's also a known fact that many hormonal contraceptives used by women are greatly polluting our environment, especially our water supply. The release of high amounts of synthetic steroids into our sewage system is even causing hormonal changes in nature. It's a huge problem, and Planned Parenthood, possibly the most anti-maternal organization in the world, chooses to ignore the facts and continues to poison the minds of women across the world by operating under the disguise of being concerned about women's health.

Yet, contrary to the lies put forth by Planned Parenthood, all women surrender to the God-given anthropology of their femininity when they see a baby in a stroller. It's because every woman was once a little girl and played mommy with her dolls, just like all little girls do. Babies are a constant reminder to the modern emancipated woman that she was once an innocent young girl with dreams of being a mommy. Every young girl dreams of being a mommy someday; even tomboys on a farm dream of this. And in her deepest feminine desires, the dream of maternity still lingers.

Even after a woman has aged beyond the years of childbearing through menopause, she still delights in and wants to be around babies. Did you ever see an older woman's reaction when she found out she was going to be a grandmother? She is ecstatic with joy because it's the closest she can come to having a baby herself. Women were made for babies, and it doesn't matter what sociological survey or Women's Studies professor teaches differently. Even women who profess a vow of chastity (celibacy) and are consecrated to God are called *sisters* and *mothers*. They spiritually mother souls, cooperating with God in bringing about the spiritual birth of God's children — and they can actually be more fruitful in childbearing than physical mothers.

Thus, it is so sad when a woman turns away from her vocation to motherhood — whether physical or spiritual. If she becomes childless by choice, she becomes miserable and self-implodes. Being closed to life and choosing not to be a bearer of life is the death of a woman.

Men can't have babies. For one thing, their biology doesn't allow it. But also men do not have the strength and skills necessary for that particular vocation, that particular mission. Yes, St. Peter described women as the weaker sex (cf. 1 Pet 3:7), but he certainly didn't intend to degrade women or consider them less in value than men. He knew better than anyone that women are generally much stronger than men when it pertains to the things that really matter. Saint Peter knew very well that it was Mary and the other women who stood at the foot of the Cross, when Peter himself and almost all of the other men except John had run away.

Women may be physically weaker than men, but they are not morally weaker than men. I can chuck a rock further than a woman and chop wood quicker than a woman, but that doesn't make me better than a woman. A woman has great strength, but not in the same way a man does. Women are strong enough to be bearers of new life, while men are not. The very title of the Sacrament that describes the blessed equality between men and women actually gives priority to the woman. It is called the Sacrament of Matrimony. In other words, it is the Sacrament of motherhood. *Matrimony means maternity or motherhood.*

Men's strength is meant to be at the service of the feminine-maternal mystery. Men are called to protect, defend, and honor this great mystery. Maternity is what furthers the human race. Motherhood is special and brings about great blessings. God's Word tells us, "Whoever glorifies his mother is like one who lays up treasure" (Sir 3:4). Thus, it's no wonder Satan hates motherhood so much. The devil doesn't want us having treasure, and he knows very well that it is through motherhood that he is defeated. The child in Mary's womb conquers darkness and death itself. Therefore, all mothers and children in the womb are a perpetual reminder to Satan that he has been conquered by motherhood.

Motherhood is a blessing and brings about great blessings to the world *and* women. Again, the Word of God tells us that "women will be saved through bearing children" (1 Tim 2:15). Remember: *Salvation* translates as *eternal health*. Indeed, motherhood is a great source of healing for a woman. Even science now affirms this.

Have you ever heard of fetal microchimerism, sometimes also called fetomaternal microchimerism? It's a long, complicated term, I know. But it's amazing stuff. Fetal microchimerism basically describes the process by which the fetal cells of a child remain in the mother after her pregnancy. Science has recently discovered that when a woman becomes pregnant, there are many cells from the baby that remain in the mother's body, and some of these living cells even remain with her for the rest of her life. Science has also discovered that cells of the mother are also exchanged with her children and remain with her children for life. And in something that is sure to bring tears to the face of every mother, it has been scientifically verified by the Department of Obstetrics and Gynecology at the University of Washington that even if a mother experiences a miscarriage or has an abortion, living cells of those children, too, remain in her body. Isn't that amazing!

This gives a whole new understanding of a "mother's intu ition." Indeed, in one article I read, a scientist quipped about how science has now come to understand how a mother intuitively knows things about her children, not because she is looking over their shoulder, but because she is in their shoulder!

But there's more!

It has also been scientifically verified that when a mother experiences certain illnesses, the living cells of her children that remain in her body have been found in the area of illness. Initially, the researchers thought that the cells might be the cause of the mother's illness, but now they are of the belief that the cells of a mother's children that are in the area of her illness are trying to fight off the illness and protect the life of the mother. That's incredible! Thus, having babies really is healing for a woman. Ironically, even if a woman killed the child in her womb through having an abortion, the child she killed fights for the life of the mother when she is sick.

Motherhood is such an incredible mystery!

And the Blessed Virgin Mary, the masterpiece of mother-hood, experienced all of its blessings. After having been courted by God and swept off her feet in the divine romance, she becomes the *Theotokos* (the God-bearer) and the New Eve and mother of all the living. Never was there a mother so fruitful. Theologically, Mary is even the spiritual mother of Eve and the spiritual mother of the Old Testament prophets! Yes, even Adam and Eve call her mother. Mary's spiritual maternity is elastic, stretching all the way back to the beginning of time, because God made her the spiritual mother of all in light of the fact that she is the originally intended mother in the divine plan.

Can you imagine the joy her heart must have experienced at the announcement of her cousin Elizabeth: "And why is this granted me, that the mother of my Lord should come to me?" (Lk 1:43). Mary is blessed among all women (cf. Lk 1:42) because she has been called to be the Mother of God and the spir-itual mother of men. And she delights in her maternity, treasuring it with every beat of her heart. She loves her femininity and her motherhood, and her heart is free to sing the *Magnificat* of praise — she has been created to be the most fruitful human person who ever lived! She is the model of fruitful Christianity.

But, once again, there's more.

Remember fetal microchimerism? Let's consider this scientifically verifiable reality in light of the divine maternity of Mary. What we learn is what the Church has always said about the complementarity of faith and science. Namely, faith and science are not opposed. It's just that faith is way ahead of science, and science is racing to catch up with, and will eventually affirm, everything the Church dogmatically teaches.

Here's what I mean: Did you know that the Church has never dogmatically stated that Mary died? There have been many theories put forth by saints and theologians about the possibility of Mary dying. There have even been personal statements by popes on the matter, but the Church has never held an official position. Catholics are free to speculate about whether Mary died or not. I personally do not believe Mary died.

The basic reasoning for the argument that Mary did not experience death is because death is the result of sin (cf. Rom 5:12; 6:23), and Mary was not a sinner. Theologically and anthropologically, there really is no solid reason, in light of Mary's not being a sinner, for why she would experience death.

On the other hand, for those who think that Mary did experience death, their argument rests solely on the basis of "fittingness." That is, since Jesus died, it was fitting that she experience death also. But it's important to make the distinction that Jesus experienced death because he was killed; he died because he was murdered. What would have happened had he not been crucified? We simply do not know. And the same logic applies to Our Lady. Though not God, Mary had the privilege of being the Immaculate Conception (she was not a sinner). But, unlike Jesus, she was not physically killed. She underwent a mystical and spiritual crucifixion, but she was not murdered. Therefore, any theory, even in ancient writings, about how her life on earth ended, is purely speculative.

However, in light of the recent discoveries in science put forth through fetal microchimerism, the argument in favor of Mary not experiencing death has a new theological and biological foundation.

Think about it: If Mary has in her body living cells of her divine Son all throughout her life, cells that fight for a mother's life and protect her against sickness, illness, and disease, how could she ever die? The cells of her Son inside her are divine cells! She is a living monstrance, a walking tabernacle. No wonder demons flee at her presence — she doesn't come alone! God lives in her. She is, in fact, the terror of demons and the conqueror of all heresies.

Don't get me wrong, though: Most certainly she experienced some passage from this life to the next, but it was not a death like you and I will experience. To illustrate this, the early Church called Mary's passage to heaven the *Transitus Mariae* ("the transition of Mary"), and the Eastern Church has always called it the *Dormition* ("falling asleep") of Mary. As a matter of fact, the Western Church has never celebrated a feast of the resurrection of Mary because resurrection implies death. Rather, the Church celebrates the Assumption of Mary. A resurrection implies death, while an assumption does not. And according to the ancient theological principle of *lex orandi, lex credendi* ("the law of prayer is the law of belief") on August 15 every year, we liturgically celebrate a mother who never experienced death.

Long live our mother who never dies!

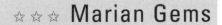

☆ ☆ ☆ Marian Gems

☆ If every woman were an image of the Mother of God, a spouse of Christ and an apostle of the divine Heart, she would fulfill her feminine vocation no matter in what circumstances she lived and what her external activities might be. *St. Edith Stein*

☆ For women called to virginal chastity, Mary reveals the lofty meaning of so special a vocation. Thus she draws attention to the spiritual fruitfulness which it produces in the divine plan: a higher order of motherhood, a motherhood according to the Spirit. *St. John Paul II*

☆ Glory of virgins, the joy of mothers, the support of the faithful, the diadem of the Church, the model of the true Faith, the seat of piety, the dwelling place of the Holy Trinity. *St. Proclus of Constantinople*

☆ At the present moment it seems to be clearly in the plans of God, whose plans reveal themselves daily more and more, to glorify his Mother in a special manner, to show her to the nations as the Mediatrix of all Graces, and as the great Victress over the anthropological heresies. *Servant of God (Fr.) Joseph Kentenich*

☆ Mary calls herself *ancilla Domini*, the handmaid of the Lord. Not to be this for any woman lowers her dignity. Woman's unhappiest moments are when she is unable to give; her most hellish moments are when she refuses to give. *Venerable Fulton J. Sheen*

☆ O holy Mother of God, remember us, I say, who make our boast in you, and who in august hymns celebrate your memory, which will ever live, and never fade away. *St. Methodius of Philippi*

☆ Every woman who wants to fulfill her destiny must look to Mary as the ideal. *St. Edith Stein*

☆ Mary is the image and model of all mothers, of their great mission to be guardians of life, of their mission to be teachers of the art of living and of the art of loving. *Pope Benedict XVI*

☆ She [Mary] is so beautiful that to see her again one would be willing to die. *St. Bernadette Soubirous*

☆ Mary, as the pattern both of maidenhood and maternity, has exalted woman's state and nature, and made the Christian virgin and the Christian mother understand the sacredness of their duties in the sight of God. *Blessed John Henry Newman*

☆ Accept me, O Mary, for thine own, and as thine, take charge of my salvation. I will no longer be mine; to thee do I give myself. If, during the time past I have served thee ill, and lost so many occasions of honoring thee, for the future I will be one of thy most loving and faithful servants. *St. Alphonsus Liguori*

☆ I beseech the Virgin Mary that she may keep you under the protection of her tender maternity. *St. Francis de Sales*

☆ No one knows the good Mother she has been to me. *Venerable Matt Talbot*

☆ She existed in the Divine Mind as an Eternal Thought before there were any mothers. She is the Mother of mothers — she is the world's first love. *Venerable Fulton J. Sheen*

☆ In Paradise, Mary is as the Mother of a family. Give me an energetic mother, one well attentive to her house: she alone keeps an eye on everything; no matter how numerous the family is, she thinks of everything; she provides everyone with what is necessary; she does not even wait for one of the children to ask, she thinks of it; in fact, even before a thing becomes necessary, she prepares it so that it will be ready at the opportune moment. Isn't it true that a good mother does this? And this is precisely what Mary does. All of us form a large family of which God is the Head, the Father; the Mother of this great family, then, is Mary Most Holy. God has deposited all graces in her hands; and she, as a good mother, is always attentive to all our needs. She goes about distributing this grace to one and that to another, according to each one's particular needs: and at times she gives them to us without our asking for them. *St. Joseph Cafasso*

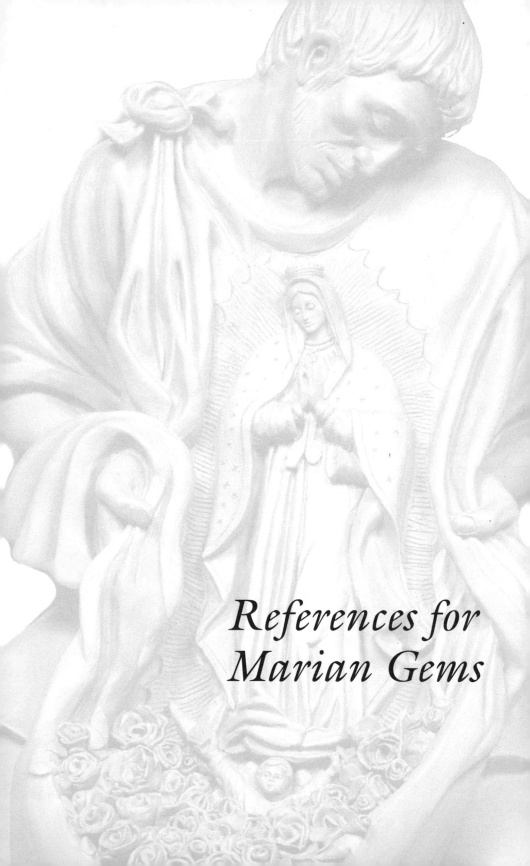

References for
Marian Gems

AAS   *Acta Apostolicae Sedis* (Vatican City, 1909-)

PL   *Patrologia Latina.J.P. Migne* (ed.) 221 vols. (Paris, 1841-1864)

PG   *Patrologia Graeca.J.P. Migne* (ed.) 161 vols. (Paris, 1857-1866)

1) The Virgin Mary: God's Masterpiece

The Woman of Our Dreams

- Venerable Fulton J. Sheen, *The World's First Love: Mary, Mother of God* (San Francisco: Ignatius Press, 1996), 20. Used with permission.
- St. John Paul II, "For the 12th World Day of the Sick – February 11, 2004 – Message to Cardinal Javier Lozano Barragan, President of the Pontifical Council for Health Pastoral Care," December 1, 2003. *L'Osservatore Romano*, English Edition, January 21, 2004.
- Pope Innocent III, as quoted in Pamela Moran (ed.), *A Marian Prayer Book: A Treasury of Prayers, Hymns, and Meditations* (Ann Arbor, Mich.: Servant Publications, 1991), 63.
- Luke 1:48 (RSVCE).
- St. Bernard of Clairvaux, as quoted in Bruce M. Metzger and Michael D. Coogan (ed.), *The Oxford Guide to Ideas & Issues of the Bible* (New York: Oxford University Press, 2001), 303.
- Servant of God (Fr.) Joseph Kentenich, *Mary, Our Mother and Educator: An Applied Mariology.* Trans. Jonathan Niehaus (Waukesha, Wis.: Schoenstatt Sisters of Mary, 1987), 57. Original text in German: Copyright 1973, under the title *Maria-Mutter und Erzieherin. Eine angewandte Mariologie*, Schönstatt-Verlag, Vallendar, Schönstatt, West Germany. Used with permission.
- Venerable Fulton J. Sheen, *The World's First Love: Mary, Mother of God* (San Francisco: Ignatius Press, 1996), 15. Used with permission.
- St. Therese of Lisieux, as quoted in Charles P. Connor, *The Saint for the Third Millennium: St. Therese of Lisieux* (New York: Alba House, 2007), 164. Used with permission.
- Venerable Pope Pius XII, as quoted in Fr. Stefano M. Manelli, FI, *Devotion to Mary: The Marian Life as Taught by the Saints* (New Bedford, Mass.: Academy of the Immaculate, 2001), 50.
- St. John Eudes, *The Admirable Heart of Mary.* Trans. Charles di Targiani & Ruth Hauser (Buffalo, N.Y.: Immaculate Heart Publications, 1947), 4.
- St. Peter Chrysologus, *Sermon* 140, 6: PL 52, 577.
- Blessed Pope Paul VI, "To Marian Congregations" (Sept. 12, 1963) in *Mary, God's Mother and Ours* (Boston, Mass.: Daughters of St. Paul, 1979), 12.
- Pope Benedict XVI (*Angelus* message, June 11, 2006), as quoted in *Pope Benedict XVI: Mary [Spiritual Thoughts Series]* (Washington, D.C.: USCCB Publishing, 2008), 59.
- Blessed James Alberione, *Mary, Hope of the World.* Trans. Hilda Calabro (Boston, Mass.: Daughters of St. Paul, 1981), 10.
- St. John Vianney, as quoted in Rev. Charles G. Fehrenbach, CSsR (ed.), *Mary, Day By Day: Marian Meditations for Every Day taken*

from the Holy Bible and the Writings of the Saints (New York: Catholic
Book Publishing Corp., 1987), 8.

- St. John Paul II, "For the Opening of the 150th Anniversary of the
Immaculate Conception – Angelus Message," December 8, 2003.
L'Osservatore Romano, English Edition, December 10, 2003.

The Immaculate Blueprint

- St. Maximilian Kolbe, as quoted in Fr. Angelo M. Geiger, FI, "Marian
Mediation as Presence and Transubstantiation into the Immaculate,"
in *Mary at the Foot of the Cross III: Mater Unitatis: Acts of the Third
International Symposium on Marian Coredemption* (New Bedford,
Mass.: Academy of the Immaculate, 2003), 157-158.
- St. Alphonsus Ligouri, as quoted in Bonaventure Hammer, OFM,
*Mary, Help of Christians and the Fourteen Saints Invoked as Holy
Helpers* (New York: Benziger Brothers, 1909), 362.
- Blessed Michael Sopocko, *The Mercy of God in His Works: Volume IV.*
Trans. R. Batchelor. (Hereford: Marian Apostolate, 1972), 78.
- St. Marguerite Bourgeoys, as quoted in Ronda De Sola Chervin,
Quotable Saints (Oak Lawn, Ill.: CMJ Marian Publishers, 1992), 95.
- St. John Damascene, *De fide orthodoxa* 3, 12; PG 94, 1029-1030.
- St. Augustine of Hippo, as quoted in Pamela Moran (ed.), *A Marian
Prayer Book: A Treasury of Prayers, Hymns, and Meditations* (Ann
Arbor, Mich.: Servant Publications, 1991), 32.
- St. Louis de Montfort, *True Devotion to the Blessed Virgin* (Bay Shore,
N.Y.: Montfort Publications, 1980), 113-114. Used with permission.
- St. Anselm of Canterbury, *De virginali conceptu* 18; PL 158, 451 A.
- Blessed John Duns Scotus, as quoted in Fr. Stefano M. Manelli, FI,
Blessed John Duns Scotus: Marian Doctor (New Bedford, Mass.:
Academy of the Immaculate, 2011), 88.
- St. Faustina Kowalska, *Diary of Saint Maria Faustina Kowalska:
Divine Mercy in My Soul.* (Stockbridge, Mass.: Marian Press, 2002),
no. 1413. Used with permission.
- Blessed James Alberione, *Glories and Virtues of Mary.* Trans. Hilda
Calabro (Boston, Mass.: Daughters of St. Paul, 1982), 18.
- St. Maximilian Kolbe, as quoted in Fr. Stefano M. Manelli, FI,
Devotion to Our Lady: The Marian Life as Taught by the Saints (New
Bedford, Mass.: Academy of the Immaculate, 2001), 53.
- Blessed George Matulaitis, *Journal.* Fontes Historiae Marianorum 17.
Trans. Sr. Ann Mikaila, MVS (Stockbridge, Mass.: Marian Fathers,
2003), 60. Used with permission.
- Servant of God Mother Auxilia de la Cruz, *The Eucharistic Life.*
Trans. Maria Victoria Hernandez, OP (Washington, D.C.: Oblate
Sisters, 2001), 68.
- St. Lawrence of Brindisi, *Mariale: Opera Omnia [Collected Sermons
and Homilies of St. Lawrence of Brindisi].* Trans. Vernon Wagner,
OFM Cap. (Delhi, India: Media House, 2007), 39.

- St. Stanislaus Papczynski, as quoted in Tadeusz Rogalewski, MIC, *Stanislaus Papczynski (1631-1701): Founder of the Order of Marians and Inspirer of the Marian School of Spirituality.* Trans. Paul & Ewa St. Jean (Stockbridge, Mass.: Marian Press, 2001), 255. Used with permission.

Total Consecration

- St. Louis de Montfort, *True Devotion to the Blessed Virgin* (Bay Shore, N.Y.: Montfort Publications, 1980), 59. Used with permission.
- St. Padre Pio, *Padre Pio's Words of Hope.* Ed. Eileen Dunn Bertanzetti (Huntington, Ind.: Our Sunday Visitor, Inc., 1999), 117.
- St. Maximilian Kolbe, as quoted in Jill Haak Adels, *The Wisdom of the Saints: An Anthology* (New York: Oxford University Press, 1987), 18.
- St. John Paul II, "Homily of Pope John Paul II at Fatima," May 13, 1982, as quoted in Timothy Tindal-Robertson, *Fatima, Russia & Pope John Paul II* (United Kingdom: Gracewing, 1998), 247.
- St. Faustina Kowalska, *Diary of Saint Maria Faustina Kowalska: Divine Mercy in My Soul.* (Stockbridge, Mass.: Marian Press, 2002), no. 79. Used with permission.
- St. Odilo of Cluny, *Vita Odilonis* 2, 1; PL 142, 915-916.
- Servant of God Frank Duff, as quoted at www.legionofmary.ie.
- St. John Eudes, *The Wondrous Childhood of the Most Holy Mother of God* (Albany, N.Y.: Preserving Christian Publications, Inc., 2000), 286.
- Blessed Dina Belanger, *The Autobiography of Dina Belanger.* Trans. Mary St. Stephen, RJM (Canada: Religious of Jesus and Mary, 1997), 64-65.
- St. Luigi Guanella, as quoted in *Magnificat* (Vol. 14, No.3, May 2012), 44.
- St. Vincent Pallotti, as quoted in *Sayings of a Saint: Selections from the Writings of St. Vincent Pallotti.* (ed.) Augustine Kolencherry, SAC (Bangalore, India: Asian Trading Corporation, 1989), 116.

2) To Jesus Through Mary

Who Do You Say That I Am? (Mt 16:15)

- Venerable Fulton J. Sheen, *The World's First Love: Mary, Mother of God* (San Francisco: Ignatius Press, 1996), 103. Used with permission.
- Pope St. Pius X, *Ad Diem Illum Laetissimum*, 6.
- Pope Leo XIII, *Octobri Mense*, 4.
- Blessed Pope Pius IX, *Ineffabilis Deus* (Boston, Mass.: St. Paul Books & Media), 17.
- Venerable Fulton J. Sheen, *The World's First Love: Mary, Mother of God* (San Francisco: Ignatius Press, 1996), 73-74. Used with permission.
- Blessed Pope Paul VI, "*Ingente Christifidelium multitudini habita, in sacra Aede B. Mariae Virginis v. 'Nostra Signora di Bonaria' Calari dicata, Beatissimo Patre Sacrum peragente,*" 24 April, AAS62 (1970): 300-301.

- Servant of God Frank Duff, "Everyone must pour himself into another soul," (1956), as quoted at www.catholicpamphlets.net.
- St. Maximilian Kolbe, as quoted in Fr. Stefano M. Manelli, FI, *Devotion to Our Lady: The Marian Life as Taught by the Saints* (New Bedford, Mass.: Academy of the Immaculate, 2001), 15.
- Blessed John Henry Newman, Discourses, as quoted in Michael O'Carroll, CSSp, *Theotokos: A Theological Encyclopedia of the Blessed Virgin Mary* (Collegeville, Minn.: Liturgical Press, 1982), 264.
- Blessed Anne Catherine Emmerich, *The Life of the Blessed Virgin Mary.* Trans. Sir Michael Palairet (London: Burns & Oates, 1954), 145.
- St. John Paul II, *Rosarium Virginis Mariae*, 14.
- Pope Benedict XVI (Joseph Cardinal Ratzinger) & Vittorio Messori. *The Ratzinger Report: An Exclusive Interview on the State of the Church.* Trans. Salvator Attanasio & Graham Harrison. (San Francisco: Ignatius Press, 1985), 105.
- Servant of God Mother Auxilia de la Cruz, *Broken Bread.* Trans. Leonard P. Fitzpatrick, MSsA (Stockbridge, Mass.: Marian Press, 1983), 49. Used with permission.

Mary Christmas

- Blessed William Joseph Chaminade, "Society of Mary Considered as a Religious Order," in *Spirit of Our Foundation: Volume I* (Dayton, Ohio: St. Mary's Convent, 1911), 144.
- Blessed Michael Sopocko, *God Is Mercy: Meditations on God's Most Consoling Attribute.* (Stockbridge, Mass.: Marian Fathers, 1965), 53. Used with permission.
- Blessed Pope Paul VI, *Marialis Cultus*, 19.
- Servant of God Mother Auxilia de la Cruz, *The Eucharistic Life.* Trans. Maria Victoria Hernandez, OP (Washington, D.C.: Oblate Sisters, 2001), 68.
- Blessed Guerric of Igny, *In Assumpt.* I, 2: PL 185, 188.
- Servant of God (Fr.) Joseph Kentenich, *Called, Consecrated, Sent: Selected Texts of Father Joseph Kententich about the Priesthood.* (ed.) Peter Wolf (Waukesha, Wis.: Schoenstatt Editions USA, 2009), 116. Original German text, Berufen-geweiht-gesandt, copyright 2009, Schönstatt-Verlag, Vallendar, Used with permission.
- St. Anthony of Padua, as quoted in *Magnificat* (Vol. 14, No.10, December 2012), 433
- Venerable Fulton J. Sheen, *Three to Get Married* (Princeton, N.J.: Scepter Publishers, 1951), 161. Used with permission.
- St. Proclus of Constantinople, *Homily* I, 3; PG 65, 684 B.
- St. Leo the Great, *Sermon* 24, 3; PL 54, 206.
- Pope Benedict XVI (Joseph Cardinal Ratzinger) & Hans Urs von Balthasar, *Mary: The Church at the Source.* Trans. Adrian Walker (San Francisco: Ignatius Press, 2005), 46-47.

- St. Albert the Great, as quoted in Luigi Gambero, SM, *Mary in the Middle Ages: The Blessed Virgin Mary in the Thought of Medieval Latin Theologians*. Trans. Thomas Buffer (San Francisco: Ignatius Press, 2005), 226.
- Pope St. Pius X, *Ad Diem Illum Laetissimum*, 15.
- St. Josemaria Escriva, *Friends of God: Homilies by Josemaria Escriva* (Manila: Sinag-tala, 2000), Chapter 17, No. 276.
- St. Lawrence of Brindisi, *Mariale: Opera Omnia [Collected Sermons and Homilies of St. Lawrence of Brindisi]*. Trans. Vernon Wagner, OFM Cap. (Delhi, India: Media House, 2007), 243.
- Blessed Guerric of Igny, as quoted in Rev. Charles G. Fehrenbach, CSsR (ed.). *Mary, Day By Day: Marian Meditations for Every Day taken from the Holy Bible and the Writings of the Saints* (New York: Catholic Book Publishing Corp., 1987), 156.
- Pope St. Pius X, as quoted in Francis Edward Nugent, *Fairest Star Of All: A Little Treasury of Mariology* (Patterson, N.J.: St. Anthony Guild Press, 1956), 1. Used with permission.
- Servant of God Mother Auxilia de la Cruz, *Broken Bread*. Trans. Leonard P. Fitzpatrick, MSsA (Stockbridge, Mass.: Marian Press, 1983), 49. Used with permission.
- Pope Benedict XVI (Joseph Cardinal Ratzinger), "Hail, Full of Grace: Elements of Marian Piety According to the Bible," in *Mary: The Church at the Source*, trans. Adrian Walker (San Francisco: Ignatius Press, 1997), 62.
- Venerable Fulton J. Sheen, *Moods and Truths*. (Garden City, N.Y.: Garden City Books, 1950), 100-101.

Eat My Flesh and Drink My Blood (Jn 6:54)

- St. Peter Julian Eymard, *Our Lady of the Blessed Sacrament: Readings for the Month of May* (Cleveland, Ohio: Emmanuel Publications, 1930), 68-69.
- St. Hilary of Poitiers, as quoted in Pope Benedict XVI, "*Message of His Holiness Benedict XVI for the Sixteenth World Day of the Sick*"(January 11, 2008), 2.
- St. Peter Damian, *Sermo XLV In Nativitate Beatissimae Virginis Mariae*: PL 144, 740-748.
- Venerable Fulton J. Sheen, *The World's First Love: Mary, Mother of God* (San Francisco: Ignatius Press, 1952), 37. Used with permission.
- Blessed James Alberione, as quoted in Fr. Stefano Manelli, FI, "Marian Coredemption in the Hagiography of the 20th Century," in *Mary at the Foot of the Cross: Acts from the International Symposium on Marian Coredemption* (New Bedford, Mass.: Academy of the Immaculate, 2001), 225.
- Venerable Fulton J. Sheen, *Three to Get Married*. (Princeton, N.J.: Scepter Publishers, 1951), 168. Used with permission.

- St. Peter Julian Eymard, *Our Lady of the Blessed Sacrament: Readings for the Month of May* (Cleveland, Ohio: Emmanuel Publications, 1930), 31.
- St. Peter Damian, *Sermo XLV In Nativitate Beatissimae Virginis Mariae*: PL 144, 743C.
- St. Anthony of Padua, as quoted in Luigi Gambero, SM, *Mary in the Middle Ages: The Blessed Virgin Mary in the Thought of Medieval Latin Theologians*. Trans. Thomas Buffer (San Francisco: Ignatius Press, 2005), 204.
- St. Augustine of Hippo, as quoted in Fr. Paul Segneri, SJ, *The Devout Client of Mary: Instructed in the Motives and Means of Serving Her Well*. (London: Burns & Lambert, 1857), 32.
- St. John Paul II, *Ecclesia de Eucharistia*, 55.
- St. Peter Damian, *Sermo XLV In Nativitate Beatissimae Virginis Mariae*: PL 144, 743B.
- St. Mary Euphrasia Pelletier, as quoted in *Magnificat* (Vol. 14, No.8/ October 2012), 169.

3) The Catholic Church

Mystical Body

- Pope Benedict XVI (Joseph Cardinal Ratzinger), "Hail, Full of Grace: Elements of Marian Piety According to the Bible," in *Mary: The Church at the Source*, trans. Adrian Walker (San Francisco: Ignatius Press, 1997), 66.
- Blessed Isaac of Stella, *Sermo* 51; PL 194, 1862-1863.
- St. Augustine of Hippo, as quoted in Francis Edward Nugent, *Fairest Star Of All: A Little Treasury of Mariology* (Patterson, N.J.: St. Anthony Guild Press, 1956), 20. Used with permission.
- Venerable Pope Pius XII, *Mystici Corporis*, 111.
- Venerable Fulton J. Sheen, *The World's First Love: Mary, Mother of God* (San Francisco: Ignatius Press, 1996), 75-76. Used with Permission.
- St. Lawrence of Brindisi, *Mariale: Opera Omnia [Collected Sermons and Homilies of St. Lawrence of Brindisi]*. Trans. Vernon Wagner, OFM Cap. (Delhi, India: Media House, 2007), 534.
- St. Bernardine of Siena, *Quadrag. De Evangel. aetern. Sermo X., a.3, c. iii*, as quoted in Pope St. Pius X, *Ad diem illum laetissimum*, 13.
- St. John Paul II, *Mulieris Dignitatem*, 22.
- St. John Eudes, *The Wondrous Childhood of the Most Holy Mother of God* (Albany, N.Y.: Preserving Christian Publications, Inc., 2000), 132.
- St. Thomas of Villanova, *The Works of Saint Thomas of Villanova: Marian Sermons*. Trans. Daniel Hobbins & Matthew J. O'Connell. (Villanova, Penn.: Augustinian Press, 2001), 63. Used with permission.
- St. Ephrem the Syrian, as quoted in Luigi Gambero, SM, *Mary and the Fathers of the Church: The Blessed Virgin Mary in Patristic Thought*.

Trans. Thomas Buffer (San Francisco: Ignatius Press, 1999), 115.

- St. Augustine of Hippo, as quoted in Luigi Gambero, SM, *Mary and the Fathers of the Church: The Blessed Virgin Mary in Patristic Thought.* Trans. Thomas Buffer (San Francisco: Ignatius Press, 1999), 224.

- St. Anthony Mary Claret, as quoted in Jill Haak Adels, *The Wisdom of the Saints: An Anthology* (New York: Oxford University Press, 1987), 18.

- St. Robert Bellarmine, as quoted in Rev. Charles G. Fehrenbach, CSsR (ed.), *Mary, Day By Day: Marian Meditations for Every Day taken from the Holy Bible and the Writings of the Saints (New York: Catholic Book Publishing Corp., 1987), 136.*

- Pope Benedict XVI (Joseph Cardinal Ratzinger) & Hans Urs von Balthasar, *Mary: The Church at the Source.* Trans. Adrian Walker (San Francisco: Ignatius Press, 2005), 16-17.

Ark of Salvation

- St. Thomas Aquinas, *In Salutationem Angelica* (On the Angelic Salutation). Trans. from the Latin text of the Marietti Edition, 1954, no. 13.

- St. Ephrem the Syrian, as quoted in Ronald N. Beshara, *Mary: Ship of Treasures* (Lebanon: Diocese of Saint Maron – USA, 1988), 35.

- St. Lawrence of Brindisi, *Mariale: Opera Omnia [Collected Sermons and Homilies of St. Lawrence of Brindisi].* Trans. Vernon Wagner, OFM, Cap. (Delhi, India: Media House, 2007), 307.

- Pope Benedict XVI (Joseph Cardinal Ratzinger) & Hans Urs von Balthasar, *Mary: The Church at the Source.* Trans. Adrian Walker (San Francisco: Ignatius Press, 2005), 59-60.

- Blessed William Joseph Chaminade, *"Aux Predicateurs de Retraites,"* (24 août 1839), *Lettres de M Chaminade,* Tome V, pp. 69-80 (No 1163) English translation: W. Joseph Chaminade, "Letter to the Retreat Masters of 1839, or Circular on the Vow of Stability," trans. Carl Dreisoerner, SM, (Kirkwood, Mo.: Maryhurst Press, 1937).

- St. Alphonsus Ligouri, *The Glories of Mary* (Brooklyn, N.Y.: Redemptorist Fathers, 1931), 125-126.

- Blessed James Alberione, *Mary, Hope of the World.* Trans. Hilda Calabro (Boston, Mass.: Daughters of St. Paul, 1981), 36.

- Servant of God (Fr.) Joseph Kentenich, *Marian Instrument Piety* (Waukesha, Wis.: International Schoenstatt Center, 1992), 127. Complete German edition – Marianische Werkzeugsfrömmigkeit, written in Dachau, 1944, copyright 1974, Schönstatt – Verlag, Vallendar-Schönstatt, Germany. Used with permission.

- St. Louis de Montfort, *True Devotion to the Blessed Virgin* (Bay Shore, N.Y.: Montfort Publications, 1980), 88. Used with permission.

- St. John Bosco, as quoted in Pamela Moran (ed.), *A Marian Prayer Book: A Treasury of Prayers, Hymns, and Meditations* (Ann Arbor, Mich.: Servant Publications, 1991), 57.

- St. John Eudes, *The Wondrous Childhood of the Most Holy Mother of God* (Albany, N.Y.: Preserving Christian Publications, Inc., 2000), 42.

- St. Peter Damian, as quoted in Deyanira Flores, "Virgin Mother of Christ: Mary, The Church, and the Faithful Soul: Patristic and Medieval Testimonies on This Inseparable Trio." *Marian Studies*, Vol. LVII (2006), 101.

- St. Thomas of Villanova, *The Works of Saint Thomas of Villanova: Marian Sermons*. Trans. Daniel Hobbins & Matthew J. O'Connell. (Villanova, Penn.: Augustinian Press, 2001), 117. Used with permission.

- St. Francis of Assisi, as quoted in Fr. Peter Damian M. Fehlner, FI, "Virgo Ecclesia Facta: The Immaculate Conception, St. Francis of Assisi, and the Renewal of the Church," in *The Immaculate Conception in the Life of the Church: Essays from the International Mariological Symposium in Honor of the 150th Anniversary of the Proclamation of the Dogma of the Immaculate Conception*. (ed.) Donald H. Calloway, MIC (Stockbridge, Mass.: Marian Press, 2004), 84. Used with permission.

- Pope Benedict XVI *(Homily at First Vespers, Solemnity of Mary, Mother of God, December 31, 2007)*, as quoted in Pope Benedict XVI: Mary [Spiritual Thoughts Series] (Washington, D.C.: USCCB Publishing, 2008), 99.

- St. Lawrence of Brindisi, *Mariale: Opera Omnia [Collected Sermons and Homilies of St. Lawrence of Brindisi]*. Trans. Vernon Wagner, OFM Cap. (Delhi, India: Media House, 2007), 172.

- St. Alphonsus Ligouri, *The Glories of Mary* (Brooklyn, N.Y.: Redemptorist Fathers, 1931), 85-86.

- St. Bernard of Clairvaux, as quoted in Rev. Charles G. Fehrenbach, CSsR (ed.), *Mary, Day By Day: Marian Meditations for Every Day taken from the Holy Bible and the Writings of the Saints* (New York: Catholic Book Publishing Corp., 1987), 63.

God's Rehabilitation Center

- St. Lawrence of Brindisi, *Mariale: Opera Omnia [Collected Sermons and Homilies of St. Lawrence of Brindisi]*. Trans. Vernon Wagner, OFM Cap. (Delhi, India: Media House, 2007), 370.

- Blessed William Joseph Chaminade, as quoted in *From A Full Heart: Thoughts from Father Chaminade* (North American Center for Marianist Studies, NACMS). Compiled by Francis J. Greiner, SM (St. Meinard, Ind.: The Grail Press, 1949), entry for September 8.

- St. John Paul II, *Redemptoris Mater*, 21.

- St. Gemma Galgani, as quoted in Fr. Stefano Manelli, FI, "Marian Coredemption in the Hagiography of the 20th Century," in *Mary at the Foot of the Cross: Acts of the International Symposium on Marian Coredemption* (New Bedford, Mass.: Academy of the Immaculate, 2001), 179.

- Venerable Fulton J. Sheen, *Three to Get Married*. (Princeton, N.J.: Scepter Publishers, 1951), 162. Used with permission.

- St. Bernard of Clairvaux, *Sermo in nativ. B.V.M.,* 7.,as quoted in Servant of God (Fr.) Joseph Kentenich, *Mary, Our Mother and Educator: An Applied Mariology.* Trans. Jonathan Niehaus (Waukesha, Wis.: Schoenstatt Sisters of Mary, 1987), 64. Used with permission.

- Servant of God (Fr.) Joseph Kentenich, *Mary, Our Mother and Educator: An Applied Mariology.* Trans. Jonathan Niehaus (Waukesha, Wis.: Schoenstatt Sisters of Mary, 1987), 24-25. Original text in German: Copyright 1973, under the title *Maria-Mutter und Erzieherin. Eine angewandte Mariologie,* Schönstatt-Verlag, Vallendar, Schönstatt, West Germany. Used with permission.

- St. Lawrence of Brindisi, *Mariale: Opera Omnia [Collected Sermons and Homilies of St. Lawrence of Brindisi].* Trans. Vernon Wagner, OFM Cap. (Delhi, India: Media House, 2007), 369.

- St. John Vianney, as quoted in Rev. Charles G. Fehrenbach, CSsR (ed.), *Mary, Day By Day: Marian Meditations for Every Day taken from the Holy Bible and the Writings of the Saints* (New York: Catholic Book Publishing Corp., 1987), 161.

- Blessed Ildefonso Schuster, as quoted in *Magnificat* (Vol. 14, No.8, October 2012), 290.

4) Confession (The Sacrament of Reconciliation)

The Curtain of Mercy

- St. John Damascene, *Homily 2 on the Dormition* 16; PG 96, 744 C-D.

- St. Thomas of Villanova, *The Works of Saint Thomas of Villanova: Marian Sermons.* Trans. Daniel Hobbins & Matthew J. O'Connell. (Villanova, Penn.: Augustinian Press, 2001), 222. Used with permission.

- Servant of God (Fr.) Joseph Kentenich, *Marian Instrument Piety* (Waukesha, Wis.: International Schoenstatt Center, 1992), 136. Complete German edition – Marianische Werkzeugsfrömmigkeit, written in Dachau, 1944, copyright 1974, Schönstatt–Verlag, Vallendar-Schönstatt, Germany. Used with permission.

- St. Vincent Pallotti, as quoted in Rev. Charles G. Fehrenbach, CSsR (ed.), *Mary, Day By Day: Marian Meditations for Every Day taken from the Holy Bible and the Writings of the Saints* (New York: Catholic Book Publishing Corp., 1987), 17.

- St. Germanus of Constantinople, *Homily on the Cincture,* PG 98, 380 B.

- St. Luigi Orione, as quoted in Fr. Stefano Manelli, FI, "Marian Coredemption in the Hagiography of the 20th Century," in *Mary at the Foot of the Cross: Acts of the International Symposium on Marian Coredemption* (New Bedford, Mass.: Academy of the Immaculate, 2001), 209.

- St. Teresa of Calcutta, *Letter to Vox Populi Mariae Mediatrici,* August 14, 1993, *Vox Populi Mariae Mediatrici* Archives. Hopedale, Ohio.

- St. Bonaventure, as quoted in Luigi Gambero, SM, *Mary in the Middle Ages: The Blessed Virgin Mary in the Thought of Medieval Latin*

Theologians. Trans. Thomas Buffer (San Francisco: Ignatius Press, 2005), 211.

- St. Peter Canisius, as quoted in Rev. Charles G. Fehrenbach, CSsR (ed.), *Mary, Day By Day: Marian Meditations for Every Day taken from the Holy Bible and the Writings of the Saints* (New York: Catholic Book Publishing Corp., 1987), 16.

Spiritual Diaper Change

- St. Louis de Montfort, *True Devotion to the Blessed Virgin* (Bay Shore, N.Y.: Montfort Publications, 1980), 12. Used with permission.
- Servant of God (Fr.) Patrick J. Peyton, *Father Peyton's Rosary Prayer Book* (San Francisco: Ignatius Press, 2003), 230.
- Blessed Michael Sopocko, *God Is Mercy: Meditations on God's Most Consoling Attribute.* (Stockbridge, Mass.: Marian Fathers, 1965), 52. Used with permission.
- St. Germanus of Constantinople, *Homilia in Sanctae Mariae zonam*; PG 98, 379-380.
- St. Bernard of Clairvaux, *In Vigilia Nativitatis Domini Sermo 3*; PL 183, 100.
- St. Bernardine of Siena, *Sermo 5 de Nativitate Beatae Mariae Virginis* (cap. 8), as quoted in Paul Haffner, *The Mystery of Mary* (England: Gracewing, 2004), 259.
- St. John Paul II, "General Audience, May 11, 1983," *L'Osservatore Romano*, May 16, 1983.
- Servant of God (Fr.) Joseph Kentenich, *Mary, Our Mother and Educator: An Applied Mariology.* Trans. Jonathan Niehaus (Waukesha, Wis.: Schoenstatt Sisters of Mary, 1987), 19. Original text in German: Copyright 1973, under the title *Maria-Mutter und Erzieherin. Eine angewandte Mariologie*, Schönstatt-Verlag, Vallendar, Schönstatt, West Germany Used with permission.
- St. Peter Damian, *Sermo* 44; PL 144, 740 C.
- St. Albert the Great, as quoted in Luigi Gambero, SM, *Mary in the Middle Ages: The Blessed Virgin Mary in the Thought of Medieval Latin Theologians.* Trans. Thomas Buffer (San Francisco: Ignatius Press, 2005), 229.
- Pope Benedict XVI (*Homily at Mass for the canonization of St. Anthony of St. Anne Galvao, Aparecida, Brazil, May 11, 2007*), as quoted in *Pope Benedict XVI: Mary [Spiritual Thoughts Series]* (Washington, D.C.: USCCB Publishing, 2008), 133.

Ongoing Conversion

- Pope Leo XIII, *Augustissimae Virginis Mariae*, 9.
- St. Anselm of Canterbury, *Oratio* 51; PL 158, 951 B.
- St. John Paul II, *Insegnamenti di Giovanni Paolo II,* as quoted in

Arthur Burton Calkins, *Totus Tuus: John Paul II's Program of Marian Consecration and Entrustment* (New Bedford, Mass.: Academy of the Immaculate, 1992), 266.

- Servant of God (Fr.) Joseph Kentenich, *Marian Instrument Piety* (Waukesha, Wis.: International Schoenstatt Center, 1992), 77. Complete German edition – Marianische Werkzeugsfrömmigkeit, written in Dachau, 1944, copyright 1974, Schönstatt–Verlag, Vallendar-Schönstatt, Germany. Used with permission.

- Pope Benedict XVI (*Message for the Sixteenth World Day of the Sick, January 11, 2008*), as quoted in *Pope Benedict XVI: Mary [Spiritual Thoughts Series]* (Washington, D.C.: USCCB Publishing, 2008), 129.

- Venerable Casimir Wyszynski, as quoted in Zygmunt Proczek, MIC, *The Servant of Mary Immaculate: Father Casimir Wyszynski* (Stockbridge, Mass.: Marians of the Immaculate Conception, 1997), 71. Used with permission.

- Venerable Pope Pius XII, Letter *Neminem profecto*, February 11, 1950 in AAS 42 (1950): 390-391.

- St. Louis de Montfort, *True Devotion to the Blessed Virgin* (Bay Shore, N.Y.: Montfort Publications, 1980), 19. Used with permission.

- Blessed Pope Paul VI, "General Audience (May 30, 1973)" in *Mary, God's Mother and Ours* (Boston, Mass.: Daughters of St. Paul, 1979), 92.

- St. Bridget of Sweden, as quoted in John Cook, *The Book of Positive Quotations*. 2nd Edition. (Minneapolis: Fairview Press, 2007), 189.

- Blessed Ildefonso Schuster, as quoted in *Magnificat* (Vol. 14, No.3, May 2012), 65.

- St. Bernard of Clairvaux, as quoted in Msgr. Joseph Clifford Fenton, "Our Lady and the Extirpation of Heresy," in *Studies in Praise of our Blessed Mother: Selections from the American Ecclesiastical Review.* (ed.) Msgr. Joseph C. Fenton & Edmond D. Benard (Washington, D.C.: Catholic University of America Press, 1952), 232.

- St. John Eudes, *The Wondrous Childhood of the Most Holy Mother of God* (Albany, N.Y.: Preserving Christian Publications, Inc., 2000), 239.

5) The Holy Priesthood

Knights of the Holy Queen

- Blessed William Joseph Chaminade, as quoted in *From A Full Heart: Thoughts from Father Chaminade* (North American Center for Marianist Studies, NACMS). Compiled by Francis J. Greiner, SM, (St. Meinard, Ind.: The Grail Press, 1949), entry for September 5.

- St. Maximilian Kolbe, *Scritti di Massimiliano Kolbe* (Rome: Editrice Nazionale Milizia dell'Immacolata, 1997): 1334.

- St. Ephrem the Syrian, *Oratio ad Santissimam Dei Matrem*, in *Enchiridion Marianum Biblicum Patristicum*. D. Casagrande (ed.) Rome: "Cor Unum" 1974, 346.

- Servant of God (Fr.) Joseph Kentenich, *Marian Instrument Piety* (Waukesha, Wis.: International Schoenstatt Center, 1992), 152. Complete German edition – Marianische Werkzeugsfrömmigkeit, written in Dachau, 1944, copyright 1974, Schönstatt–Verlag, Vallendar-Schönstatt, Germany Used with permission.

- Pope Benedict XVI (Joseph Cardinal Ratzinger) & Hans Urs von Balthasar, *Mary: The Church at the Source*. Trans. Adrian Walker (San Francisco: Ignatius Press, 2005), 88.

- Blessed William Joseph Chaminade, as quoted in *From A Full Heart: Thoughts from Father Chaminade* (North American Center for Marianist Studies, NACMS). Compiled by Francis J. Greiner, SM, (St. Meinard, Ind.: The Grail Press, 1949), entry for January 2.

- St. Maximilian Kolbe, as quoted in Fr. Stefano M. Manelli, FI, *The Marian Vow* (New Bedford, Mass.: Academy of the Immaculate, 2010), 111.

- Servant of God (Fr.) Joseph Kentenich, *Marian Instrument Piety* (Waukesha, Wis.: International Schoenstatt Center, 1992), 166. Complete German edition – Marianische Werkzeugsfrömmigkeit, written in Dachau, 1944, copyright 1974, Schönstatt–Verlag, Vallendar-Schönstatt, Germany. Used with permission.

- St. Peter Julian Eymard, *Our Lady of the Blessed Sacrament: Readings for the Month of May* (Cleveland, Ohio: Emmanuel Publications, 1930), 142.

- St. Francis de Sales, *The Sermons of St. Francis de Sales on Our Lady* (Rockford, Ill.: TAN Books, 1985), 148.

- St. John Eudes, *The Admirable Heart of Mary*. Trans. Charles di Targiani & Ruth Hauser (Buffalo, N.Y.: Immaculate Heart Publications, 1947), 201.

- St. John Damascene, as quoted in Jill Haak Adels, *The Wisdom of the Saints: An Anthology* (New York: Oxford University Press, 1987), 21.

- Blessed James Alberione, *Glories and Virtues of Mary*. Trans. Hilda Calabro (Boston, Mass.: Daughters of St. Paul, 1982), 237.

- Pope Benedict XVI (*Meeting with clergy of the Dioceses of Belluno-Feltre and Treviso, July 24, 2007*), as quoted in *Pope Benedict XVI: Mary* [*Spiritual Thoughts Series*] (Washington, D.C.: USCCB Publishing, 2008), 146.

- St. Philip Neri, as quoted in *Magnificat* (Vol. 14, No.3, May 2012), 355.

- St. Maximilian Kolbe, as quoted in H.M. Manteau-Bonamy, OP, *Immaculate Conception and the Holy Spirit: The Marian Teachings of St. Maximilian Kolbe*. Trans. Richard Arnandez, FSC (Libertyville, Ill.: Franciscan Marytown Press, 1977), 108.

Fishers of Men

- St. Catherine of Siena, *Dialogue of St. Catherine of Siena* (paragraph 139). The translation offered here is my own. The Latin version, as given by St. Alphonsus de Liguori in *The Glories of Mary* (Brooklyn: Redemptorist Fathers, 1931), p. 204 (Chapter VI, Section III), reads: "*Ipsa est a me velut esca dulcissima electa pro capiendis hominibus ... .*" Unfortunately, most modern translations of the *Dialogue* in circulation today are only available in an abridged version and do not contain this section at all. Therefore, I have attempted to render a more literal translation for the reader based off of the Latin as provided by St. Alphonsus.

- Servant of God (Fr.) Joseph Kentenich, *Mary, Our Mother and Educator: An Applied Mariology.* Trans. Jonathan Niehaus (Waukesha, Wis.: Schoenstatt Sisters of Mary, 1987), 105. Original text in German: Copyright 1973, under the title *Maria-Mutter und Erzieherin. Eine angewandte Mariologie,* Schönstatt-Verlag, Vallendar, Schönstatt, West Germany. Used with permission.

- Servant of God (Fr.) Joseph Kentenich, *Marian Instrument Piety* (Waukesha, Wis.: International Schoenstatt Center, 1992), 155. Complete German edition – Marianische Werkzeugsfrömmigkeit, written in Dachau, 1944, copyright 1974, Schönstatt–Verlag, Vallendar-Schönstatt, Germany Used with permission.

- St. Lawrence of Brindisi, *Mariale: Opera Omnia [Collected Sermons and Homilies of St. Lawrence of Brindisi].* Trans. Vernon Wagner, OFM Cap. (Delhi, India: Media House, 2007), 175.

- St. Louis de Montfort, *True Devotion to the Blessed Virgin* (Bay Shore, N.Y.: Montfort Publications, 1980), 17. Used with permission.

- St. Ildelphonsus of Toledo, *De virginitate sanctae Mariae* 12; PL 96, 105 B – 106 B.

- St. John Eudes, *The Wondrous Childhood of the Most Holy Mother of God* (Albany, N.Y.: Preserving Christian Publications, Inc., 2000), 214.

- St. Germanus of Constantinople, *Oratio in Praesentatione B.M.V.,* as quoted in Pope Leo XIII, Adiutricem, 14.

- St. Cyril of Alexandria, *Homily IV Preached at Ephesus against Nestorius,* PG 77, 992-996.

- Pope Benedict XVI (*Address at Heiligenkreuz Abbey, Austria, September 9, 2007*), as quoted in *Pope Benedict XVI: Mary [Spiritual Thoughts Series]* (Washington, D.C.: USCCB Publishing, 2008), 120.

- Blessed Pope Pius IX, as quoted in *The Official Handbook of the Legion of Mary.* (Dublin: Concilium Legionis Mariae, 2005), 146.

- Blessed James Alberione, *Mary, Queen of the Apostles* (Derby, N.Y.: Daughters of St. Paul, 1956), 33.

- St. Padre Pio, *Padre Pio parla della Madonna,* as quoted in Fr. Stefano M. Manelli, FI, *The Marian Vow* (New Bedford, Mass.: Academy of the Immaculate, 2010), 133.

- Venerable Fulton J. Sheen, *The Priest Is Not His Own.* (New York: McGraw-Hill Book Company, Inc., 1963), 271-272.

Brothers In Arms

- St. Bonaventure, as quoted in Jill Haak Adels, *The Wisdom of the Saints: An Anthology* (New York: Oxford University Press, 1987), 18.
- St. Maximilian Kolbe, (*Scritti* 1295, III: 696), as quoted in James McCurry, OFM Conv., "The Mariology of Maximilian Kolbe," *Marian Studies: Volume 36* (1985): 96.
- Venerable Fulton J. Sheen, *Three to Get Married.* (Princeton, N.J.: Scepter Publishers, 1951), 163-164. Used with permission.
- Blessed James Alberione, *Glories and Virtues of Mary.* Trans. Hilda Calabro (Boston, Mass.: Daughters of St. Paul, 1982), 197.
- Blessed Pope Pius IX, *Ineffabilis Deus* (Boston, Mass.: St. Paul Books & Media), 22-23.
- St. Louis de Montfort, *The Secret of the Rosary.* Trans. Mary Barbour, TOP (Bay Shore, N.Y.: Montfort Publications, 1954), 91. Used with permission.
- Pope Leo XIII, *Adiutricem*, 4.
- St. Louis de Montfort, *The Secret of the Rosary.* Trans. Mary Barbour, TOP (Bay Shore, N.Y.: Montfort Publications, 1954), 61. Used with permission.
- Blessed William Joseph Chaminade, *Letters of Father Chaminade*, Vols. 1-8. (Dayton, Ohio: Marianist Resources Commission, 1976-1986), no. 188.
- St. Bonaventure, *Sermo de Purificatione B.M.V. 2, IX, 642a*, as quoted in Fr. Stefano M. Manelli, FI, *Devotion to Our Lady: The Marian Life as Taught by the Saints* (New Bedford, Mass.: Academy of the Immaculate, 2001), 28.
- Blessed Bartolo Longo, *Supplication to the Queen of the Holy Rosary*, as quoted in St. John Paul II, *Rosarium Virginis Mariae*, 43.
- St. Josemaria Escriva, *The Way: Furrow: The Forge.* (New York: Scepter, 2001), 123.

6) Prayer & Devotion(s)

Spiritual Marriage

- St. Lawrence of Brindisi, as quoted in Arturo da Carmignano, OFM Cap. *St. Lawrence of Brindisi.* Trans. Paul Barrett, OFM Cap. (Westminster, Md.: Newman Press, 1963), 129.
- St. Stanislaus Papczynski, *Templum Dei Mysticum.* Fontes Historiae Marianorum 5. (Varsaviae: Institutum Historicum Marianorum, 1998), 81.
- St. Gregory Palamas, "A Homily on the Dormition of Our Supremely Pure Lady Theotokos and Ever-Virgin Mary." (Homily 37), in PG 151, 177B, as quoted in Paul Haffner, *The Mystery of Mary* (England: Gracewing, 2004), 9-10.
- Venerable Fulton J. Sheen, *The Rainbow of Sorrow.* (Garden City, N.Y.: Garden City Books, 1953), 40.

- St. Ephrem the Syrian, as quoted in Sebastian Brock, *The Luminous Eye: The Spiritual World Vision of Saint Ephrem the Syrian.* (Kalamazoo, Mich.: Cistercian Publications, 1992), 127.

- St. Cyril of Alexandria, as quoted in *Magnificat* (Vol. 14, No.10, December 2012), 302.

- St. John Vianney, as quoted in Abbe Francois Trochu, *The Cure d'Ars: Saint Jean-Marie-Baptiste Vianney.* Trans. Dom Ernest Graf, OSB (Rockford, Ill.: TAN Books, 1977), 8.

- St. Anthony Mary Claret, as quoted in Ann Ball, *Modern Saints: Their Lives and Faces* (Rockford, Ill.: TAN Books, 1983), 65.

- St. John Eudes, *The Admirable Heart of Mary.* Trans. Charles di Targiani & Ruth Hauser (Buffalo, N.Y.: Immaculate Heart Publications, 1947), 141.

- St. John Damascene, *Homily 3 on the Dormition* I; PG 96, 753 B-C.

- St. Ildephonsus of Toledo, *De virginitate sanctae Mariae* I; PL 96, 58 A – 59 B.

- St. Bernadette Soubirous, as quoted in Patricia A. McEachern, *A Holy Life: St. Bernadette of Lourdes* (San Francisco: Ignatius Press, 2005), 18-19.

- Pope St. Gregory VII, *Ad Mathildem:* PL 148, 327A.

- Servant of God Archbishop Luis M. Martinez, *Only Jesus.* Trans. Sr. Mary St. Daniel, BVM (St. Louis, Mo.: B. Herder Book Co., 1962), 175.

- Servant of God Mother Auxilia de la Cruz, *The Eucharistic Life.* Trans. Maria Victoria Hernandez, OP (Washington, D.C.: Oblate Sisters, 2001), 69.

- St. John Paul II, "General Audience, May 11, 1983," *L'Osservatore Romano,* May 16, 1983.

After the Honeymoon

- St. Louis de Montfort, *True Devotion to the Blessed Virgin* (Bay Shore, N.Y.: Montfort Publications, 1980), 112. Used with permission.

- St. Raphaela Maria, as quoted in Ronda De Sola Chervin, *Quotable Saints* (Oak Lawn, Ill.: CMJ Marian Publishers, 1992), 101.

- St. Irenaeus of Lyons, *Adversus haereses* 3, 22; PG 7, 959-960.

- St. Pope John XXIII, *Epistle to Cardinal Agaganian*, Legate to Marian Congress in Saigon (31 Jan 1959) in AAS 51 (1959), 88.

- St. John Paul II, *Rosarium Virginis Mariae*, 5.

- St. Gabriel Possenti, as quoted in Ann Ball, *Modern Saints: Their Lives and Faces* (Rockford, Ill.: TAN Books, 1983), 33.

- St. John Vianney, as quoted in Francis Edward Nugent, *Fairest Star Of All: A Little Treasury of Mariology* (Patterson, N.J.: St. Anthony Guild Press, 1956), 26. Used with permission.

- Venerable Teresa of Jesus Quevedo, as quoted in Ann Ball, *Modern Saints: Their Lives and Faces* (Rockford, Ill.: TAN Books, 1983), 396.

- St. Pope John XXIII, as quoted in Andrew J. Gerakas, *The Rosary and Devotion to Mary* (Boston, Mass.: St. Paul Books & Media, 1992), 23.
- Blessed George Matulaitis, as quoted in *Marian Prayers* (Rome-Stockbridge: Congregation of Marian Fathers, 2010), 6. Used with permission.
- St. Maximilian Kolbe, *Maria Was His Middle Name*. Trans. Regis N. Barwig. (Altadena, Calif.: Benziger Sisters Publishers, 1977), 96-97.
- St. Fulgentius, as quoted in Francis Edward Nugent, *Fairest Star Of All: A Little Treasury of Mariology* (Patterson, N.J.: St. Anthony Guild Press, 1956), 25. Used with permission.
- Blessed Henry Suso, *Der Marienprediger*, as quoted in Servant of God (Fr.) Joseph Kentenich, *Mary, Our Mother and Educator: An Applied Mariology*. Trans. Jonathan Niehaus (Waukesha, Wis.: Schoenstatt Sisters of Mary, 1987), 144. Used with permission.

The Cross (The Wedding Ring)

- St. John Vianney, as quoted in Jill Haak Adels, *The Wisdom of the Saints: An Anthology* (New York: Oxford University Press, 1987), 19.
- St. Therese of Lisieux, as quoted in Francis W. Johnston (ed.), *The Voice of the Saints: Counsels from the Saints to Bring Comfort and Guidance in Daily Living* (Rockford, Ill.: TAN Books, 1986), 142.
- St. Veronica Giuliani, as quoted in Mother Francesca Perillo, FI, "Marian Coredemption in St. Veronica Giuliani," *Mary at the Foot of the Cross: Acts of the International Symposium on Marian Coredemption* (New Bedford, Mass.: Academy of the Immaculate, 2001), 246.
- Pope Pius XI, *Allocution to Pilgrims from Vicenza*, as quoted in Msgr. Arthur Burton Calkins, "Mary Co-Redemptrix: The Beloved Associate of Christ" in *Mariology: A Guide for Priests, Deacons, Seminarians, and Consecrated Persons* (Goleta, Calif.: Queenship Publishing, 2007), 378.
- Our Lady's words to St. Juan Diego, as quoted in *A Handbook on Guadalupe* (New Bedford, Mass.: Academy of the Immaculate, 1997), 200.
- Venerable Fulton J. Sheen, *The World's First Love: Mary, Mother of God* (San Francisco: Ignatius Press, 1996), 260. Used with permission.
- St. Bernardine of Siena, as quoted in Jill Haak Adels, *The Wisdom of the Saints: An Anthology* (New York: Oxford University Press, 1987), 18.
- St. Bonaventure, *Spec. B.M.V. lect. xi.*, as quoted in St. Alphonsus Ligouri, *The Glories of Mary* (London: Burns and Oates, Ld., 1868), 122-123.
- St. Peter Faber, as quoted in Servant of God (Fr.) Joseph Kentenich, *Mary, Our Mother and Educator: An Applied Mariology*. Trans. Jonathan Niehaus (Waukesha, Wis.: Schoenstatt Sisters of Mary, 1987), 66. Original text in German: Copyright 1973, under the title *Maria-Mutter und Erzieherin. Eine angewandte Mariologie*, Schönstatt-Verlag, Vallendar, Schönstatt, West Germany. Used with permission.

- Venerable Casimir Wyszynski, as quoted in *Marian Prayers* (Rome-Stockbridge: Congregation of Marian Fathers, 2010), 18-19. Used with permission.

7) The Divine Mercy

Message and Devotion for Our Times

- St. Faustina Kowalska, *Diary of Saint Maria Faustina Kowalska: Divine Mercy in My Soul.* (Stockbridge, Mass.: Marian Press, 2002), no. 1746. Used with permission.
- Blessed Michael Sopocko, *God Is Mercy: Meditations on God's Most Consoling Attribute.* (Stockbridge, Mass.: Marian Fathers, 1965), 53. Used with permission.
- St. John Paul II, *Dives in Misericordia*, 30.
- St. John Fisher, *Exposition of the Seven Penitential Psalms*, in modern English with an introduction by Anne Barbeau Gardiner (San Francisco: Ignatius Press, 1998), 55.
- St. John Eudes, *The Admirable Heart of Mary.* Trans. Charles di Targiani & Ruth Hauser (Buffalo, N.Y.: Immaculate Heart Publications, 1947), 290.
- Blessed Michael Sopocko, *The Mercy of God in His Works: Volume IV.* Trans. R. Batchelor. (Hereford: Marian Apostolate, 1972), 90.
- St. Anselm of Lucca, *Oratio I* as quoted in "Discovering Mary in the Middle Ages: St. Anselm of Lucca (1086); Mary's Maternal Intercession," by Deyanira Flores, STD, in *Queen of All Hearts,* May-June 1996, 26.
- Blessed Michael Sopocko, *God Is Mercy: Meditations on God's Most Consoling Attribute.* (Stockbridge, Mass.: Marian Fathers, 1965), 53. Used with permission.
- St. Madeleine Sophie Barat, as quoted in Francis W. Johnston (ed.), *The Voice of the Saints: Counsels from the Saints to Bring Comfort and Guidance in Daily Living* (Rockford, Ill.: TAN Books, 1986), 138.
- Servant of God (Fr.) Joseph Kentenich, *Mary, Our Mother and Educator: An Applied Mariology.* Trans. Jonathan Niehaus (Waukesha, Wis.: Schoenstatt Sisters of Mary, 1987), 129. Original text in German: Copyright 1973, under the title *Maria-Mutter und Erzieherin. Eine angewandte Mariologie,* Schönstatt-Verlag, Vallendar, Schönstatt, West Germany. Used with permission.
- St. Albert the Great, *De Natura Boni, 59,* as quoted in Michael O'Carroll, CSSp, *Theotokos: A Theological Encyclopedia of the Blessed Virgin Mary* (Collegeville, Minn.: Liturgical Press, 1982), 11.
- St. Thomas Aquinas, as quoted in Francis Edward Nugent, *Fairest Star Of All: A Little Treasury of Mariology* (Patterson, N.J.: St. Anthony Guild Press, 1956), 1. Used with permission.
- St. Catherine of Siena, as quoted in J.M. Perrin, OP, *Catherine of Siena.* Trans. Paul Barrett, OFM Cap. (Westminster, Md.: Newman Press, 1965), 185.

- St. John Eudes, *The Admirable Heart of Mary*. Trans. Charles di Targiani & Ruth Hauser (Fitzwilliam, N.H.: Loreto Publications, 2006), 137.

Vessels of Mercy

- St. John Paul II, *Dives in Misericordia* (Boston, Mass.: St. Paul Books & Media, 1980), 30.
- St. Lawrence of Brindisi, *Mariale: Opera Omnia [Collected Sermons and Homilies of St. Lawrence of Brindisi]*. Trans. Vernon Wagner, OFM Cap. (Delhi, India: Media House, 2007), 449-450.
- Blessed Columba Marmion, *Christ the Life of the Soul* (Bethesda, Md.: Zaccheus Press, 2005), 385.
- St. Louis de Montfort, *True Devotion to the Blessed Virgin* (Bay Shore, N.Y.: Montfort Publications, 1980), 9. Used with permission.
- St. Alphonsus Ligouri, *The Glories of Mary* (Rockford, Ill.: TAN, 1977), 136.
- St. Gregory Palamas, "A Homily on the Dormition of Our Supremely Pure Lady Theotokos and Ever-Virgin Mary." (Homily 37), in PG 151, 469-470, as quoted in Paul Haffner, *The Mystery of Mary* (England: Gracewing, 2004), 264.
- St. John Eudes, *The Admirable Heart of Mary*. Trans. Charles di Targiani & Ruth Hauser (Buffalo, N.Y.: Immaculate Heart Publications, 1947), 127.
- St. Bernard of Clairvaux, *Sermo I super Salve*, as quoted in St. John Eudes, *The Admirable Heart of Mary*. Trans. Charles di Targiani & Ruth Hauser (Buffalo, N.Y.: Immaculate Heart Publications, 1947), 127.
- Servant of God (Fr.) Joseph Kentenich, *Marian Instrument Piety* (Waukesha, Wis.: International Schoenstatt Center, 1992), 116. Complete German edition – Marianische Werkzeugsfrömmigkeit, written in Dachau, 1944, copyright 1974, Schönstatt–Verlag, Vallendar-Schönstatt, Germany. Used with permission.
- St. Faustina Kowalska, *Diary of Saint Maria Faustina Kowalska: Divine Mercy in My Soul.* (Stockbridge, Mass.: Marian Press, 2002), no. 1746. Used with permission.
- Servant of God Mother Auxilia de la Cruz, *The Eucharistic Life.* Trans. Maria Victoria Hernandez, OP (Washington, D.C.: Oblate Sisters, 2001), 67.
- Venerable Pope Pius XII, "Allocution to Catholic Relief Services," December 8, 1955. *L'Osservatore Romano*, English Edition, December 12, 1955.
- St. Catherine of Siena, as quoted in J.M. Perrin, OP, *Catherine of Siena*. Trans. Paul Barrett, OFM Cap. (Westminster, Md.: Newman Press, 1965), 186.
- Venerable Mary of Agreda, as quoted in Pamela Moran (ed.), *A Marian Prayer Book: A Treasury of Prayers, Hymns, and Meditations* (Ann Arbor, Mich.: Servant Publications, 1991), 169.

Jesus, I Trust in You!

- St. Andrew of Crete, as quoted in St. Alphonsus Ligouri, *The Glories of Mary* (Brooklyn, N.Y.: Redemptorist Fathers, 1931), 85.

- Pope Leo XIII, *Magnae Dei Matris*, as quoted in W. Lawler, OP, (ed.), *The Rosary of Mary: Translation of the Encyclicals and Apostolic Letters of Pope Leo XIII* (Paterson, N.J.: 1944): 87-88.

- St. Francis de Sales, *Introduction to the Devout Life*. Trans. John K. Ryan (New York: Doubleday, 2003), 96.

- Servant of God (Fr.) Joseph Kentenich, *Marian Instrument Piety* (Waukesha, Wis.: International Schoenstatt Center, 1992), 115. Complete German edition – Marianische Werkzeugsfrömmigkeit, written in Dachau, 1944, copyright 1974, Schönstatt –Verlag, Vallendar-Schönstatt, Germany. Used with permission.

- Venerable Fulton J. Sheen, *The World's First Love: Mary, Mother of God* (San Francisco: Ignatius Press, 1996), 266. Used with permission.

- Venerable Bernard Maria Clausi, as quoted in Fr. Paul Maria Sigl, "The Spiritual Maternity of Mary in the Lives of the Saints," in *Mary at the Foot of the Cross V: Redemption and Coredemption under the Sign of the Immaculate Conception: Acts of the International Symposium on Marian Coredemption* (New Bedford, Mass.: Academy of the Immaculate, 2005), 553.

- Blessed Michael Sopocko, *The Mercy of God in His Works: Volume IV*. Trans. R. Batchelor. (Hereford: Marian Apostolate, 1972), 83.

- St. Anselm of Canterbury, *Oratio* 52; PL 158, 957 A.

- St. John Paul II, "Papal Address in Washington, D.C., October 6, 1979," as quoted in Margaret R. Bunson (ed.), *John Paul II's Book on Mary* (Huntington, Ind.: Our Sunday Visitor, Inc., 1996), 181.

- Blessed George Matulaitis, *Journal*. Fontes Historiae Marianorum 17. Trans. Sr. Ann Mikaila, MVS (Stockbridge, Mass.: Marian Fathers, 2003), 138. Used with permission.

- St. Maximilian Kolbe, *Maria Was His Middle Name*. Trans. Regis N. Barwig. (Altadena, Calif.: Benziger Sisters Publishers, 1977), 133.

- St. John Vianney, *Thoughts of the Cure D'ars*. (Charlotte, N.C.: Tan Books, 1984), 33.

- Servant of God (Fr.) Joseph Kentenich, *Mary, Our Mother and Educator: An Applied Mariology*. Trans. Jonathan Niehaus (Waukesha, Wis.: Schoenstatt Sisters of Mary, 1987), 71. Original text in German: Copyright 1973, under the title *Maria-Mutter und Erzieherin. Eine angewandte Mariologie*, Schönstatt-Verlag, Vallendar, Schönstatt, West Germany. Used with permission.

8) Manhood

Like Father, Like Son

- Blessed William Joseph Chaminade, as quoted in *From A Full Heart: Thoughts from Father Chaminade* (North American Center for Marianist

Studies, NACMS). Compiled by Francis J. Greiner, SM, (St. Meinard, Ind.: The Grail Press, 1949), entry for March 12.

- St. John Vianney, *Thoughts of the Cure D'Ars.* (Charlotte, N.C.: TAN Books, 1984), 74.

- St. John Paul II, as quoted in Jason Evert, *Purity: 365 Daily Reflections on True Love* (Cincinnati, Ohio: Servant Books, 2009), 86.

- St. Thomas of Villanova, *The Works of Saint Thomas of Villanova: Marian Sermons.* Trans. Daniel Hobbins & Matthew J. O'Connell. (Villanova, Penn.: Augustinian Press, 2001), 52. Used with permission.

- Blessed Guerric of Igny, as quoted in Deyanira Flores, "Forming Her Only-Begotten In The Sons By Adoption: The Marian Spirituality of Bl. Guerric of Igny (1157)," *Marian Studies*, Vol. LII (2001), 106.

- Venerable Fulton J. Sheen, *The World's First Love: Mary, Mother of God* (San Francisco: Ignatius Press, 1996), 171. Used with permission.

- Pope Benedict XVI *(Homily as Mass for the canonization of St. Anthony of St. Anne Galvao, Aparecida, Brazil, May 11, 2007)*, as quoted in *Pope Benedict XVI: Mary [Spiritual Thoughts Series]* (Washington, D.C.: USCCB Publishing, 2008), 147.

- St. John Vianney, *Thoughts of the Cure D'Ars.* (Charlotte, N.C.: TAN Books, 1984), 32.

- Servant of God Catherine de Hueck Doherty, as quoted in *The Air We Breathe: The Mariology of Catherine de Hueck Doherty* by Fr. Denis Raymond Lemieux. (New Bedford, Mass.: Academy of the Immaculate, 2011), 77.

- Servant of God (Fr.) Joseph Kentenich, *Mary, Our Mother and Educator: An Applied Mariology.* Trans. Jonathan Niehaus (Waukesha, Wis.: Schoenstatt Sisters of Mary, 1987), 122. Original text in German: Copyright 1973, under the title *Maria-Mutter und Erzieherin. Eine angewandte Mariologie*, Schönstatt-Verlag, Vallendar, Schönstatt, West Germany. Used with permission.

- St. Vincent Pallotti, as quoted in Servant of God (Fr.) Joseph Kentenich, *Mary, Our Mother and Educator: An Applied Mariology.* Trans. Jonathan Niehaus (Waukesha, Wis.: Schoenstatt Sisters of Mary, 1987), 176. Used with permission.

- Venerable Fulton J. Sheen, as quoted in Francis Edward Nugent, *Fairest Star Of All: A Little Treasury of Mariology* (Patterson, N.J.: St. Anthony Guild Press, 1956), 55. Used with permission.

- St. John Vianney, *Thoughts of the Cure D'Ars.* (Charlotte, N.C.: TAN Books, 1984), 59.

- Blessed Timothy Giaccardo, as quoted in *Spiritual Advice from the Saints: 365 Days of Inspiration.* Compiled by Daughters of St. Paul (Boston, Mass.: Pauline Books & Media, 2004), entry for October 7.

- St. John XXIII, as quoted in Pope Paul VI, *Mary, God's Mother and Ours* (Boston, Mass.: Daughters of St. Paul, 1979), 14.

Band of Brothers

- St. Bernard of Clairvaux, *De Aquaeductu* 7; PL 183, 441 B.
- St. Bonaventure, as quoted in Fr. Patrick Greenough, OFM, Conv., *The Immaculate Conception and Other Teachings on the Blessed Virgin Mary* (Libertyville, Ill.: Marytown Press, 2005), 101.
- St. John Eudes, *Kingdom of Jesus* (Part VI, Chapter XI), as quoted at www.piercedhearts.org.
- Pope Leo XIII, *Adiutricem*, 17.
- St. Maximilian Kolbe, *Maria Was His Middle Name*. Trans. Regis N. Barwig. (Altadena, Calif.: Benziger Sisters Publishers, 1977), 72.
- St. John Eudes, *The Admirable Heart of Mary*. Trans. Charles di Targiani & Ruth Hauser (Buffalo, N.Y.: Immaculate Heart Publications, 1947), 126.
- St. Anselm of Canterbury, *Oratio* 52; PL 158, 956 B – 957 A.
- St. Bernard of Clairvaux, *De Aquaeductu* I, 7; PL 183, 441 C.
- Vatican Council II (*Lumen Gentium*, Chapter 8)
- Pope St. Pius X, as quoted in Francis Edward Nugent, *Fairest Star Of All: A Little Treasury of Mariology* (Patterson, N.J.: St. Anthony Guild Press, 1956), 53. Used with permission.
- St. Maximilian Kolbe, as quoted in Fr. Stefano M. Manelli, FI, *The Marian Vow* (New Bedford, Mass.: Academy of the Immaculate, 2010), 65.

All For Beauty

- Venerable Fulton J. Sheen, *The World's First Love: Mary, Mother of God* (San Francisco: Ignatius Press, 1996), 171. Used with permission.
- Pope Benedict XVI (Joseph Cardinal Ratzinger), *God and the World: A Conversation with Peter Seewald* (San Francisco: Ignatius Press, 2002), 302.
- St. Louis de Montfort, *True Devotion to the Blessed Virgin* (Bay Shore, N.Y.: Montfort Publications, 1980), 12. Used with permission.
- St. Francis Anthony Fasani, as quoted in Fr. Patrick Greenough, OFM Conv., *The Immaculate Conception and Other Teachings on the Blessed Virgin Mary* (Libertyville, Ill.: Marytown Press, 2005), 104.
- St. Lawrence of Brindisi, *Mariale: Opera Omnia [Collected Sermons and Homilies of St. Lawrence of Brindisi]*. Trans. Vernon Wagner, OFM Cap. (Delhi, India: Media House, 2007), 382.
- St. Thomas of Villanova, *The Works of Saint Thomas of Villanova: Marian Sermons*. Trans. Daniel Hobbins & Matthew J. O'Connell. (Villanova, Penn.: Augustinian Press, 2001), 108. Used with permission.
- St. John Damascene, *Homily*, PG 94, 1161.
- St. Proclus of Constantinople, *Homily* 5, 2; PG 65, 717 C – 720 A.

- St. Ambrose Autpert, *De Assumptione sanctae Mariae* 5; PL 39, 2131.
- Pope Benedict XVI (*Angelus* message, December 8, 2005), as quoted in *Pope Benedict XVI: Mary [Spiritual Thoughts Series]* (Washington, D.C.: USCCB Publishing, 2008), 65.
- Blessed James Alberione, *Mary, Queen of the Apostles* (Derby, N.Y.: Daughters of St. Paul, 1956), 250.

9) Femininity

Daddy's Princess

- St. John Eudes, *The Wondrous Childhood of the Most Holy Mother of God* (Albany, N.Y.: Preserving Christian Publications, Inc., 2000), 237.
- Servant of God (Fr.) Joseph Kentenich, *Marian Instrument Piety* (Waukesha, Wis.: International Schoenstatt Center, 1992), 39. Complete German edition – Marianische Werkzeugsfrömmigkeit, written in Dachau, 1944, copyright 1974, Schönstatt –Verlag, Vallendar-Schönstatt, Germany. Used with permission.
- Venerable Fulton J. Sheen, *The World's First Love: Mary, Mother of God* (San Francisco: Ignatius Press, 1996), 85. Used with permission.
- Servant of God (Fr.) Joseph Kentenich, *Marian Instrument Piety* (Waukesha, Wis.: International Schoenstatt Center, 1992), 142. Complete German edition – Marianische Werkzeugsfrömmigkeit, written in Dachau, 1944, copyright 1974, Schönstatt–Verlag, Vallendar-Schönstatt, Germany. Used with permission.
- St. Lawrence of Brindisi, *Mariale: Opera Omnia [Collected Sermons and Homilies of St. Lawrence of Brindisi]*. Trans. Vernon Wagner, OFM Cap. (Delhi, India: Media House, 2007), 123.
- St. Francis of Assisi, *The Office of the Passion*, as quoted in Marion A. Habig (ed.), *St. Francis of Assisi, Writings and Early Biographies: English Omnibus of the Sources for the Life of St. Francis* (Chicago, 1983), 142.
- Blessed Mary of Agreda, *City of God: The Conception: The Divine History and Life of the Virgin Mother of God*. Trans. Fiscar Marison. (Washington, N.J.: Ave Maria Institute, 1971), 220.
- Blessed Gabriel Maria Allegra, *Mary's Immaculate Heart: A Way to God*. Trans. Joachim Daleiden, OFM (Chicago: Franciscan Herald Press, 1985), 22.
- St. John Eudes, *The Wondrous Childhood of the Most Holy Mother of God* (Albany, N.Y.: Preserving Christian Publications, Inc., 2000), 99-100.
- St. Bernardine of Siena, as quoted in Jill Haak Adels, *The Wisdom of the Saints: An Anthology* (New York: Oxford University Press, 1987), 20.
- St. Phillip Neri, as quoted in Jill Haak Adels, *The Wisdom of the Saints: An Anthology* (New York: Oxford University Press, 1987), 18.
- St. John Eudes, *The Admirable Heart of Mary*. Trans. Charles di Targiani & Ruth Hauser (Buffalo, N.Y.: Immaculate Heart Publications, 1947), 169.
- Pope Benedict XVI, *Deus Caritas Est*, no. 12.

- Blessed Pope Paul VI, "Sermon in the parish church of Castel Gandolfo" (Aug. 15, 1964), in *Mary, God's Mother and Ours* (Boston, Mass.: Daughters of St. Paul, 1979), 18.
- Servant of God (Fr.) Patrick J. Peyton, *The Ear of God* (New York: Doubleday & Company, Inc., 1951), 82.

Capture Her Heart

- Venerable Fulton J. Sheen, *The World's First Love: Mary, Mother of God* (San Francisco: Ignatius Press, 1996), 83. Used with permission.
- St. Ambrose, as quoted in Jill Haak Adels, *The Wisdom of the Saints: An Anthology* (New York: Oxford University Press, 1987), 20.
- St. Lawrence of Brindisi, *Mariale: Opera Omnia [Collected Sermons and Homilies of St. Lawrence of Brindisi]*. Trans. Vernon Wagner, OFM Cap. (Delhi, India: Media House, 2007), 131.
- Servant of God (Fr.) Joseph Kentenich, *Mary, Our Mother and Educator: An Applied Mariology*. Trans. Jonathan Niehaus (Waukesha, Wis.: Schoenstatt Sisters of Mary, 1987), 104. Original text in German: Copyright 1973, under the title *Maria-Mutter und Erzieherin. Eine ungewandte Mariologie*, Schönstatt-Verlag, Vallendar, Schönstatt, West Germany. Used with permission.
- St. Amadeus of Lausanne, as quoted in Michael O'Carroll, CSSp, *Theotokos: A Theological Encyclopedia of the Blessed Virgin Mary* (Collegeville, Minn.: Liturgical Press, 1982), 15.
- Venerable Fulton J. Sheen, *The World's First Love: Mary, Mother of God* (San Francisco: Ignatius Press, 1996), 171. Used with permission.
- St. Leonard of Port Maurice, as quoted in Fr. Patrick Greenough, OFM Conv., *The Immaculate Conception and Other Teachings on the Blessed Virgin Mary* (Libertyville, Ill.: Marytown Press, 2005), 104.
- St. John Paul II, *Letter to Women* (June 29, 1995).
- Venerable Fulton J. Sheen, as quoted in Jason Evert, *Purity: 365 Daily Reflections on True Love* (Cincinnati, Ohio: Servant Books, 2009), 53.
- Servant of God (Fr.) Joseph Kentenich, *Marian Instrument Piety* (Waukesha, Wis.: International Schoenstatt Center, 1992), 138. Complete German edition – Marianische Werkzeugsfrömmigkeit, written in Dachau, 1944, copyright 1974, Schönstatt–Verlag, Vallendar-Schönstatt, Germany. Used with permission.
- St. Lawrence of Brindisi, *Mariale: Opera Omnia [Collected Sermons and Homilies of St. Lawrence of Brindisi]*. Trans. Vernon Wagner, OFM Cap. (Delhi, India: Media House, 2007), 187.

The Blessings of Motherhood

- St. Edith Stein, *Writings of Edith Stein* (London: P. Owen, 1956), 170.
- St. John Paul II, "Mary Sheds Light on Role of Women," General Audience of December 6, 1995 as quoted in *L'Osservatore Romano* [English Edition], December 13, 1995, p.11

- St. Proclus of Constantinople, as quoted in Jill Haak Adels, *The Wisdom of the Saints: An Anthology* (New York: Oxford University Press, 1987), 21.
- Servant of God (Fr.) Joseph Kentenich, *Marian Instrument Piety* (Waukesha, Wis.: International Schoenstatt Center, 1992), 153. Complete German edition – Marianische Werkzeugsfrömmigkeit, written in Dachau, 1944, copyright 1974, Schönstatt–Verlag, Vallendar-Schönstatt, Germany. Used with permission.
- Venerable Fulton J. Sheen, *The World's First Love: Mary, Mother of God* (San Francisco: Ignatius Press, 1996), 83-84. Used with permission.
- St. Methodius of Philippi, *Oration on Simeon and Anna*, as quoted in Jimmy Akin, *The Fathers Know Best: Your Essential Guide to the Teachings of the Early Church* (San Diego, CA: Catholic Answers, 2010), 345-346.
- St. Edith Stein, as quoted in Jason Evert, *Purity: 365 Daily Reflections on True Love* (Cincinnati, Ohio: Servant Books, 2009), 82.
- Pope Benedict XVI (*Homily at Mass for the Fifth World Meeting of Families, July 9, 2006)*, as quoted in *Pope Benedict XVI: Mary* [*Spiritual Thoughts Series*] (Washington, D.C.: USCCB Publishing, 2008), 70.
- St. Bernadette Soubirous, as quoted in Jill Haak Adels, *The Wisdom of the Saints: An Anthology* (New York: Oxford University Press, 1987), 18.
- Blessed John Henry Newman, *Mary: The Virgin Mary in the Life and Writings of John Henry Newman.* (ed.) Philip Boyce (Leominster, Herefordshire: Gracewing Publishing, 2001), 344.
- St. Alphonsus Liguori, *Hail Holy Queen! An Explanation of the 'Salve Regina' and the Role of the Blessed Mother in Our Salvation* (Rockford, Ill.: TAN Books, 1995), 18-19.
- St. Francis de Sales, as quoted in *Magnificat* (Vol. 14, No.3, May 2012), 156.
- Venerable Matt Talbot, as quoted in Mary Purcell, *Remembering Matt Talbot* (Dublin: M.H. Gill and Sons, Ltd., 1990), 38.
- Venerable Fulton J. Sheen, *The World's First Love: Mary, Mother of God* (San Francisco: Ignatius Press, 1996), 13. Used with permission.
- St. Joseph Cafasso, as quoted in Fr. James Alberione, *Mary, Queen of the Apostles* (Derby, N.Y.: Daughters of St. Paul, 1956), 319.

About the Author

Father Donald Calloway, MIC, a convert to Catholicism, is a member of the Congregation of the Marian Fathers of the Immaculate Conception. Before his conversion to Catholicism, he was a high school dropout who had been kicked out of a foreign country, institutionalized twice, and thrown in jail multiple times. After his radical conversion, he earned a B.A. in Philosophy and Theology from the Franciscan University of Steubenville, Ohio; M.Div. and S.T.B. degrees from the Dominican House of Studies in Washington, D.C.; and an S.T.L. in Mariology from the International Marian Research Institute in Dayton, Ohio. In addition to *Under the Mantle*, he has also written the best-selling books *Champions of the Rosary: The History and Heroes of a Spiritual Weapon* (Marian Press, 2016) and *No Turning Back: A Witness to Mercy* (Marian Press, 2010), a bestseller that recounts his dramatic conversion story. He also is the author of the book *Purest of All Lilies: The Virgin Mary in the Spirituality of St. Faustina* (Marian Press, 2008). He introduced and arranged *Marian Gems: Daily Wisdom on Our Lady* (Marian Press, 2014). Further, he has written many academic articles and is the editor of two books: *The Immaculate Conception in the Life of the Church* (Marian Press, 2004) and *The Virgin Mary and Theology of the Body* (Marian Press, 2005).

Father Calloway is the Vicar Provincial and Vocation Director for the Mother of Mercy Province.

To learn more about Marian vocations, visit
marian.org/vocations
or visit
Fr. Calloway's website,
fathercalloway.com.

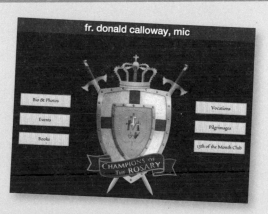

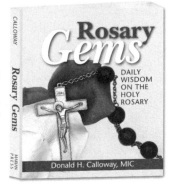

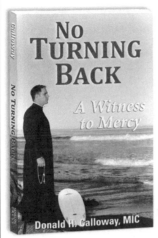

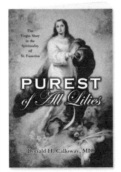

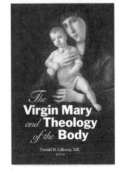

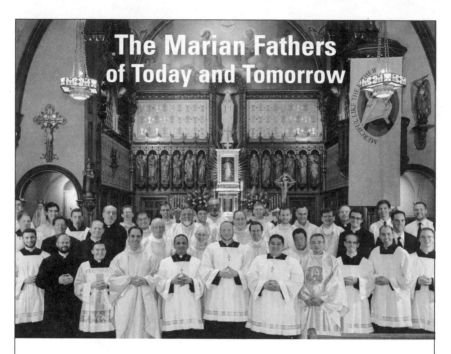

What are you looking for in the priests of tomorrow?

- ☑ Zeal for proclaiming the Gospel
- ☑ Faithfulness to the Pope and Church teaching
- ☑ Love of Mary Immaculate
- ☑ Love of the Holy Eucharist
- ☑ Concern for the souls in Purgatory
- ☑ Dedication to bringing God's mercy to all souls

These are the top reasons why men pursuing a priestly vocation are attracted to the Congregation of Marian Fathers of the Immaculate Conception.

Please support the education of these future priests. Nearly 150 Marian seminarians are counting on your gift.

THIRTEENTH
OF THE MONTH CLUB

Father Donald Calloway, MIC, Marian Vocation Director, participates in a recurring feature in the Thirteenth of the Month Club newsletter.

I'm honored and delighted to do this for the club, since it's a good way for me to help people come to a better place in their relationship with Our Lady. I want to let people know that by being in the Thirteenth of the Month Club, they're part of the Marian family. They are praying for us [the Marian Fathers of the Immaculate Conception], and we are praying for them.

Thirteenth of the Month Club members are a group of special friends who help support the work of the Marians of the Immaculate Conception. On the thirteenth of each month, members pray the Rosary for the intentions of the Club. The Marians residing in Fatima offer a special Mass on the thirteenth of the month for members' intentions. All members pledge a monthly gift and receive the Club newsletter published by the Association of Marian Helpers, Stockbridge, MA 01263.

**For more information call: 1-800-671-2020
Online: marian.org/13th   E-mail: thirteenth@marian.org**

MARY 101 Kit

A book, a DVD, and a treasure trove of pamphlets, prayercards, and more:

Y30-MKIT

This is your one-stop introduction to the Blessed Virgin Mary. Get to know our spiritual mother better with information on the basic Church dogmas about Mary Immaculate, key prayers such as the Rosary, and answers to common Protestant objections to devotion to Mary.

In our special 100th Anniversary of Fatima pack (included in the kit), we provide resources to help you learn about the apparitions and calls of Our Lady at Fatima, why these apparitions are still relevant today, and what we can do to bring about peace in the world.

Join the
Association of Marian Helpers,
headquartered at the
National Shrine of The Divine Mercy,
and share in special blessings!

An invitation from
Fr. Joseph, MIC, the director

Marian Helpers is an Association of Christian faithful of the Congregation of Marian Fathers of the Immaculate Conception. By becoming a member, you share in the spiritual benefits of the daily Masses, prayers, and good works of the Marian priests and brothers.

This is a special offer of grace given to you by the Church through the Marians. Please consider this opportunity to share in these blessings, along with others whom you would wish to join into this spiritual communion.